Far East Everyday

遠東生活華語

Book I

主編	葉德明	**Yeh, Teh-Ming**
編者	劉咪咪	**Liu, Mi-Mi**
	潘蓮丹	**Pan, Lian-Tan**
	陳惠玲	**Chen, Huei-Ling**
	林千惠	**Lin, Chien-Hwei**

遠東圖書公司

The Far East Book Co., Ltd.

Published by

The Far East Book Co., Ltd.

66-1 Chungking South Road, Section 1

Taipei, Taiwan

http://www.fareast.com.tw

遠東圖書公司出版發行 版權所有 翻印必究

Distributed by

US International Publishing Inc.

39 West 38th Street

New York, New York 10018

U.S.A.

ISBN 957-612-482-4

前言

　　遠東生活華語教材系列，是配合光碟與書面一同發行而設計的。本教材提供教師在課室授課及學生自學的材料。

　　本教材宗旨是以真實生活語料為主，讓學生學習有意義的華語文，在聽、說、讀、寫四項語文能力上，都能達到與人溝通的目的。因此在語音、語法、語意與語用上，均考慮到學生語言習得的因素，加強認知能力的練習，以期達到以華語文為第二語言學習的目的。

　　全教材一套三冊，每冊包括課本、學生作業簿（第一冊另加編寫字簿）、教師手冊、錄音帶、光碟等附件。

　　每冊共十二課，每課項目分為本課學習目標（包括生詞與語法要點）、課文、生詞、注釋、文法、聽力練習、綜合練習、實用語料等。

　　第一冊內容著重在日常實用口語會話的表達，採用真實的語料與基本功能語法，期使學生能用基本華語達到交際的目的。全冊漢字共457個，新詞共609個，語法要點118條。

　　第二冊內容漸進到現代生活資訊方面的語料，增加書面語，進一步介紹書面語中的文法結構。語用上使學生熟識現代各地通用的社會語言。全冊漢字共569個，新詞1148個，語法要點179條。

　　第三冊內容由目前流行的經濟話題漸進至新聞、歷史文化等層面，使學生能了解更多中國人的思想方式與文化內涵。全冊漢字共435個，新詞共912個，語法要點171條。

　　全書語音系統是用漢語拼音為注音符號，語法解釋方式是參照耶魯大學華語教材語法詞類系統，與中國呂叔湘著作＜現代漢語八百語料＞等為依據。

　　本教材在編輯時為了使內容資料豐富，提供給學生更多的語料，篇幅較長，在配合上課時數的前題下，教師可以自由選用，以利教學。

　　本教材由台灣師大國語教學中心劉咪咪、潘蓮丹、陳惠玲、林千惠、吳彰英、蔡顏秀、鄭嘉俶、王文娟、陳瑩漣等九位老師共同編寫。由羅凱（Frank Kenneth Ross II）與金包伯(Robert Kinney)兩位美籍人士翻譯為英文。全書經過美國威廉大學東方語文學系主任顧百里博士(Dr. Cornelius C. Kubler)，台灣師範大學華語文研究所所長鄧守信博士審查指正，於此一併致謝。敬希華語文教學界各位先進給予指教。

葉德明

一九九九年九月

編 輯 大 意

一、目標

本套教材包括課本、作業簿、寫字簿、錄音帶及光碟等部分。

教材內容係按照學生問卷調查結果編寫而成。以學生學習性向為編輯重心。希望學生學會使用中文應付生活中的各種狀況。聽、說、讀、寫四種技能同時發展，為本書的理想。第一冊共十二課。每課最前面有學習要點，使學生了解每課學習目標，同時列出生詞和文法要點，供學生複習、整理之用。〔有的生詞後面有括弧，表示這個生詞是由括弧內的詞組成。如：白菜（白、菜）〕

為因應新世代學生講究迅速有效的需求，本教材力求真實、自然、實用，使學生學了就立刻能用。本書每課有兩段或三段對話，每段對話後面有生詞、注釋、文法、聽力練習，最後有綜合練習（包括遊戲、角色扮演等）、猜猜猜和實用語料。

本書各部分設計是為幫助學生學習。老師可以依照學校規定授課時間、學生學習情形採用，不一定每個部分都必須教完。

二、每課內容結構

1. 對話

每個對話均力求簡單自然而且實用。學生對趣味盎然的內容覺得有用、有興趣，才容易學會，所以老師可以依照學生的需要增減書上的對話。

2. 生詞

除了拼音、詞類、英文意思，還有用學過的詞做的例句，讓學生透過實際的例子了解該生詞的意思和用法。例句下有英文翻譯。請老師建議學生先自己看例句，看不懂才看英文翻譯。前面有＊號的生詞沒有出現在對話中，但與對話中的生詞相關。

3. 注釋

針對對話中所提文化方面的習慣或語言及詞類縮略語加以說明。

4. 文法

先用對話中的句子引出句型，再加上句型用法說明。說明之後有練習，為了強調語言的溝通功能，這些練習都是對話式的。學生應該在家裡先預習，課堂上做練習時不要讓學生照著書念，先練習聽、說，有時間再讓學生看著書念，或是要求學生回家念。"Q"表示「問題(Question)」，"A"表示「回答(Answer)」。這種練習的回答比較沒有彈性。有方框的練習，表示學生需要自己選擇、組合。另外，後面幾課多為小李、小王兩人對話形式。在每個完成對話或句子的練習下面，有個黃色長方框，裡面是可能的答案，並非唯一的標準答案；我們希望學生可以根據自己的生活經驗作答，實在想不出來時才看方框裡的答案。補充生詞加注在當頁下方，是生詞表內沒有，但做練習可能需要的詞，在這個階段學生只要會說就可以了，不必會寫，所以將漢字列在拼音後面。有的時候配合遊戲、活動加強學生使用該句型的能力。

5. 聽力練習

在每段最後，都是配合對話內容所編寫的生活化對話，其中可能有學生沒學過的辭彙。我們希望學生注意語境，從上下文來了解內容，掌握語意重點，而不是逐字翻譯。

6. 綜合練習

有各種聽與說的活動，包括遊戲、問卷調查、角色扮演等。老師和學生可以選擇需要的部分來做。有些活動參考Penny Ur跟Andrew Wright合著之 *Five-Minute Activities* 及 Penny Ur 所著 *Grammar Practice Activities*。

7. 猜猜猜

除了第一課、第三課之外，每課都有。這個部分設計的目的是讓學生有機會了解中文辭彙組成的特色，培養學生對中文的語感。

8. 實用語料

根據課文內容，將真實生活中可能看到的相關文字資料提供給學生，希望學生能逐漸培養閱讀中文資料的方法和能力。但是其中第八課的實用語料是用來練習聽力的，都是電話錄音。

9. 課文翻譯

將課文翻成英文，放在每課最後。學生除了了解課文內容，也可比較英文中文說法的不同。

三、學生作業簿

包括聽力練習（發音、聲調、聽寫、句子理解、對話理解）、寫字、部首整理、重組、完成對話、克漏字、對話翻譯、看圖回答問題、讀實用語料回答問題、撰寫有關主題之短文。

四、寫字簿

簡單介紹六書、中國字筆畫、結構、部件、筆順規則、常用部首等。後面是每課生字練習，包括筆順、發音、字義等。

五、教師手冊

包括教學要點、課室活動說明、課本內練習解答、聽力練習內容及解答，後半部為學生作業簿解答。

Foreword

I. Purpose

Designed for English-speaking people to learn Chinese as a second language, the Far East Everyday Chinese (Book I) consists of a textbook, a student workbook, a teacher's manual, a character guide, tape cassettes, and multi-media material.

This textbook, with its 12 chapters, provides the learners with texts in modern standard Chinese. Each of its chapters is equipped with a variety of exercises in phonetics, grammar, contextual meaning and usage to help the learners improve their communicative skills in listening, speaking, reading and writing, and achieve the objective of second language acquisition.

II. Structure

1. Dialogues: The dialogues are simple and practical. The conversations include interesting, meaningful content which promotes learning.
2. Vocabulary: Each vocabulary provides pronunciation, identification of parts of speech, and meaning with examples of usage, followed by an English translation. An "*" precedes each new word that does not appear in the dialogue, but is related to the vocabulary in the dialogue.
3. Notes: Notes explain special uses of expressions and structures used in the dialogues.
4. Grammar: The grammar section explains the correct use of sentence patterns in both English and Chinese. Various drills are used for practice. The drills are designed for students to prepare before class so that they can practice in class without looking at the book. "Q" represents question and "A" represents answer. Several chapters use dialogues between Little Li and Little Wang. Each drill is followed by an additional vocabulary used only in the drills. Students need only possess speaking ability for this section, as writing is not required, so pinyin is included for the new words. Some patterns are used to strengthen practical language skills.
5. Aural Comprehension Drill: The section is designed to enable students to understand meanings through the context. Starting with chapter 7, the second listening section emphasizes vocabulary used in public notices or documents.

6. Variety Exercises: This section includes listening and speaking activities, such as games, questions and answers, and role-playing. The teacher and students can choose the activities which are most suitable. *Grammar Practice Activities* by Penny Ur and *Five-Minute Activities* by Andrew Wright are sometimes used as reference.

7. Try to Guess: This section is designed to help students understand the Chinese word combinations and acquire a good sense of the Chinese language.

8. Authentic Material: This section provides words and expressions in daily spoken Chinese to help students understand commonly encountered situations such as telephone conversations.

9. Translation of the Dialogues: At the end of each chapter an English translation of the dialogues helps students better understand the dialogues as well as how certain phrases are translated into English.

III. Student Workbook

The workbook includes exercises for listening(pronunciation, intonations, dictation, sentence comprehension, and dialogue comprehension), character writing, character distinction, character correction, matching, multiple choices, fill in the blanks, dialogue completion, translation, choosing the correct phrases, answering questions, and writing short essays.

IV. Character Guide

This guide provides brief introductions to the six categories of Chinese characters, stroke order, structure, radicals, and commonly used radicals. Exercises for each chapter's vocabulary stroke order and pronunciation are also included.

V. Teacher's Manual

The Teacher's Manual includes important teaching points, suggestions for classroom activities, exercise answer key, as well as the Student's Workbook answer key.

CONTENTS
目　錄

第一課　多少錢？

LESSON 1 HOW MUCH?

Key Study Points

numbers 1-99／asking prices／counting money／verifying amounts／forms of address for men and women／expressing thanks／ordering food

Vocabulary	Pronunciation	Grammar
Dialogue I	**Dialogue I**	**Dialogue I**
多少，錢，小姐，這個(這，個)，那，〇，一，二，三，四，五，六，七，八，九，十，塊	**Initials**: b, d, g, j, k, l, n, q, s, sh, x, zh **Finals**: an, er, iao, ing, iu, u, uai, uo	S + Nu + M (+N) (The verb can be omitted.) SP + Nu + M + (N) (If Nu is "1", it can be omitted.) QW 多少
Dialogue II	**Dialogue II**	**Dialogue II**
先生，你，我，他，她，您，吃，什麼，兩，包子，杯(杯子)，茶，一共，謝謝	**Initials**: b, ch, g, l, m, n, sh, t, x, z, **Finals**: a, ao, e, ei, en, eng, i, -i, ian, iang, ie, in, o, ong	S + V + O QW 什麼 Nu + M + N 一共

Dialogue I Asking Prices

A：小姐[1]，這個 多少 錢？
Xiǎojiě, zhèi·ge duōshǎo qián?

B：六十 塊。[2]
Liùshí kuài.

Vocabulary [3](The words with * in the front are not used in the dialogue.)

1. 多少 duōshǎo QW : how much/many

2. 錢 qián N : money

3. 小姐 xiǎojiě N : Miss, Ms. (M：wèi 位 person)

4. 這個 zhèi·ge[4] PN : this one
   這 zhè SP[5] : this
   個 ·ge M[6] : general measure word

*5. 那 nà SP : that

*6. ○ líng Nu : zero

*7. 一　　yī　　Nu : one

*8. 二　　èr　　Nu : two

*9. 三　　sān　　Nu : three

*10. 四　　sì　　Nu : four

*11. 五　　wǔ　　Nu : five

12. 六　　liù　　Nu : six

*13. 七　　qī　　Nu : seven

*14. 八　　bā　　Nu : eight

*15. 九　　jiǔ　　Nu : nine

16. 十　　shí　　Nu : ten

17. 塊　　kuài　　M : (for money) a dollar; (for things) a piece of

Notes

1. In Taiwan, "小姐" is not only used to address an unmarried woman. It may also be used to address a woman who does not have to change her family name and title after marriage. Therefore a woman is addressed as "小姐"or "X 小姐" ("X" is the woman's maiden name).

2. "。" is the Chinese period. It is a circle, not a dot.

3. Characters and words: Chinese characters, "字" (zì), are monosyllabic. A character can be pronounced differently in different dialects. The language taught in this book is Mandarin Chinese, which is the official language both in Mainland China and Taiwan. One character can have more than one meaning. Some characters can only be used in combination with some other character(s) never used alone. A "詞" (cí) is the smallest unit of meaning. A "詞" (cí) has either one syllable or two syllables, i.e. one or two characters, but most "詞" are disyllabic. Sentences are composed of "詞" (cí).

4. When the number after "這(zhè)" is "one", the vowel of "這", è, combines with the vowel of "一", i, and it is pronounced as "zhèi". "一" is omitted in writing.

5. "SP" stands for Specifier. It is used to point out the person or thing referred to. Usually it is placed in front of a numbered noun, e.g. "這個".

6. "M" stands for "Measure Word". It is used to show the quantity of a noun. It goes after a number and before the corresponding noun. The measure word in a phrase can help people distinguish

among homophones, e.g. "一只錶" (yì zhǐ biǎo, one watch) and "一張表" (yì zhāng biǎo, one form). "個" is the most commonly used measure word, and is applicable to many nouns. However, a number of nouns require specific measure words, e. g. "一本書" (yì běn shū, one book) "一輛車"(yí liàng chē, one car) "一斤白菜" (yì jīn bái cài, one catty of cabbage). It is best to memorize them together with their measure words.

1.0 Numbers

0	1	2	3	4	5
líng	yī	èr	sān	sì	wǔ

6	7	8	9	10
liù	qī	bā	jiǔ	shí

Exercises

I. Circle the numbers you hear.

1.   0   1   2   3   4   5   6   7   8   9   10
2.   0   1   2   3   4   5   6   7   8   9   10
3.   0   1   2   3   4   5   6   7   8   9   10
4.   0   1   2   3   4   5   6   7   8   9   10
5.   0   1   2   3   4   5   6   7   8   9   10

II. Write down the numbers you hear (including some telephone numbers.)

1. ____ 2. ____ 3. ____ 4. ____ 5. ____ 6. _____ 7. _____

1.0-1 Pronunciation

Pinyin

"Hanyu Pinyin" is the transcription system used in this book.

Syllable

A Chinese syllable has three components: the initial, the final, and the tone. Sometimes there is no initial. Take the numbers from zero to ten as examples:

Number / Feature	0 líng	1 yī	2 èr	3 sān	4 sì	5 wǔ	6 liù	7 qī	8 bā	9 jiǔ	10 shí
Initial	l	*		s	s	*	l	q	b	j	sh
Final	ing	i	er	an	-i	u	iu	i	a	iu	-i
Tone	′	–	ヽ	–	ヽ	˅	ヽ	–	–	˅	′

※ See rules of phonetic spelling.

Many new concepts and grammatical rules are introduced in the first few lessons of this book and may initially seem confusing. If at first you do not completely understand everything, do not lose heart. Chinese is not a simple language to master, and these rules and concepts are being introduced at this point in your study of Mandarin for your benefit. As you progress, continue to use these few chapters as a reference tool, consulting their contents whenever necessary, thereby methodically comprehending the fundamental aspects of Mandarin Chinese over a period of time. In other words, do not feel you have to be an expert right away.

Note

The vowel sounds in "si" and "shi" are written as "-i" when they stand alone. "-i" has no pho-netic value. (This vowel has two unique sounds: "-i" in "si" is a blade-alveolar vowel. It is more frontal than the vowel "-i" in "shi", which is blade-palatal.) Care should be given to differentiate "-i" from "i" in "liù", "qī", "jiǔ" and "líng". "-i" cannot be pronounced as the simple final "i", which is never found after "s", "sh", and other initials like "zh", "ch", "r", "z", and "c", which will be covered in future lessons.

Tones

Tones refer to pitches of individual syllables. There are four tones in the Mandarin Chinese. Usually, a syllable has a different meaning when it is pronounced with a different tone. However, there are a number of syllables which are short and spoken lightly called the neutral tone. The main four tones in Mandarin are marked as follows: – (1st), ′ (2nd), ˅ (3rd), ヽ (4th), and no mark to indi-cate the neutral tone. Marks are placed above the main vowel of a syllable, i.e. the one which is pronounced with the mouth wide open.

Note

In an effort to help students study, in this book, a "·" is placed in front of the syllable which should/can be pronounced light and short. If a character can be spoken either in the neutral tone or some other tone, and they share the same meaning, both a tone mark and "·" are indicated.

Tone	Tone Marks	Description	Pitch	Tone-graph
1st tone	–	high level	55:	
2nd tone	′	high rising	35:	
3rd tone	˅	falling and rising	214:	
4th tone	‵	falling	51:	

Tone Graphs

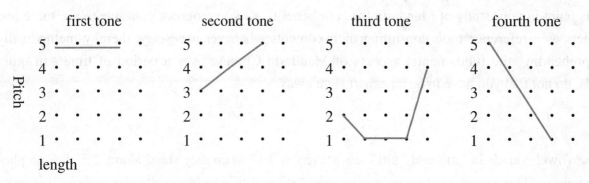

Tone Change

When a 3rd tone is followed by a 1st, 2nd or 4th tone or most neutral tones, it usually becomes a half 3rd tone; the second half, the rising part, is dropped. When a 3rd tone is followed by another 3rd tone, it should be pronounced as a 2nd tone. However, the tone mark remains unchanged.

Exercises

Repeat after the teacher:

五十、九個、兩塊、兩包、小姐、kěkǒu、lǎoshǔ、dǎsǎo、biǎoyǎn、bǎoxiǎn

Exercises

I. Listen and check the correct tones.

	ˉ	ˊ	ˇ	ˋ
1.	☐	☐	☐	☐
2.	☐	☐	☐	☐
3.	☐	☐	☐	☐
4.	☐	☐	☐	☐
5.	☐	☐	☐	☐

II. Mark tones.

1. _____	6. _____	11. _____
2. _____	7. _____	12. _____
3. _____	8. _____	13. _____
4. _____	9. _____	14. _____
5. _____	10. _____	15. _____

III. Circle the character which has a different tone from the other two in each group.

1. a. 一　　b. 錢　　c. 八
2. a. 少　　b. 姐　　c. 六
3. a. 這　　b. 塊　　c. 小
4. a. 十　　b. 三　　c. 七
5. a. 九　　b. 四　　c. 五

6. a. 十一　b. 十三　　c. 十五
7. a. 二十　b. 一共　　c. 十四
8. a. 什麼　b. 一杯　　c. 一個
9. a. 三個　b. 謝謝　　c. 先生
10. a. 四季　b. 送信　　c. 明年

Rules of Phonetic Spelling

1. When at the beginning of a syllable, "i" is written as "y", e.g. "ia" → "ya". When "i" forms an independent syllable, it is written as "yi". The dot over the vowel "i" should be replaced by the tone mark when it is the main vowel of the syllable, e.g. "yī".

2. When at the beginning of a syllable, "u" is written as "w", e.g. "ua" → "wa" and "u" is written as "wu" when it forms an independent syllable, e.g. "wǔ".

3. When "in" and "ing" form independent syllables, they are written as "yin" and "ying".

4. "-iou" is written as "-iu" when it comes after an initial. The tone mark should be placed over "u", e.g. "liù".

5. An apostrophe (') is used to clarify potential confusions, e.g. xiān(先) versus Xī'ān (西安).

Pronunciation Drill 1

Repeat the following syllables and pay attention to the tones:

· bā bá bǎ bà　bān bǎn bàn　bī bí bǐ bì　bú bǔ bù　bīng bǐng bìng

· jī jí jǐ jì　jiǔ jiù　jīng jǐng jìng

· lā lǎ là　lí lǐ lì　lán lǎn làn　liū liú liǔ liù　līng líng lǐng lìng　lú lǔ lù

· qī qí qǐ qì　qiū qiú　qīng qíng qǐng qìng

· sā sǎ sà　sān sǎn sàn　sī sǐ sì　sū sú sù

· shā shǎ shà　shān shǎn shàn　shī shí shǐ shì　shū shú shǔ shù

· ér ěr èr

(More drills can be found in the teacher's manual.)

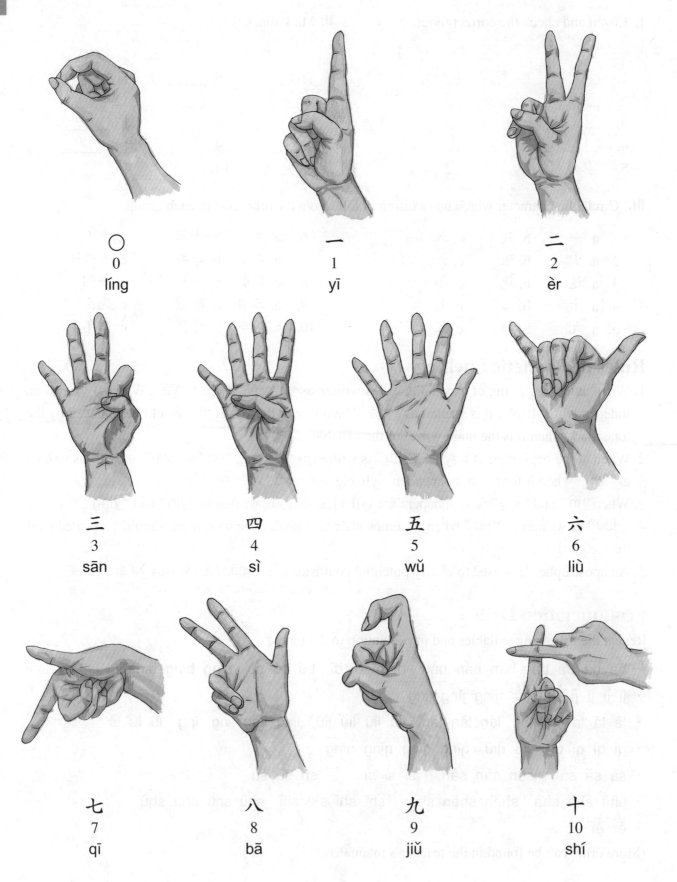

Chinese Numbers

0
líng

1
yī

二
2
èr

三
3
sān

四
4
sì

五
5
wǔ

六
6
liù

七
7
qī

八
8
bā

九
9
jiǔ

十
10
shí

0 = ○	10 = 十	20 = 二十	30 = 三十
1 = 一	11 = 十一	21 = 二十一	40 = 四十
2 = 二	12 = 十二	22 = 二十二	50 = 五十
3 = 三	13 = 十三	23 = 二十三	60 = 六十
4 = 四	14 = 十四	24 = 二十四	70 = 七十
5 = 五	15 = 十五	25 = 二十五	80 = 八十
6 = 六	16 = 十六	26 = 二十六	90 = 九十
7 = 七	17 = 十七	27 = 二十七	......
8 = 八	18 = 十八	28 = 二十八	......
9 = 九	19 = 十九	29 = 二十九	99 = 九十九

Notes

1. When "十" is in the middle of three syllables, it can be pronounced in the neutral tone.

2. For information on the Chinese writing system please refer to the Character Practice Guide.

Exercises

I. Circle the Numbers You Hear.

1.	10	20	30	40	50	60	70	80	90
2.	11	12	13	14	15	16	17	18	19
3.	11	22	33	44	55	66	77	88	99

II. Circle the Numbers You Hear.

1. 一　　二　　三　　四　　五　　六　　七　　八　　九　　十
2. 七　　四　　三　　五　　九　　二　　六　　八　　十　　一
3. 二十　三十　四十　五十　六十　七十　八十　九十
4. 十一　十二　十三　十四　十五　十六　十七　十八
5. 三十八　四十五　六十八　九十二　五十一　八十六
6. 七十七　二十四　八十五　三十一　六十九　四十三

III. Ball Game

Make up numbered cards, one for each student, such as 1-25, and distribute them to the students in your class. The teacher should also have a numbered card, which in this case would be number 26. The teacher can begin by saying, "我的26球碰5球" (Wǒ·de èrshí liù qiú pèng wǔ qiú; My #26 ball hits #5 ball), whereupon, the student holding number 5 card should immediately respond, "我的5球碰14球" (Wǒ·de wǔ qiú pèng shísì qiú; My #5 ball hits #14 ball), and so forth. Once students become familiar with the game, encourage them to play even faster. Any student who answers incorrectly or pronounces a number wrong must say the correct number five times.

Pronunciation Drill II

Repeat the following syllables and pay attention to the tones:

- dā dá dǎ dà dān dǎn dàn dāo dǎo dào dé děi dī dí dǐ dì diān diǎn diàn diāo diào diē dié dīng dǐng dìng diū dū dú dǔ dù duō duó duǒ duò
- gān gǎn gàn gāo gǎo gào gē gé gě gè gěi gū gǔ gù guāi guǎi guài guō guó guǒ guò
- kǎ kān kǎn kàn kǎo kào kē ké kě kè kū kǔ kù kuǎi kuài kuò
- ná nǎ nà nán nàn ·ne nèi ní nǐ nì nián niǎn niàn niǎo niào niē níng nǐng nìng niú niǔ niù nú nǔ nù nuò
- qiān qián qiǎn qiàn qiāo qiáo qiǎo qiào qiē qiě qiè
- shuō shāo shǎo shào shē shé shě shè shuāi shuǎi shuài
- xī xí xǐ xì xiān xián xiǎn xiàn xiāo xiǎo xiào xiē xié xiě xiè xīng xíng xǐng xìng xiū xiǔ xiù
- zhā zhá zhǎ zhà zhān zhǎn zhàn zhāo zháo zhǎo zhào zhē zhé zhě zhè zhī zhí zhǐ zhì zhū zhú zhǔ zhù zhuō zhuó zhuǎi zhuài

cf. jiān jiǎn jiàn jiāo jiǎo jiào jiē jié jiě jiè jī jí jǐ jì

(More drills can be found in the teacher's manual.)

Grammar

1-1 多少錢？   How much does it cost?

Explanation: When expressing amounts or quantities in Chinese, one must add the corresponding measure word after the number. For QW (question words) which serve to ask a specific number, the measure word after "多少" may be omitted.

A：多少 + N？   B：Nu + M + N。

A：多少 錢？   B：二十二塊 錢。

$ 500

$ 100

$ 50

$ 100

$ 10

$ 5

$ 50

$ 50

$ 10

$ 5

$ 1

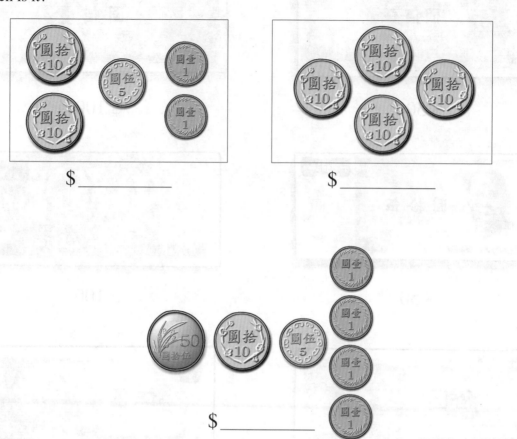

Exercises

How much is it?

$ _____

$ _____

$ _____

$ _____

$ _____

1-2 這個多少錢？　　How much is this?

Explanation: (1) In Chinese, the word order of questions containing QW is the same as that of the statements. By substituting a QW for the word or phrase in the statement to be asked about, the statement thereby becomes a question. (2) In the Chinese Sp-Nu-M pattern, if the number is 1, then it may be omitted. (3) When a sentence's predicate is an amount or quantity (to indicate price, age, date, time, etc.), then a verb is not needed, e.g. "我十八歲。" meaning "I am eighteen years old." and "今天二號。" meaning "It is the 2nd today."

A：(Sp + Nu + M) 多少　　錢？　　　B：　　Nu + 塊　錢。

　　 S　+　　多少+(M)+N ？　　　　　(S)+ Nu + M + (N)

A：這　　三　個　多少　　　錢？　　B：　　十八　塊　錢。

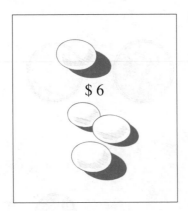

$ 6

$ 10

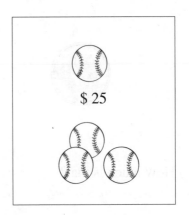

$ 25

$ 10

$ 18

$ 7

Aural Comprehension Drill

The following dialogues may contain some unfamiliar vocabulary. Do not be concerned if you have not yet learned the vocabulary or do not understand its meaning. Try to figure out the meaning from the context, then answer the questions.

Choose the correct answer.

1. (   ) Which picture best portrays the conversation?

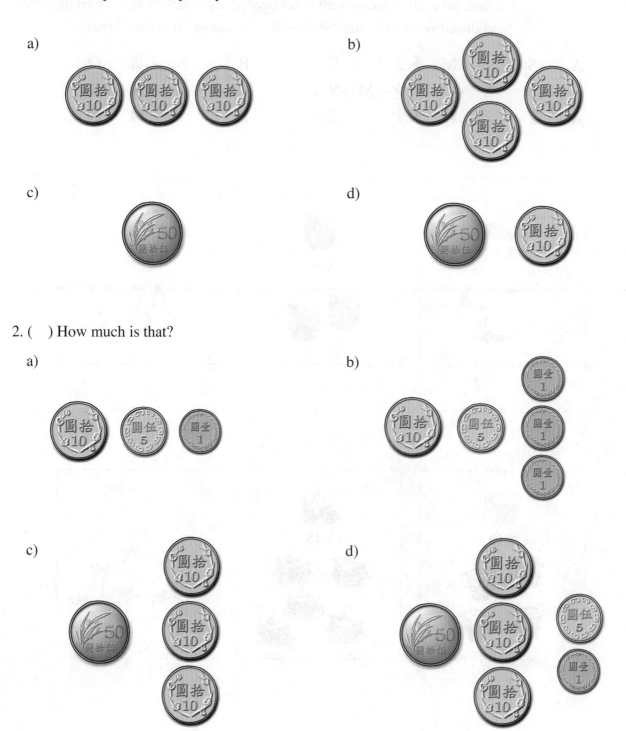

a)

b)

c)

d)

2. (   ) How much is that?

a)

b)

c)

d)

Dialogue II Buying from a Food Stand

A： 先生，你吃 什麼？
Xiān·sheng, nǐ chī shén·me?

B： 兩 個 包子、¹ 一 杯 茶。多少 錢？
Liǎng ·ge bāo ·zi, yì bēi chá. Duōshǎo qián?

A： 一共 四十 八 塊。
Yígòng sìshí bā kuài.

(B pays.)²

A： 謝謝。
Xiè ·xiè ·

Vocabulary

1. 先生　　xiān·sheng　　PN : Mr., Sir　　(M：wèi 位)

2. 你　　nǐ　　PN : you

*3. 我　　wǒ　　PN : I, me

*4. 他　　tā　　PN : he, him

*5. 她　　tā　　PN : she, her

*6. 您³　　nín　　PN : polite form of you　(你)

7. 吃　　chī　　V : to eat⁴

8. 什麼　　shén·me　　QW : what

A：你吃什麼？

B：我吃包子。

A: What do you eat?

B: I eat steamed buns.

9. 兩　　liǎng　　Nu : two

10. 包子　　bāo·zi　　N : steamed bun with meat or vegetable filling　　(M：個)

11. 杯　　bēi　　M/N : a cup of / cup

　　杯子　　bēi·zi　　N : cup　　(M：個)

12. 茶　　chá　　N : tea　　(M：杯)

13. 一共　　yígòng　　Adv : altogether

包子、茶，一共三十五塊錢。

steamed bun and tea, altogether $35.

14. 謝謝　　xiè·xiè　　IE : thanks

謝謝您。

Thank you.

Notes

1. "、" is used to separate noun phrases when they are mentioned successively.

2. In Taiwan, many cashiers say "收你 X 塊錢，找你 Y 塊錢。" (shōu nǐ X kuàiqián, zhǎo nǐ Y kuàiqián.) when receiving money from customers. What they are saying is: "I'm taking X dollars from you, and I should give you Y dollars change".

3. "您" is the polite form of "你". It is used to address people who are older or of a higher social rank. If it is for the sake of courtesy, "您" can also be used to address people of the same age. Nowadays, fewer young people are using "您" as a form of address.

4. There are no inflectional endings in Chinese. In other words, there are no endings to show tense, person, gender, number, or case. For example, "eat", "eats", "ate", "eating", and "eaten" are all "吃" in Chinese. Therefore, the word order is extremely important. A change in the word order can change the meaning of a sentence, and express various grammatical relationships.

Pronunciation Drill III

Repeat the following syllables and pay attention to the tones:

· chā chá chà   chān chán chǎn chàn   chāo cháo chǎo   chē chě chè   chén chèn chēng chéng chěng chèng   chī chí chǐ chì   chōng chóng chǒng chòng   chū chú chǔ chù   chuǎi chuài   chuō chuò

· mā má mǎ mà   mán mǎn màn   māo máo mǎo mào   méi měi mèi   mén mèn méng měng mèng   mī mí mǐ mì   mín mǐn   mián miǎn miàn   miáo miǎo miào miè   míng mìng   mō mó mǒ mò   mú mǔ mù

· tā tǎ tà   tān tán tǎn tàn   tāo táo tǎo tào   tè téng   tī tí tǐ tì   tiān tián tiǎn tiāo tiáo tiǎo tiào   tiē tiě tiè   tīng tíng tǐng tìng   tū tú tǔ tù   tuō tuó tuǒ tuò

· zā zá zán zàn   zāo záo zǎo zào   zé zè   zéi   zēn zěn zēng zèng   zī zǐ zì zōng zǒng zòng   zū zú zǔ   zuó zuǒ zuò

(More drills can be found in the teacher's manual.)

Grammar

2-1 你吃什麼？　　What do you eat?

Explanation: S + V + O is the most basic sentence pattern. "什麼" can function as a subject or an object.

Q：S　+　V + 什麼？　　　　A：S　+　V　+　O。

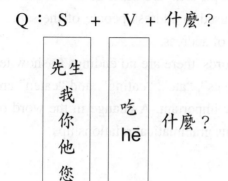

先生我你他您	吃 hē	什麼？

| 他你我他我 | 吃 hē | 包子
茶
miànbāo
niúnǎi
dàn'gāo
dòujiāng 。 |

2-2 一個包子多少錢？　　How much is one steamed bun?

Explanation: Nu + M + N can function as a subject.

Q：Nu + M　+　N　　多少錢？　　A：Nu + M + N　。

一	個	包子		
兩	杯	茶	多少錢？	$15
三	塊	dàn'gāo		$40
五	杯	niúnǎi		$60
				$75

Additional Vocabulary

hē(喝)：to drink　　　　miànbāo(麵包)：bread　　　　niúnǎi(牛奶)：milk

dàn'gāo(蛋糕)：cake　　　dòujiāng(豆漿)：soybean milk

2-3 我吃兩個包子。 I (will) eat two steamed buns.

Explanation: Nu + M + N can function as an object.

Q： S ＋ V＋什麼？ A： S ＋ V ＋Nu＋M＋N 。

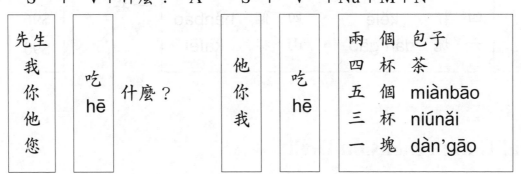

| 先生
我
你
他
您 | 吃
hē | 什麼？ | 他
你
我 | 吃
hē | 兩 個 包子
四 杯 茶
五 個 miànbāo
三 杯 niúnǎi
一 塊 dàn'gāo | 。 |

2-4 一共多少錢？ How much is the steamed bun and tea altogether?

Explanation: "一共" must be followed by a number to represent the total amount.

a) Q： N₁ ， N₂ 一共多少錢？ A：N₁, N₂ 一共 Nu＋M＋N。

包子 ， 茶		$35
niúnǎi ， dàn'gāo		$45
miànbāo ， dòujiāng	一共多少錢？ 一共	$60
dòujiāng ， 包子		$55
茶 ， miànbāo		$74

b) Q：Nu＋M ＋ N ， Nu＋M ＋ N 一共多少錢？

兩 杯 茶 ， 一 個 包子	
三 個 包子 ， 五 杯 茶	一共多少錢？
四 杯 kělè ， 四 個 hànbǎo	
六 塊 dàn'gāo ， 兩 杯 kāfēi	

Additional Vocabulary

hē(喝) : to drink　　　　miànbāo(麵包) : bread　　　　niúnǎi(牛奶) : milk

dàn'gāo(蛋糕) : cake　　　dòujiāng(豆漿) : soybean milk　　kělè(可樂) : cola

hànbǎo(漢堡) : hamburger　kāfēi(咖啡) : coffee

A：Nu + M + N 　　 , 　Nu +M + N 　　 一共　Nu + M + N 。

兩	杯	茶	,	一	個	包子		$32
三	個	包子	,	五	杯	茶	一共	$85
四	杯	kělè	,	四	個	hànbǎo		$96
六	塊	dàn'gāo	,	兩	杯	kāfēi		$90

Aural Comprehension Drill

The following dialogues may contain some unfamiliar vocabulary. Do not be concerned if you have not yet learned the vocabulary or do not understand its meaning. Try to figure out the meaning from the context, then answer the questions.

Listen to the following dialogues and choose the best answers.

1. (　) How much does one steamed bun cost?

    a) $10   b) $15   c) $20   d) $25

2. (　) How much is a cup of coffee and a sandwich?

    a) $24   b) $70   c) $74   d) $94

Additional Vocabulary

    kělè (可樂) : cola   hànbǎo (漢堡) : hamburger

    dàn'gāo (蛋糕) : cake   kāfēi (咖啡) : coffee

Variety Exercises

I. Connect the dots

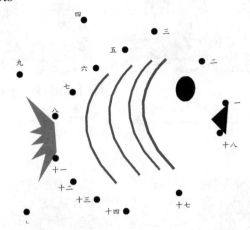

II. Complete the dialogues on the basis of the pictures given.

1.

小姐：____ ____，這個____ ____ ____？
先生：八十五____ ____。

2.

小姐：_____？　小姐：_____。　小姐：_____。
先生：一塊三十。　　　　先生：一共六十塊錢。

3.

先生：太太，你吃什麼？

B：＿＿＿＿＿＿。

　　＿＿＿＿＿＿？

先生：＿＿＿＿＿＿。

(B hands over the money.)

先生：＿＿＿＿＿＿。

4.

A：＿＿＿＿＿＿

B：＿＿＿＿＿＿

B：＿＿＿＿＿＿

III. Read each sentence or question. Circle the correct response.

1. 先生：多少錢？

　　小姐：a) 八十八塊。　　　b) 兩杯茶。　　　c) 謝謝。

2. 小姐：你吃什麼？

　　先生：a) 這個多少錢？　　b) 一個包子。　　c) 一共五十。

3. 先生：我吃一個，他吃三個。

　　小姐：a) 一共九十九塊錢。　　b) 一共多少錢？　　c) 你吃什麼？

IV. Role Play

One person is the customer and the other the store attendant. (Either the teacher or the students may decide upon the setting)

Authentic Material

Look at the picture and identify the characters.

A：老闆，兩個包子、一杯茶。

B：一共二十塊錢。

Can you guess what "元" means ?

Translation of the Dialogues

Dialogue I

A: Miss, how much is this?

B: Sixty dollars.

Dialogue II

A: Sir, what would you like to eat?

B: Two steamed buns and a cup of tea. How much is that?

A: Altogether forty-eight dollars.

   (B pays.)

A: Thank you.

第二課　買東西

LESSON 2　SHOPPING

Key Study Points

greetings／shopping／asking unit prices／bargaining／consulting／apologizing and politely refusing／absolutely rejecting

Vocabulary	Pronunciation	Grammar
Dialogue I	**Dialogue I**	**Dialogue I**
買，東西(東，西)，早，啊，太太，白菜(白，菜)，好吃(好)，嗎，斤，幾，要，給	**Initials**: c, h (ch, m, t, z, b, g, l, n, sh, x, d, j, k, q, s, zh) **Finals**: ai (ei, en, eng, iang, in, o, ong, a, ao, e, i, -i, ian, ie, an, er, iao, ing, iu, u, uai, uo)	S + SV 疑問助詞 - 嗎 QW 幾 (S) + V + IO + DO
Dialogue II	**Dialogue II**	**Dialogue II**
你們，我們，他們/她們，有，沒，日本，美國(國)，中國，車，對不起，不，賣，種，很，萬，千，百，零，太，了，貴，便宜，一點兒(點)，行	**Initials**: p, r (c, h, ch, m, t, z, b, g, l, n, sh, x, d, j, k, q, s, zh) **Finals**: ou, ui (ai, ei, en, eng, iang, in, o, ong, a, ao, e, i, -i, ian, ie, an, er, iao, ing, iu, u, uai, uo)	地名 + N (no "的") A - not - A S + neg + V + O S + adv + SV

Dialogue | In a Traditional Chinese Market

A：早 啊，太太[1]。你買 什麼？
　　Zǎo ·a, tài·tài. Nǐ mǎi shén·me?

B：白菜 好吃 嗎？一斤 幾 塊 錢？
　　Báicài hǎochī ·ma? Yì jīn jǐ kuài qián?

A：好吃，一斤 十七 塊 錢。你要 幾個？
　　Hǎochī, yì jīn shíqī kuài qián. Nǐ yào jǐ ·ge?

B：你 給 我 兩 個。
　　Nǐ gěi wǒ liǎng ·ge.

Vocabulary

1. 買　　mǎi　　V : to buy
　　　A：你買什麼？
　　　B：我買兩個包子。
　　　A: What do you buy?
　　　B: I buy two steamed buns.

2. 東西　　dōng·xi　　N : thing, object　　(M：個)
　　東　　dōng　　N : east
　　西　　xī　　N : west

3. 早　　zǎo　　IE : Good morning.
　　你早。
　　Good morning.

4. 啊　　·a　　P : ah, an exclamation

5. 太太　　tài·tài　　N : Mrs., wife

6. 白菜　　báicài　　N : Chinese cabbage
　　白　　bái　　SV : to be white
　　菜　　cài　　N : vegetable; dish, course

7. 好吃　　hǎochī　　SV[2] : to be delicious
　　好　　hǎo　　SV : to be good, nice, well, OK
　　1)你好[3]。
　　2)這個好。
　　1) Hello.
　　2) This one is good.

8. 嗎　　·ma　　P : question particle
　　那兩個包子好吃嗎？
　　Do those two steamed buns taste good?

9. 斤　　jīn　　M : catty, Chinese pound

10. 幾   jǐ   QW : how many

你買幾斤白菜？

How many catties of cabbage do you buy?

11. 要   yào   V/AV : to want; would like

1)他們要五杯茶。

2)我要吃包子。

1) They want five cups of tea.

2) I want to eat steamed buns.

12. 給   gěi   V : to give

Notes

1. "太太" is used to address a married woman, or a woman who is a stranger and appears to be married. When addressing a friend's wife, "X 太太" is used. "X" is the husband's family name.

2. SV stands for Stative Verb. Stative verbs are verbs which describe a quality or condition. A stative verb = to be + adjective, e.g. "他 (很) 好。" = "He is fine." When a SV is in a descriptive sentence, there is no need for another verb, which means that this SV is functioning as a verb. However, a SV can also be used to modify a noun, e.g. "好茶", good tea.

3. "你好" means "Hello", or "How do you do?", and it is used to greet people you meet for the first time, or have not seen each other for a long time. Another situation is answering phone calls at work places. Chinese people usually do not greet acquaintances by saying "你好"; they greet each other by commenting on what the other person is doing, e.g. "出去(chūqù)啊？" (Are you going out?), "回家啦 (huíjiā ·la)？" (Are you going home?), "上街(shàngjiē)啊？" (Going out?), etc. The speaker does not necessarily expect an extended answer. Usually a simple "是 (shì) 啊！" (Yes.) is considered satisfactory.

Pronunciation Drill 1

Repeat the following syllables and pay attention to their tones:

· cā   cāi   cái   cǎi   cài   cān   cán   cǎn   càn   cāo   cáo   cǎo   cào   cè   cēn   cén   céng

   cèng   cī   cí   cǐ   cì   cōng   cóng   cū   cù   cuō   cuò

· hā   hān   hán   hǎn   hàn   hái   hǎi   hài   háo   hǎo   hào   hē   hé   hè   hēi   hén   hěn   hèn

   hēng   héng   hèng   hōng   hóng   hǒng   huō   huó   huǒ   huò   hū   hú   hǔ   hù   huái   huài

(More drills can be found in the teacher's manual.)

Rules of Phonetic Spelling

"uei" is written as "ui" when preceded by an initial, and the tone mark is placed over "i", e.g. "guì". The dot on the top of "i" is replaced by the tone mark.

Grammar

1-1 早啊！   Good morning!

Explanation: In Chinese, apart from the use of "早" and "早啊" for morning greetings, "你好" may be used as a general greeting for the rest of the day.

A：早啊！太太。
B：早。

A：你好。
B：你好。

A：早，先生。
B：你好。

1-2a 白菜好吃嗎？   Does (your) cabbage taste good?

Explanation: (1) A subject plus a stative verb is one kind of the Chinese statement.(2) Statements with the ending particle "嗎" immediately turn the sentence into a yes/no question. This type of question carries with it the implication for affirmation. Replying by using the original sentence minus its "嗎" particle is considered standard. In the reply the subject is usually omitted. If the subject is a pronoun, it should be changed according to the situation.

A：   S   +   SV   +   嗎？   B：（S）+   SV。
A：   白菜   好吃   嗎？   B：   好吃。

茶
包子
hànbǎo
kāfēi

好
guì
hǎohē

嗎？

Additional Vocabulary

hànbǎo(漢堡)：hamburger   kāfēi （咖啡）：coffee

guì(貴)：expensive   hǎohē (好喝)：taste good (to drink)

1-2b 你買白菜嗎？　Do (Will) you buy any cabbage?

Explanation: In response to this type of question, one must, as in the above, use only the original statement without its "嗎". If the subject is a pronoun, it should be changed according to the situation. Sometimes people respond with "是的", "duì (對)" (right) "對了", "mm (嗯)", "bú duì(不對)" "bú shì(不是)" (no).

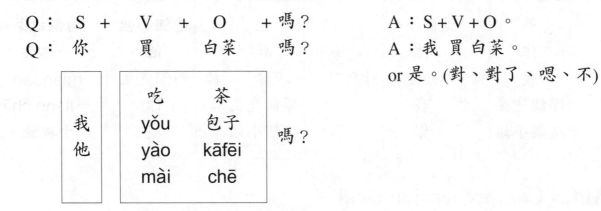

Q：S ＋ V ＋ O ＋嗎？　　　A：S＋V＋O。
Q：你 買 白菜 嗎？　　　A：我 買白菜。
　　　　　　　　　　　　　　or 是。(對、對了、嗯、不)

| 我 他 | 吃　　茶 yǒu　包子 yào　kāfēi mài　chē | 嗎？ |

1-3 QW 幾　　how many

Explanation: (1) The words "幾" and "多少" both request an amount or quantity; the appropriate measure words must be used after "幾". Generally speaking, amounts smaller than ten usually employ "幾", while greater amounts are used in conjunction with "多少". (2) When inquiring about prices, it is customary to add the respective item's measure word before the question word (QW).

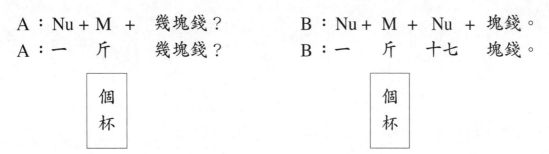

A：Nu ＋ M ＋ 幾塊錢？　　　B：Nu ＋ M ＋ Nu ＋ 塊錢。
A：一 斤 幾塊錢？　　　B：一 斤 十七 塊錢。

| 個 杯 | | 個 杯 |

Additional Vocabulary

yǒu(有) : to have　　　　yào(要) : to want to　　　　kāfēi(咖啡) : coffee
mài(賣) : to sell　　　　chē(車) : vehicle, car, automobile

1-4 給我兩個。　Give me two (of these).

Explanation: The verb 給 takes double objects.

(Nu+M+N)

Q：S　＋給＋　IO　＋什麼？　　A：S　＋給＋　IO　＋　　DO。

他 你 我 那個先生 這個小姐	給	這個小姐 他 那個先生 我 你	什麼？	他 我 你 那個先生 這個小姐	給	這個小姐 他 那個先生 你 我	兩個白菜 一杯茶 miànbāo 一 liàng chē 十塊錢

Aural Comprehension Drill

The following dialogues may contain some unfamiliar vocabulary. Do not be concerned if you have not yet learned the vocabulary or do not understand its meaning. Try to figure out the meaning from the context, then answer the question.

Choose the correct answer.

(　) What time of day does this dialogue take place?

   a) in the morning   b) at noon   c) in the evening

Additional Vocabulary

    miànbāo (麵包) : bread   liàng (輛) : M for vehicles

    chē (車) : vehicle, car, automobile

Dialogue II   Bargaining at the Car Dealership

A： 先生， 你們 有 沒有 日本 車？
　　Xiān·sheng,　　nǐ·men yǒu méiyǒu Rìběn chē?

B：對不起，我們 不賣 日本車。 這種　 美國車 很 好。
　　Duì·bùqǐ,　　wǒ·men bú mài Rìběn chē. Zhèizhǒng Měiguó chē hěn hǎo.

　　你要 不要 ？
　　Nǐ yào búyào?

A： 多少 錢？
　　Duōshǎo qián?

B：五十 九 萬　 九千 五百 塊。
　　Wǔshí jiǔ wàn　jiǔqiān wǔbǎi kuài.

A：太貴 了[1] ! 便宜 一點兒[2]，五十萬， 好 不好？
　　Tài guì ·le! 　Piányí yìdiǎnr,　　wǔshíwàn ,　hǎo bùhǎo ?

B：對不起，不 行。
　　Duì·bùqǐ,　　bù xíng.

Vocabulary

2

1. 你們[3]   nǐ·men   PN : you (pl.)

2. 我們   wǒ·men   PN : we, us

*3. 他們／她們

    tā·men   PN : to have

4. 有   yǒu   V : to have

他有錢。

He has money.

5. 沒   méi   Adv : not

你們有沒有錢？

Do you have any money?

6. 日本   Rìběn   N : Japan

7. 美國   Měiguó   N : U.S.A.

   國   guó   M/N : country

*8. 中國   Zhōngguó   N : China

9. 車   chē   N : car, vehicle   (M : liàng 輛)

他沒有日本車。

He does not have a Japanese car.

10. 對不起   duì·bùqǐ   IE : Excuse me.   Sorry.

11. 不   bù／bú[4]   Adv : not

我們不買美國白菜。

We do not buy any American cabbage.

12. 賣   mài   V : to sell

你們賣日本車嗎？

Do you sell Japanese cars?

13. 種   zhǒng   M : kind, variety, type

這種白菜好吃嗎？

Does this kind of cabbage taste good?

14. 很　　hěn　　Adv : very

白菜包子很好吃嗎？

Do cabbage steamed buns taste good?

15. 萬　　wàn　　Nu : ten thousand

16. 千　　qiān　　Nu : thousand

17. 百　　bǎi　　Nu : hundred

*18. 零　　líng　　Nu : zero

19. 太　　tài　　Adv : too

20. 了　　·le　　P : (often used after stative verbs, preceded by 太)

21. 貴　　guì　　SV : to be expensive

這種美國車太貴了。

This kind of American car is too expensive.

22. 便宜　　piányí　　SV : inexpensive

日本茶很便宜。

Japanese tea is cheap.

23. 一點兒　　yìdiǎnr　　Nu-M/Adv : a little

這個東西太貴。便宜一點兒，好嗎？

This thing is too expensive. A little cheaper, is it okay?

點　　diǎn　　N/M : dot, point

24. 行　　xíng　　SV : to be acceptable

A：你給我一百萬，行不行？

B：不行，我沒有錢。

A: Give me 1,000,000, okay?

B: I cannot. I do not have any money.

Notes

1. "太貴了。" When the particle "了" is at the end of a sentence like this one, it is always relevant to the moment when the sentence is spoken. If "太" is also used in the same sentence to form a pattern such as "太 SV 了", this "了" indicates the situation has reached a certain point which concerns the SV, e.g. "這個包子太貴了" means "This steamed bun is too expensive." i.e. the price of the steamed bun is higher than expected.

2. "一點兒。" "兒", er, is a retroflex final and is sometimes attached to another final, so that the syllable "er" is no longer independent. "r" is added to the final in Pinyin, and "兒" is added to the character in actual writing. However, "兒" is not commonly used in Taiwan and most southern parts of Mainland China.

3. "們" is a suffix, indicating plurality. It can be added to the end of a pronoun or, occasionally, to a noun which denotes more than one person. This plural noun refers to a certain group of people which is understood by the speaker and the listener. "們" cannot be used when the noun is preceded by a numeral or an intensifier, such as "兩個太太" (two wives) and "很多太太" (many wives).

4. The original pronunciation of "不" is a fourth tone, but when it is followed by another fourth tone it becomes a second tone. In natural or fast speaking, "不" is spoken neutral. This rule also applies to "一". The original tone of "一" is first tone, and this remains the case when it is used alone, as a number, or at the end of a phrase or a sentence. The tone of "一" changes to second tone when followed by a fourth tone. When "一" precedes a word with a first tone, second tone, or third tone, "一" is spoken as a fourth tone.

Pronunciation Drill II

Repeat the following syllables and pay attention to their tones:

- pā pá pà pāi pái pài pān pán pàn pāo páo pǎo pào pēi péi pèi pēn pén pēng péng pěng pèng pī pí pǐ pì piān pián piàn piāo piáo piǎo piào piē piě pīn pín pǐn pìn pīng píng pìng pō pó pǒ pò pōu póu pǒu pū pú pǔ pù
- rì rán rǎn ráo rǎo rào rě rè rén rěn rèn rēng réng róng rǒng róu rǒu ròu rú rǔ rù ruò ruí ruǐ ruì

(More drills can be found in the teacher's manual.)

Grammar

2-1 五十九萬九千五百塊　five hundred, ninety-nine thousand and five hundred dollars

Explanation: (1) "二" and "兩" both mean "2." Only "兩" should be used with a measure word. However, numbers containing "2" with two digits (i.e.12, 20, 22), should always use "二", regardless of whether or not it is used in conjunction with a measure word. (2) When reading numbers, any zero which appears before (to the left of) the smallest unit must be read. If more than one zeroes are present in continuing order in the number, then only one should be read.

100 = 一百	1000 = 一千	10000 = 一萬
101 = 一百零一	1001 = 一千零一	10012 = 一萬零一十二
111 = 一百一十一	1010 = 一千零一十	10200 = 一萬零兩百
120 = 一百二(十)	1100 = 一千一(百)	20000 = 兩萬
12000 = 一萬兩千(一萬二)	222222 = 二十二萬兩千兩百二十二	

Exercises

I. Dictation

_____ _____ _____ _____

_____ _____ _____ _____

II. 這個多少錢？

2-2 日本車　Japanese cars

Explanation: In Chinese, modifiers are always placed before the noun they modify, while "的" is placed between the modifier and its corresponding noun. However, whenever a place name (country, town, etc.) is used as the modifier, this "的" is omitted.

Q： S ＋V＋什麼＋N？ A： S ＋V＋ PW ＋ N。
你 買 什麼 車 ？ 我 買 美國 車。

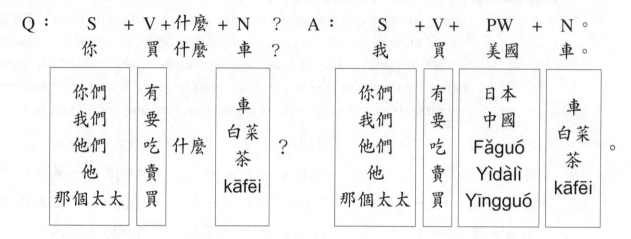

| 你們
我們
他們
他
那個太太 | 有
要
吃
賣
買 | 什麼 | 車
白菜
茶
kāfēi | ？ | 你們
我們
他們
他
那個太太 | 有
要
吃
賣
買 | 日本
中國
Fǎguó
Yìdàlì
Yīngguó | 車
白菜
茶
kāfēi | 。 |

2-3 你們有沒有日本車？　Do you have any Japanese cars?

Explanation: This type of question is referred to as a choice-type question (A-not-A) due to the fact that two possible forms of the predicate are presented, one affirmative and the other negative. Therefore, when using this type of question, the individual being questioned is given two choices, both of equal probability. When replying, the entire sentence may be used or simply its corresponding verb. (Including the stative verb.)

a)　Q： S ＋VnotV＋ (O) ？ A： S ＋ V ＋ O。
　　　　　　　　　　　　　　　　　　or　　not V
　　你 吃不吃 包子？ 我 吃 包子。

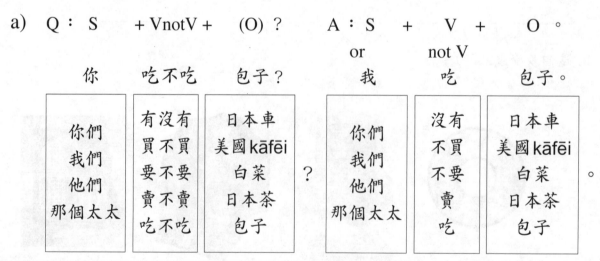

| 你們
我們
他們
那個太太 | 有沒有
買不買
要不要
賣不賣
吃不吃 | 日本車
美國kāfēi
白菜
日本茶
包子 | ？ | 你們
我們
他們
那個太太 | 沒有
不買
不要
不賣
不吃 | 日本車
美國kāfēi
白菜
日本茶
包子 | 。 |

Additional Vocabulary

kāfēi(咖啡)：coffee　　　　　Fǎguó(法國)：France

Yìdàlì(義大利)：Italy　　　　Yīngguó(英國)：England

b) Q：S + V not V + (O) ? A：(S) + V + (O) 。
　　　　　　　　　　　　　　　　　　　or　　 not V

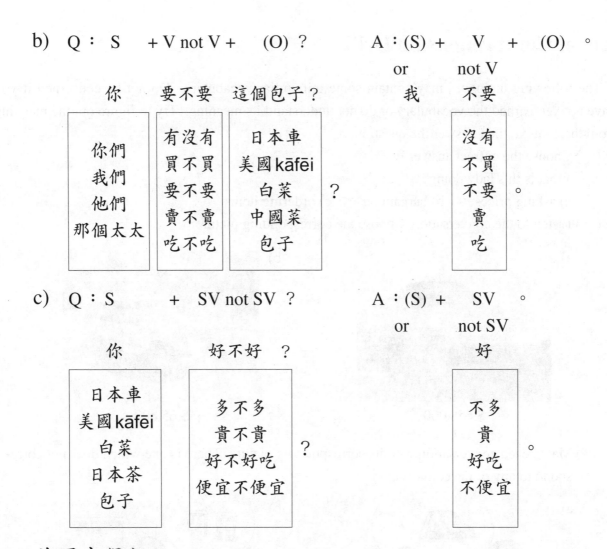

| 你 | 要不要 | 這個包子? | | 我 | 不要 |

b) boxes:

| 你們
我們
他們
那個太太 | 有沒有
買不買
要不要
賣不賣
吃不吃 | 日本車
美國kāfēi
白菜
中國菜
包子 ? | 沒有
不買
不要
賣
吃 |

c) Q：S + SV not SV ? A：(S) + SV 。
　　　　　　　　　　　　　　　　　or　 not SV

| 你 | 好不好 ? | | 好 |

c) boxes:

| 日本車
美國kāfēi
白菜
日本茶
包子 | 多不多
貴不貴
好不好吃
便宜不便宜 ? | 不多
貴
好吃
不便宜 |

2-4 美國車很好。　　American cars are good.

Explanation: When the predicate of an affirmative statement is a stative verb, it is customary to add the adverb "很" in front of the stative verb. Unless noticeably heavy inflection is added, the adverb "很" does not usually indicate "very".

Q：	S	+ SV + 嗎?	A：	S	+ 很 + SV 。
		or SV not SV			
	美國車	貴 嗎?		美國車	很 貴。
	你	好不好?		我	很 好。
	他們	好不好?		他們	很 好。
	Yīngguó 茶	hǎohē 嗎?		Yīngguó 茶	很 hǎohē。
	包子	好吃嗎?		包子	很 好吃。
	中國白菜	便宜嗎?		中國白菜	很 便宜。

Additional Vocabulary

　　kāfēi(咖啡) : coffee　　Yīngguó(英國) : England　　hǎohē(好喝) : taste good (to drink)

Aural Comprehension Drill

The following dialogues may contain some unfamiliar vocabulary. Do not be concerned if you have not yet learned the vocabulary or do not understand its meaning. Try to figure out the meaning from the context, then answer the question.

1. (   ) Choose the correct answer.

What is this lady doing?

a) asking prices   b) bargaining   c) ordering items

2. (   ) Listen to the conversation. Choose the corresponding picture.

a)

$ 658,000

b)

$ 65,800

3. (   ) Match each conversation with its corresponding picture. There is one which does not correspond to any of the conversations.

a)

b)

c)

d)

1. _____ 2. _____ 3. _____

Variety Exercises

I. What would you say?

1. If you are not careful and accidentally step on another person's foot, what would you say?

2. If someone gives you something to eat that you find delicious, how would you reply?

3. How would you greet people in the morning?

4. You would like to know how much a cup of coffee costs. How would you go about asking?

5. You would like to ask your father for a car. What should you say to him?

6. Your child asks for some candy, but you don't give it to her/him. What should you say in response?

7. Your friend wants to borrow something which you really do not wish to lend him. What should you say?

II. Role Play

One person plays the role of a store owner, the other a customer. The customer first asks prices of individual items/objects and afterwards begins to bargain.

Words you might need:

lǎobǎn (老闆) : store owner biǎo (錶) : watch yìtiáo qún·zi (一條裙子) : one skirt

yíjiàn chènshān (一件襯衫) : one shirt yìtiáo niúzǎikù (一條牛仔褲) : a pair of jeans

Try to Guess

1. ( ) What do you think "不三不四" means?

　　a) not three not four

　　b) incongruities in shape, appearance or manner

　　c) just a little bit

2. ( ) What do you think "三三兩兩" means?

　　a) in twos and threes

　　b) two threes and two twos

　　c) three groups of three and two groups of two

3. ( ) What do you think "零錢" means?

　　a) no money

　　b) small change

　　c) a loan

4. ( ) What do you think "萬一" means?

　　a) ten thousand and one

　　b) one ten thousandth

　　c) just in case; if by any chance

Authentic Material

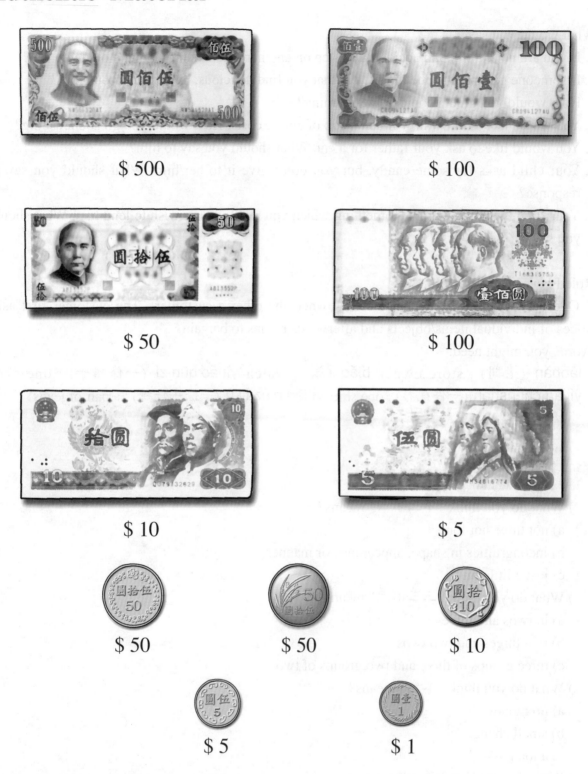

$ 500

$ 100

$ 50

$ 100

$ 10

$ 5

$ 50

$ 50

$ 10

$ 5

$ 1

1. Take a guess. How much money is this?

2. Do you know what "圓" means? What numbers do the characters "壹", "伍", "佰", "仟", and "拾" represent? What do the formal characters for the numbers 0,2,3,4,6,7,8 and 9 look like? What about that of "10000"?

Translation of the Dialogues

Dialogue I

A: Good morning, Ma'am. What would you like?

B: Does your cabbage taste good? How much per catty?

A: It's quite good. 17 dollars a catty. How many heads would you like?

B: Give me two heads.

Dialogue II

A: Sir, do you have any Japanese cars?

B: I'm sorry, we don't sell Japanese cars. This type of American car is good. Do you want it?

A: How much?

B: Five hundred, ninety-nine thousand and five hundred dollars.

A: That's too expensive! A little cheaper? Will five-hundred thousand be okay?

B: Sorry, that won't do.

第三課　付錢

LESSON 3 PAYMENT

Key Study Points

methods of payment ╱ polite refusal ╱ seeking an opinion ╱ telephone conversations ╱ counting ╱ names ╱ currency exchange ╱ decimal points

Vocabulary	Pronunciation	Grammar
Dialogue I	**Dialogue I**	**Dialogue I**
付，打折，可以，刷卡，收，信用卡，那麼，現金	**Initials**: f (p, r, c, h, ch, m, t, z , b, g, l, n, sh, x, d, j, k, q, s, zh) **Finals**: ua (ou, ui, ai, ei, en, eng, iang, in, o, ong, a, ao, e, i, -i, ian, ie, an, er, iao, ing, iu, u, uai, uo)	可以 那麼
Dialogue II	**Dialogue II**	**Dialogue II**
支票，噢，對了(對)，本，新，舊，書，來了(來)，給(CV)，打電話(打，電話)，的，號，是，姓，錢書宜，叫，不客氣(客氣)	no new ones	SV (的) N N + 的 + N N₁ + 是 + N₂ CV(給) + N + V + O N₁ 姓 N₂，N₁ 叫 N₂
Dialogue III	**Dialogue III**	**Dialogue III**
換，美金，台幣，點(point)，請，先，填表（填，表），張(M)，都，旅行支票(旅行)，等，一下，點(to count)	**Initials**:(f, p, r, c, h, ch, m, t, z , b, g, l, n, sh, x, d, j, k, q, s, zh) **Finals**: ang, ia, uan, ü (ua, ou, ui, ai, ei, en, eng, iang, in, o, ong, a, ao, e, i, -i, ian, ie, an, er, iao, ing, iu, u, uai, uo)	都 V 一下 Nu + M + (N) + 的 (+N)

Dialogue | Making Payments in a Store

A：一共 多少 錢？
　　Yígòng duōshǎo qián?

B：兩千 九百 五十塊。打八折[1]，兩千 三百六。
　　Liǎngqiān jiǔbǎi wǔshí kuài. Dǎ bā zhé, liǎngqiān sānbǎiliù.

A：可以刷卡 嗎？
　　Kěyǐ shuākǎ ·ma?

B：對不起，我們 不 收 信用卡。
　　Duì·bùqǐ, wǒ·men bù shōu xìnyòngkǎ.

A：那麼[2]，我 給你 現金。
　　Nà·me, wǒ gěi nǐ xiànjīn.

Vocabulary

3

1. 付   fù   V : to pay

你買這個東西，要付四千四百四十塊錢。

To buy this thing, you must pay $4,440.

2. 打折   dǎ//zhé[3]   VO[4] : to discount

1) A：這個打折嗎？

  B：這個不打折。

2) 一萬塊打七折，便宜多少？

1) A: Can this be discounted?

   B: This cannot be discounted.

2) How much cheaper is $10,000 with 30% off?

3. 可以   kěyǐ   Aux : may, can

你有錢。你可以買這種日本車。

You have money. You can buy this kind of Japanese car.

4. 刷卡   shuā//kǎ   VO : to pay with a credit card

我要買一杯茶。可以刷卡嗎？

I want to buy a cup of tea. Can I use a credit card?

5. 收   shōu   V : to receive

我收你三千五百塊錢。

I've received your $3,500.

6. 信用卡   xìnyòngkǎ   N : credit card   (M：zhāng 張)

你們收不收信用卡？

Do you accept credit cards?

7. 那麼   nà·me   Adv : then; in that case; that being the case

A：三千塊太貴了。

B：那麼，打八折，兩千四百。

A: Three thousand dollars is too expensive.

B: Then, with 20% off it is two thousand four hundred.

8. 現金   xiànjīn   N : cash

Notes

1. "打八折" means "to take 20% off." That is, only 80% of the price should be paid. Since "一折" is 10 %, if something is "三折", then only 30% of the price should be paid.

2. "那麼" means "in that case, then." Most people omit the second syllable "麼", as is very often practiced by young people in Taiwan nowadays.

3. "//" refers to separable VO compounds, i.e. there are word(s) that can be inserted into this "詞", e.g. a number can be inserted into "打折"—"打八折".

4. VO stands for verb-object compound. Some Chinese verbs are commonly associated with generalized objects, e.g. "睡覺"(shuì//jiào, to sleep), "唱歌"(chàng//gē, to sing), etc. They usually can be translated into a single English intransitive verb. Chinese verbs do not imply their object, as English verbs usually do. Therefore, the object of a verb must be expressed by the speaker, otherwise the listener will not understand. For example, "I want to eat" will be "我要吃飯 (chī//fàn)" in Chinese. If only "我要吃" is spoken, the listener will wonder what one wants to eat, unless there is a clear context. Another example: "I like to sing" will become "我喜歡唱歌 (Wǒ xǐhuān chànggē)" in Chinese. Without a context, it is incorrect to say "我喜歡唱".

Pronunciation Drill

Repeat the following syllables and pay attention to their tones:

· fā fá fǎ fà fó fēi féi fěi fèi fǒu fān fán fǎn fàn fēn fén fěn fèn fēng féng fěng fèng fū fú fǔ fù

· wā wá wǎ wà guā guǎ guà kuā kuǎ kuà huā huá huà zhuā zhuǎ shuā shuǎ

Grammar

1-1 可以刷卡嗎？   May I use a credit card?

Explanation: The "可以VP嗎？" question form carries with it an expression of seeking another individual's opinion or consultation. This may also be used with an affirmative-negative question. The correct response is often "可以", "可以啊", "不可以", or "不行". A negative answer may be prefaced with "對不起" for a softer, more polite feel.

Q：可以 + VP + 嗎？　　　　　A：(Neg) 可以。

or　可以不可以 + VP？

Q：可以　刷卡　嗎？　　　　　A：不　可以　　　　　。

| 便宜一點兒 |
| 吃東西 |
| 打七折 |
| 給我一杯茶 |

| 可以 |
| 可以啊 |
| 不行 |
| 對不起，不行 |
| 對不起，不可以 |

1-2 那麼，我給你現金。　　In that case, I will give you cash.

Explanation: "那麼" is an adverb used to bring in a sentence as a result of a previous utterance. After accepting the situation of the previous statement, the speaker may use this expression to put forward a consequential proposal.

A：對不起，我們不收信用卡。

B：那麼，＿＿＿＿＿＿＿＿。(現金)

A：這個不好吃。

B：那麼，＿＿＿＿＿＿＿＿。(那個)

A：一個七塊，三個二十塊。

B：那麼，＿＿＿＿＿＿＿＿。(三個)

A：對不起，我們沒有日本車。

B：那麼，＿＿＿＿＿＿＿＿？(美國車)

A：打七折，不行。

B：那麼，＿＿＿＿＿＿＿＿，好不好？(打八折)

Aural Comprehension Drill

The following dialogues may contain some unfamiliar vocabulary. Do not be concerned if you have not yet learned the vocabulary or do not understand its meaning. Try to figure out the meaning from the context, then answer the questions.

Listen to the question or statement, then circle the correct response.

1.(　) a) 對不起，不行。　　b) 對不起，沒有。　　c) 謝謝，很便宜。

2.(　) a) 你買什麼車？　　b) 你要買什麼？　　c) 那麼我給你打九折。

Dialogue II   Ordering Items in a Bookstore

A：你給我現金，給我支票[1]？
　　Nǐ gěi wǒ xiànjīn,　gěi wǒ zhīpiào?

B：我給你支票。噢[2]，對了[3]，那本新書來了[4]，給我打個
　　Wǒ gěi nǐ zhīpiào.　Òu,　duì·le,　nèiběn xīn shū lái·le,　gěi wǒ dǎ·ge

　　電話，可以嗎？
　　diànhuà,　kěyǐ ·ma?

A：好。你的電話幾號[5]？
　　Hǎo.　Nǐ·de diànhuà jǐ hào?

B：我的電話是三二六八四五七。我姓錢，我叫
　　Wǒ·de diànhuà shì sān èr liù bā sì wǔ qī.　wǒ xìng Qián, wǒ jiào

　　錢書宜[6]。謝謝。
　　Qián Shūyí.　Xiè·xiè.

A：不客氣[7]。
　　Bú kèqì.

Vocabulary

1. 支票   zhīpiào   N : check   (M：zhāng 張)

     我可以給你支票嗎？

     Can I give you a check?

2. 噢   òu   I : Oh! (indicating sudden realization)

     噢！你是錢書宜的太太。

     Oh! You are Qian Shuyi's wife.

3. 對了   duì·le   IE : by the way (indicating one has just thought of something)

     對了，你有車嗎？

     By the way, do you have a car?

   對   duì   SV : to be right, correct

     A：兩杯茶六十塊，對不對？

     B：對。

     A: Two cups of tea are $60, right?

     B: Right.

4. 本   běn   M : for books, magazines, etc.

     一本，兩本……一共二十本。

     One book, two books..., altogether 20 books.

5. 新   xīn   SV : to be new

     他要新車。我們沒有新車。

     He wants a new car. We do not have a new car.

*6. 舊   jiù   SV : to be old, used

     舊車便宜。他要買舊車。

     Used cars are cheap. He wants to buy a used car.

7. 書   shū   N : book   (M：本)

     一本書多少錢？

     How much is one book?

8. 來了   lái·le   V : to have come, to have been brought

     茶來了嗎？

     Has the tea been brought?

來　　　lái　V : to come

他要來台北。

He is coming to Taipei.

9. 給　　gěi　CV/V[8] : for; to give

10. 打電話　dǎ//diànhuà　VO : to make a phone call

他給我打電話。

He called me on the telephone.

打　　　dǎ　V : to hit

他不好，他打我。

He was not good; he hit me.

電話　　diànhuà　N : telephone

我沒有電話。

I do not have a telephone.

11. 的　　·de　P : suffix indicating modification

你們的美國車好不好？

How is your American car?

12. 號　　hào　N : number

你的車幾號？

What is your license plate number?

13. 是　　shì　V : be

1) 我的電話是2551249。

2) 他的新車是日本車。

1) My telephone number is 2551249.

2) His new car is a Japanese car.

14. 姓　　xìng　N/V : surname; be surnamed　(M：個)

1)「錢」是一個中國姓。

2) A：那個小姐姓什麼？

　　B：那個小姐姓錢。

1) "Qian" is a Chinese surname.

2) A: What is that lady's surname?

　　B: That lady is surnamed Qian.

15. 錢書宜　　Qián Shūyí　　Proper N : a Chinese name

16. 叫　　　jiào　　V : to be called, named

A：那個先生叫什麼？

B：他叫書宜。

A: What is that man's name?

B: He is called Shuyi.

17. 不客氣　　bú kèqì　　IE : You are welcome.

A：謝謝。

B：不客氣。

A: Thank you.

B: You are welcome.

客氣　　　kèqì　　SV : to be courteous, to stand on ceremony

我給他書。他謝謝我。他很客氣。

I gave him a book. He thanked me. He was very polite.

Notes

1. "支票" are personal checks. People in Taiwan prefer to make transactions in cash. They use checks primarily when doing business or dealing with large sums of money.

2. "噢" is an interjection, indicating sudden realization or understanding.

3. "對了" is used independently with a comma to separate it from the rest of the sentence, indicating something has suddenly come to the speaker's mind. This indicates the speaker possibly wants to change the subject and ask for the listener's attention.

4. "書來了" means "When the book arrives, or when the book is here." "來" means to come or to get closer to the speaker. "了" is used at the end of the sentence, indicating change of status. Therefore "來了" means the subject is here, or is coming.

5. "你的電話幾號？" The verb of this sentence "是" is omitted, because the predicate of the sentence is expected to be a number, and it is not necessary to have a verb in this kind of sentence. It is also correct to say "你的電話多少號？"

6. "我叫錢書宜" means "My name is Qián Shūyí." In Chinese the surname is put before the given name. Given names may either be one or two syllables. In this case, Qián is the surname, and Shūyí is the given name. When Chinese parents or grandparents choose a name for a child, they select characters which express their expectations for the child or their aspirations of his future. However, given names are usually only used by one's family members and close friends. It is not considered polite to use someone's full name. It is better to call someone by "X 先生" or "X 小姐" if they are not familiar.

7. "不客氣" is used to respond to "謝謝". It is also acceptable to respond to "謝謝" with "不謝", which means there is no need to say thanks.

8. "CV" stands for "Coverb". A coverb always takes a verbal object and is put before the main verb to provide a setting for the action taking place. A coverb phrase usually functions as an English prepositional phrase, e. g. 我給你打電話。他跟我說對不起。我用信用卡付錢。

Pronunciation Drill II

Repeat the following words and pay attention to their tones:

1. ˅ – (third tone & first tone)

   měitiān huǒchē hǎochī jǐjiān shǒudū Běijīng lǎoshī pǔtōng hǎibiān jiǔbēi dǎzhēn jiǎngshū

2. ˅ ˊ (third tone & second tone)

   bǎipíng yǐqián liǎngtiáo jiǎnzhí zhǎoqián běnlái yǒumíng jiǎnchá xiǎohái Běipíng qiǎnlán mǎixié

3. ˅ ˅ (two third tones)

   bǎoxiǎn běihǎi shuǐguǎn dǎsǎo diǎnhuǒ zǎowǎn gǎnjǐn liǎnglǐ zhǐyǒu kěyǐ shuǐguǒ suǒyǐ

4. ˅ ˋ (third tone & fourth tone)

   yǐhòu jǐhào wǔhuì chǎocài hǎoxiàng kǒngpà fǎnzhèng kǎoshì lěngrè cǎomào wǎnfàn běndì

5. neutral tones

   – · wū·zi tiān·qi dāo·zi shū·fu xiū·xi dōng·xi qīng·chu xīn·li

   ˊ · lái·ba xíng·li shén·me chuán·shang hái·zi má·fan bié·de tíng·le

   ˅ · yǐ·zi xiǎo·de jiǎo·zi zǎo·shang kě·shi wǒ·men liǎng·ge zěn·me

   ˋ · xiè·xie yàng·zi lì·hai nèi·ge dì·fang yào·shi qì·hou kè·qi diào·le

Grammar

2-1 新書　　a new book

Explanation: The structural particle "的" is placed after the noun modifier in a phrase or sentence. However, if the modifier is a monosyllabic adjective, then "的" may be omitted. It can likewise be retained, especially if one wishes to place emphasis on the noun.

Q：S　　　　　+ Adv+ SV ，　　……？　　　　A：……SV (的) N……。

這 liàng(輛) 車	不	便宜。	你買不買？	我不要買貴的車。我沒有錢。
那本書	很	舊。	你要嗎？	我不要_____。
他的車	很	新。	貴不貴？	他的_____很貴。
這種茶	很	好。	多少錢？	那種_____，一斤兩千塊錢。
這個菜	很	好吃。	你要不要？	好，給我那個_____。

2-2 你的電話幾號?　　What is your telephone number?

Explanation: "的" as a possessive marker must not be omitted (unless referring to family relationship, cf. L.4,2-3).

Q：這是 shéi(誰)的書？　　　　　　A：那是_____。
　　那是 shéi(誰)的車？　　　　　　　　那是_____。
　　shéi(誰)有好茶？　　　　　　　　_____很好。
　　shéi(誰)的包子好吃？　　　　　　_____好吃。

> 錢太太的書　我的書　那個小姐的書　我先生的車
> 他們的車　這個先生的茶　我們的茶
> 錢小姐的茶　他的包子　我太太的包子

Additional Vocabulary

　　liàng(輛)：M for vehicles　　　shéi(誰)：who, whom

2-3 我的電話是三二一〇四五七。 My telephone number is 3210457.

Explanation: The character "是" is used to show that the preceding and following words are related in classification or equivalence. The focus of the sentence is the information following the character "是". Sentences with "是" can only use "不" as a negative. The subject can be a noun, verb, phrase, or clause.

Q： N₁ + 是 + QW + N₂ ？   A： N₁ + 是 +   N₂   。

你的電話 是 幾號 ？   我的電話 是 三二六八四五七。

他的車   什麼車   他的書   美國車

我的書 是 什麼書 ？   你的書 是 新書   。

那杯茶   什麼茶   這杯茶   日本茶

2-4 我姓錢。我叫錢書宜。 My last name is Qian. My full name is Qian Shuyi.

Explanation: (1) The word order used for Chinese names is surname first followed by given name. When used together with status nouns such as Mr., Mrs., Miss, etc., then the surname should be placed in front of them, e.g. 王太太. (2) "叫" can be used to introduce one's full name or given name.

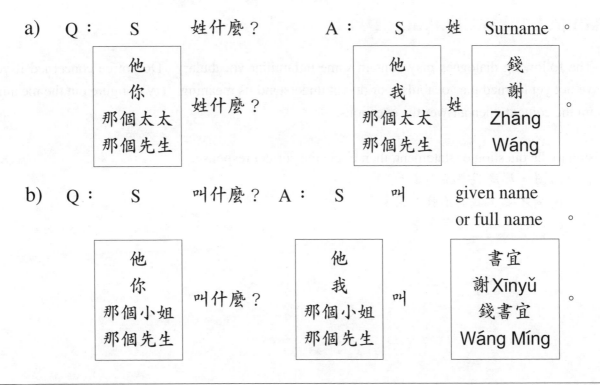

a) Q： S 姓什麼？   A： S 姓 Surname 。

他
你
那個太太   姓什麼？
那個先生

他
我   姓   錢
那個太太   謝
那個先生   Zhāng
                 Wáng

b) Q： S 叫什麼？ A： S 叫 given name or full name 。

他
你
那個小姐   叫什麼？
那個先生

他
我   叫
那個小姐
那個先生

書宜
謝 Xīnyǔ
錢書宜
Wáng Míng

Additional Vocabulary

Zhāng (張) : a Chinese surname   Wáng (王) : a Chinese surname

Xīnyǔ (新雨) : a Chinese given name   Wáng Míng (王明) : a Chinese name

2-5 給我打電話　　to give me a call

Explanation: The coverb "給" is used to indicate the recipient of an action.

Q： S　　　　給 QW　　　　VP　　　？
謝先生　　給 shéi(誰)　　打電話　　？

錢太太		
那個小姐	給 shéi(誰)	買一本書
你們		打八折

?

A： S　　　給　　　N　　＋　VP　　　。
謝先生　　給　　我　　　打電話　。

錢太太		Wáng 小姐	買一本書
那個小姐	給	他	打八折
我們		謝先生	

。

Aural Comprehension Drill

The following dialogues may contain some unfamiliar vocabulary. Do not be concerned if you have not yet learned the vocabulary or do not understand its meaning. Try to figure out the meaning from the context, then answer the questions.

Listen to the question or statement, then circle the correct response.

1. (　) a) 好，那麼我要換美金。
　　　b) 對不起，我們不收支票。
　　　c) 不行，我們沒有支票。

Additional Vocabulary

　　shéi(誰) : who, whom　　　Wáng(王) : a Chinese surname

Dialogue III Exchanging Currencies in a Bank

A： 先生，我要 換 五百美金。一塊 美金多少台幣？
Xiān·sheng, wǒ yào huàn wǔbǎi Měijīn. Yí kuài Měijīn duōshǎo Táibì?

B：二十七點 五。請 先 填表，這 兩 張 都要[1] 填。
Èrshí qī diǎn wǔ. Qǐng xiān tián biǎo, zhè liǎng zhāng dōu yào tián.

(A fills out the forms)

A： 請 給我四 張 一百的旅行支票，五 張 二十的現金。
Qǐng gěi wǒ sì zhāng yìbǎi ·de lǚxíng zhīpiào, wǔ zhāng èrshí ·de xiànjīn.

B： 好。請 等 一下。 (給錢) 請 點 一下。
Hǎo. Qǐng děng yíxià.   Qǐng diǎn yíxià.

Vocabulary

1. 換　　huàn　　V : to exchange

　　這本書不好。我要換一本。

　　This book is not good. I want to exchange it.

2. 美金　　Měijīn　　N : US Dollar　　(M：塊)

3. 台幣　　Táibì　　N : (New) Taiwan Dollar　　(M：塊)

4. 點　　diǎn　　N : point (decimal point)

5. 請　　qǐng　　V : to please

　　請給我兩本美國書。

　　Please give me two American books.

6. 先　　xiān　　Adv : first, to be the first (in doing something)

　　我沒有一千塊。先給你八百，好不好？

　　I do not have $1,000. I'll give you $800 first, okay?

7. 填表　　tián//biǎo　　VO : to fill in a form

　　填　　tián　　V : to fill in

　　表　　biǎo　　N : form　　(M：zhāng 張)

　　我要換錢。要填什麼表？

　　I want to exchange money. Which form should I fill in?

8. 張　　zhāng　　M : sheet (for a form, paper, etc.)

　　你要幾張表？

　　How many forms do you want?

9. 都　　dōu　　Adv : all, both

　　美金、台幣，我都有。

　　US dollars, (New) Taiwan dollars, I have both.

10. 旅行支票　　lǚxíng zhīpiào　　V : traveler's check　　(M：張)

　　旅行　　lǚxíng　　V/N : to travel; travel, traveling

11. 等   děng   V : to wait

他要來。我要等他。

He will come. I want to wait for him.

12. 一下   yíxià   一-M : a moment

錢小姐，請你等一下。

Miss Qian, please wait a moment.

13. 點   diǎn   V : to count

這是兩千五百塊。請你點一下。

This is $2,500. Please count it.

Note

1. "要" can mean: must; should; ought to; have to; to need; to demand; to require, etc. "這兩張都要填" means "You should fill in both of these two (forms)." Other examples are:

a. "打一個電話要一塊錢。" It costs one dollar to make a phone call. (Literally: Making a phone call needs one dollar.)

b. "從這裡到那裡要十分鐘。" (Cóng zhèlǐ dào nàlǐ yào shí fēnzhōng.) It takes ten minutes to get there. [Literally: From here to there, (it) needs ten minutes.]

c. "每個學生都要做功課。" (Měi ·ge xuéshēng dōu yào zuò gōngkè .) Every student is required to do his/her homework. Or: Every student should do homework.

Pronunciation Drill III

Repeat the following syllables and pay attention to their tones:

· yū yú yǔ yù   yuē yuè   yuān yuán yuǎn yuàn   yūn yún yǔn yùn

· lǔ lǜ lüè nǚ   nüè   jū jú jǔ jù   juē jué juè   juān juǎn juàn   jūn jùn

· qū qú qǔ qù   quē què   quān quán quǎn quàn   qún

· xū xú xǔ xù   xuē xué   xuě xuè   xuān xuán xuǎn xuàn   xūn xún xùn

· duān duǎn duàn   tuān tuán   nuǎn   luán luǎn luàn   zuān zuǎn zuàn   cuān cuán cuàn   suān suàn   zhuān zhuǎn zhuàn   chuān chuán chuǎn chuàn   shuān shuàn ruǎn   guān guǎn guàn   kuān kuǎn   huān huán huǎn huàn

· wēn wén wěn wèn   dūn dǔn dùn   tūn tún tùn   lūn lún lùn   zūn cūn cún cǔn cùn   sūn sǔn   zhūn zhǔn   chūn chún chǔn   shǔn shùn   rùn   gǔn gùn   kūn kǔn kùn   hūn hún hǔn hùn

(More drills can be found in the teacher's manual.)

Rules of Phonetic Spelling

1. "ü" is written as "yu" when it is at the beginning of a syllable or forms a syllable by itself, as "yú" in "chī yú" (to eat fish).

2. When "ü" appears after "j", "q", or "x", "ü" is written as "u", with the two dots omitted, e.g. "qù" (to go) and "xuéxí" (to study).

3. "uen" is written as "un" when it is preceded by an initial, as "cún" in "cún qián" (to save money).

Grammar

3-1 這兩張都要填。 Both of these forms need to be filled in.

Explanation: (1) "都" as an adverb indicates totality, referring to the preceding noun or pronoun. (2) If the noun(s) which "都" modifies happens to be the object of the sentence, then this object must be moved forward to its correct place before "都".

a)   Q：QW nǎ (哪) +M+(N) + VP   ?   A：   N (pl.)   + 都 + VP 。
or   QW什麼、shéi (誰)

什麼	好吃	包子、hànbǎo	好吃
Shéi (誰)	要來	謝小姐、錢小姐	要來
Nǎ (哪)本書	便宜 ?	這三本書	都 便宜 。
Nǎ (哪)張表	要填	那兩張表	要填
Nǎ (哪) liàng (輛)車	貴	我的車、他的車	貴

Additional Vocabulary

hànbǎo (漢堡) : hamburger   shéi (誰) : who, whom   nǎ (哪) : what, which
liàng (輛) : M for vehicles

b)   Q：   S ＋ V ＋   QW   ?

           or   QW nǎ (哪) ＋M＋(N)

	給	shéi (誰)
你	有	什麼
他們	要填	nǎ (哪) 張 表 ？
我	買	nǎ (哪) 本 書
	要點	什麼

       A：   N(pl.)   ＋   (S) ＋都＋ VP 。

錢先生、錢太太			給
包子、茶	你		有
那五張表	他們	都	要填。
這六本	我		買
現金、支票			要點

3-2 等一下   to wait a moment

Explanation: "V 一下" has the pattern of V ＋ Nu ＋ M. However, in this chapter, Nu is limited to use only with "一". "一下" placed behind the verb indicates a brief action in addition to a more relaxed tone.

Please complete the following sentences:

1) A：可以給我一杯茶嗎？

    B：好，請_____。

2) 這是三萬塊，請_____。

3) 我要給你一本書。你_____。

4) 這兩張表請_____。

5) 我要中國茶。這杯不是中國茶。請_____。

點一下   來一下   等一下   換一下   填一下

Additional Vocabulary

     shéi (誰)：who, whom   nǎ (哪)：what, which

3-3 四張一百的旅行支票　　four $100 traveler's checks

Explanation: Nu + M + (N) is also a kind of noun modifier form. If the noun in a question is already known, then it may be omitted.

Q：　　S　　+　V +　Nu+M+(N) + 的 + (N) ？　　Nu+M+(N) + 的 + (N) ？
　　　　你　　　要　　　五十塊　　　的　美金 ？　　　二十塊　　　的　美金 ？

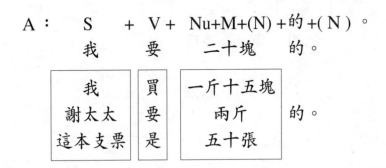

A：　　S　　+　V +　Nu+M+(N) + 的 + (N) 。
　　　　我　　　要　　　二十塊　　　的 。

Aural Comprehension Drill

The following dialogues may contain some unfamiliar vocabulary. Do not be concerned if you have not yet learned the vocabulary or do not understand its meaning. Try to figure out the meaning from the context, then answer the questions.

Listen to the question or statement, then circle the correct response.

1. (　) a) 二十七點七　　　b) 二十七點七十　　　c) 二十七點七個
2. (　) a) 對，謝謝。　　　b) 便宜一點兒，好嗎？　　　c) 可以打幾折？

- 60 -

Variety Exercises

I. Game:

Every student is given two cards. On one, students should write down a fixed price (numbers must be rounded off to the nearest ten), on the other, everyone should write a discount percentage. All cards are then separated into two corresponding bags, boxes, etc. Students and teachers then take turns drawing one card from each bag respectively. The teacher begins by asking "＃塊打＃折，多少錢？". Students should then reply with "＃塊打＃折，＃塊。". Students can also form teams and compete. In this case, divide the class into two groups. As the teacher selects cards from the bag, the first team to answer correctly gets a point. Time students to see which team gets the highest score within, say, five or ten minutes. When the time is up, the team with the most points wins. Either the teacher or an appointed student must keep the score. Once students get the hang of it, the teacher may let them play entirely on their own.

II. Questions and Answers

　1. 白菜一斤二十塊錢。打九折，多少錢？

　2. 包子一個十塊錢，買十個打八五折。我買二十個，一共多少錢？

　3. 一個東西一千塊。打三折，多少錢？

III. What would you say?

　1. Someone says "謝謝" to you. How should you respond?

　2. You would like to ask someone's telephone number. How should you phrase the question?

IV. Listening and Speaking

　1. A 問 B (A asks B)：你有電話嗎？

　　B：有／沒有。

　　全班問 A (entire class asks A)：他有電話嗎？

　　A：有／沒有。

　　A 問 B (A asks B)：你的電話幾號？

　　B：我的電話是＃。

　　全班問 A (entire class asks A)：他的電話幾號？

　　A：他的電話是＃。

2. A 對 B (A says to B)：我姓＿＿＿＿。你姓什麼？

B：我姓＿＿＿＿。我叫＿＿＿＿＿＿＿。

或 or

A 問 B (A asks B)：你姓什麼？

B：我姓＿＿＿＿。你姓什麼？

A：我姓＿＿＿＿。

A 問 B (A asks B)：你叫什麼？

B：我叫＿＿＿＿＿＿＿。你叫什麼？

A：我叫＿＿＿＿＿＿＿。

V. Role Play

You go to a bank to exchange some money. Act out a dialogue between yourself and the bank teller.

VI. Activities

1. Have students get up and walk around the classroom, using the dialogues given in **IV** & **V** above and getting to know their classmates and asking their phone numbers. Set a ten-minute limit. When the time is up, see who has met the most new people.

2. True-False

Divide students into two or more groups. Once the groups are formed, start with one person from each group and move down the line, having each classmate loudly and clearly ask one true/false question in turn. If the answer is true, then the team who has the same answer gets a point. Likewise, if the answer is false, only that team who answers so receives a point. As an added bonus, those classmates who are able to provide the correct answer to false questions will be awarded two points. At the same time, if one team answers incorrectly, the opportunity immediately goes to the opposing side. If there are only two teams participating, then move on to the next question.

Authentic Material

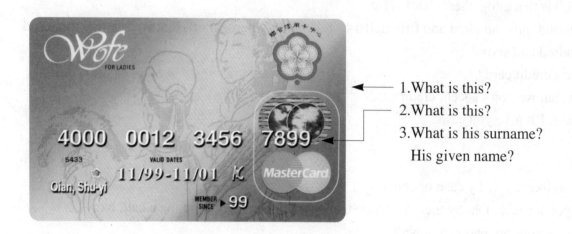

1. What is this?
2. What is this?
3. What is his surname?
   His given name?

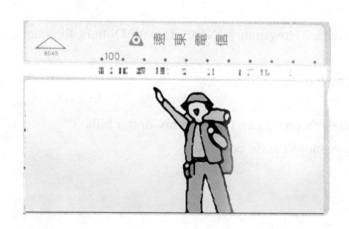

1. What is this?
2. Does a phone card have a serial number?

大東圖書公司
經理　王永強
台北市自強路二段六十六之一號
電話：（02）27128740

1. 他姓什麼？叫什麼？
2. 他的電話幾號？

Translation of the Dialogues

Dialogue I

A: How much is that altogether?

B: Two thousand, nine hundred and fifty dollars. Take twenty percent off, that will be two thousand, three hundred and sixty.

A: Can I use a credit card?

B: I'm sorry, but we don't accept credit cards.

A: In that case, I'll give you cash.

Dialogue II

A: Would you like to pay by cash or check?

B: I'll give you a check. Oh, by the way, when that new book arrives, give me a call, okay?

A: Sure, what's your telephone number?

B: My number is 3268457. My last name is Qian. My full name is Qian Shuyi. Thank you.

A: You're welcome.

Dialogue III

A: Sir, I would like to exchange 500 US Dollars. How many (New) Taiwan Dollars for one US Dollar?

B: Twenty-seven point five. Please first fill in both of these forms.
   (A fills out the forms)

A: Please give me four one-hundred dollar traveler's checks and five twenty-dollar bills.

B: Okay. One moment please. (B hands A the money) Please count it.

第四課 打電話約時間

LESSON 4

MAKING PHONE CALLS AND APPOINTMENTS

Key Study Points

making phone calls ∕ answering the phone ∕ dialing the wrong
number ∕ setting the time ∕ making an appointment

<table>
<tr><td><u>Vocabulary</u></td><td><u>Grammar</u></td></tr>
<tr><td>Dialogue I</td><td>Dialogue I</td></tr>
<tr><td>約，時間，喂，請問，謝美宜
(謝)，老師，在，誰，人，這
裡，那裡，打錯了(錯)</td><td>QW誰

PN∕N＋這裡</td></tr>
<tr><td>Dialogue II</td><td>Dialogue II</td></tr>
<tr><td>張台生(張)，哪，位，想，請(to
invite)，到，家，吃飯(飯)，
做，今天(天)，明天，昨天，晚
上，上午(早上)，中午，下午</td><td>QW哪
NP＋VP₁＋VP₂
PN∕N＋N ("的"omitted)
到＋PW＋來∕去＋V(O)
我想＋句子 (sentence)</td></tr>
<tr><td>Dialogue III</td><td>Dialogue III</td></tr>
<tr><td>就，去，看，什麼時候(時候)，
星期四(星期，星期天，星期
一，星期二，星期三，星期五，
星期六)，有空，事，呢，忙，
下(個)，上(個)，兩點半(點，
半)，分，再見(再，見)</td><td>QW什麼時候
Time - When ＋ VP
呢</td></tr>
</table>

Dialogue | Dialing the Wrong Number

A：喂，請問[1]，謝老師[2]在不在？
Wéi, qǐngwèn, Xiè lǎoshī zài búzài?

B：誰？
Shéi?

A：謝美宜老師。
Xiè Měiyí lǎoshī.

B：對不起，沒有 這個 人。
Duì·bùqǐ, méiyǒu zhèi·ge rén.

A：你那裡[3]是不是三 九五六八二五？
Nǐ nàlǐ shì búshì sān jiǔ wǔ liù bā èr wǔ?

B：不是，你打錯 了。
Búshì, nǐ dǎ cuò ·le.

A：對不起。
Duì·bùqǐ.

Vocabulary

1. 約   yuē   V : to make an appointment

   我可以約錢小姐來嗎？

   May I ask Miss Qian to come?

2. 時間   shíjiān   N : time

3. 喂   wéi[4]   P : a common telephone greeting "hello"

4. 請問   qǐngwèn   IE : May I ask...?

   請問，我可以付旅行支票嗎？

   May I ask, can I use a traveler's check?

5. 謝美宜   Xiè Měiyí   N : a Chinese full name

   謝   Xiè   N : a Chinese surname

6. 老師   lǎoshī   N : teacher   (M：wèi 位、個)

   謝老師是一個好老師。

   Teacher Xie is a good teacher.

7. 在   zài   V/CV : be in, at, on

   錢先生在美國。

   Mr. Qian is in America.

8. 誰   shéi   QW : who, whom

   你的老師是誰？

   Who is your teacher?

9. 人   rén   N : person, people   (M：個)

   錢小姐是美國人。

   Miss Qian is American.

10. 那裡   nàlǐ   N : there

    錢老師不在那裡。

    Teacher Qian is not there.

*11. 這裡   zhèlǐ   N : here

    他們都在這裡。

    They are all here.

12. 打錯了　　dǎ cuò ·le　　IE : wrong number

　　錯　　　　cuò　　　　SV : to be wrong

　　　　A：六百塊打八折是四百六嗎？

　　　　B：錯了，是四百八。

　　　　A: Is $460 20% off $600?

　　　　B: Wrong, it is $480.

Notes

1. "請問" means "Could you please tell me....", or "May I ask...." It is a polite way to ask a question about direction or information.

2. Chinese often address to each other by their surnames and titles.

3. "那裡" means the same as "那兒" (nàr), and "這裡" means the same as "這兒" (zhèr). People in northern China usually say "這兒" and "那兒", whereas "這裡" and "那裡" are common in the south. "裡" is the same as "裏", only "裡" is written horizontally and "裏" is written vertically, because both "裡" and "裏" are composed of "衣" and "里".

4. "喂" is originally pronounced with a fourth tone, but when it is used to greet people on the phone, the tone is raised to a second tone.

Grammar

1-1 誰？　　Who? Whom?

Explanation: "誰" is the interrogative word used for people, generally corresponding to "who" or "whom".

a)　Q： S ＋V＋誰 ？　　A： S ＋V＋ N 　　。

你 他 錢老師	約 請 是	誰？

我 他 錢老師	約 請 是	謝美宜 我先生 他的 Zhōngwén 老師

。

b)　Q：誰 ＋ VP ？　　A： NP ＋ VP 。

誰	有錢 在那裡 要來	？

錢太太 他們 我	有錢 在那裡 要去

。

Additional Vocabulary

　　Zhōngwén (中文) : Chinese language

c) 　Q：　S　＋給誰＋ VP 　？　A：　S　＋給＋ N 　＋　VP 　。

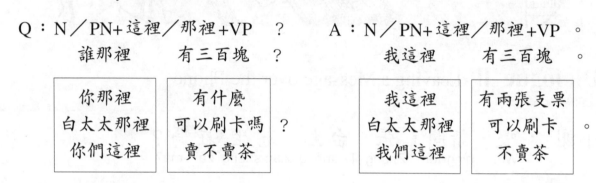

| 白先生
謝小姐
你 | 給誰 | 買書
打電話
打折 | ？ | | 白先生
謝小姐
我 | 給 | 他太太
我
錢小姐 | 買書
打電話
打折 | 。 |

1-2 你那裡是不是三九五六八二五？　　Is this 3956825?

Explanation: Upon adding a "這裡" or "那裡" after a N or PN, the word automatically becomes a place noun. This indicated place, therefore, is in some way related to the N or PN; the speaker will be able to know the actual place referred to by the context of the sentence.

Q：N／PN＋這裡／那裡＋VP 　？　　　A：N／PN＋這裡／那裡＋VP 　。

　誰那裡　　　有三百塊　　？　　　　　我這裡　　　有三百塊　　。

| 你那裡
白太太那裡
你們這裡 | 有什麼
可以刷卡嗎
賣不賣茶 | ？ | | 我這裡
白太太那裡
我們這裡 | 有兩張支票
可以刷卡
不賣茶 | 。 |

Aural Comprehension Drill

　The following dialogues may contain some unfamiliar vocabulary. Do not be concerned if you have not yet learned the vocabulary or do not understand its meaning. Try to figure out the meaning from the context, then answer the question.

(　) According to the dialogue, which is correct?
　　a) 小錢 is at home
　　b) 小錢 is not at home
　　c) we do not know whether 小錢 is at home or not

Dialogue II Leaving a Message over the Phone

小謝[1]：喂，請問，張　台生　先生　在嗎？
　　　　Wéi,　qǐngwèn, Zhāng Táishēng xiān·sheng zài ·ma?

A　：他不在。請問，您是哪位[2]？
　　　Tā búzài.　Qǐngwèn,　nín shì něiwèi?

小謝：我是謝美宜。我想　請他到我家來吃飯。
　　　Wǒ shì Xiè Měiyí.　Wǒ xiǎng qǐng tā dào wǒ jiā lái chīfàn.

　　　請他今天　晚上　打電話　給我。
　　　Qǐng tā jīntiān wǎnshàng dǎdiànhuà gěi wǒ.

A　：好。他有你的　電話嗎？
　　　Hǎo.　Tā yǒu nǐ·de diànhuà ·ma?

小謝：我　想他有。謝謝。
　　　Wǒ xiǎng tā yǒu.　Xiè·xiè.

Vocabulary

1. 張台生　　Zhāng Táishēng　　Proper N : a Chinese full name
   張　　　　Zhāng　　Proper N : a Chinese surname

2. 哪　　　　nǎ　　QW : which
   哪個包子好吃？
   Which steamed bun tastes better?

3. 位　　　　wèi　　M : (for a person, in a polite way)

4. 想　　　　xiǎng　　AV/V : would like, to want; to think
   1) 你想給王先生多少錢？
   2) 我想他是美國人。
   1) How much money would you like to give Mr. Wang?
   2) I think he is American.

5. 請　　　　qǐng　　V : to invite
   你要請幾位老師來？
   How many teachers do you want to invite?

6. 到　　　　dào　　CV/V : to; to arrive
   1) 張先生，請你到這裡來。
   2) 小姐，新車到了，請打電話給我。
   1) Mr. Zhang, please come here.
   2) Miss, when the new car arrives, please give me a call.

7. 家　　　　jiā　　N : home, house　　(M：個)
   謝老師家在美國嗎？
   Is Teacher Xie's home in America?

8. 吃飯　　　chī//fàn　　VO : to have a meal
   菜不好吃。我不想吃飯。
   The food does not taste good; I don't want to eat.

   飯　　　　fàn　　N : meal, cooked rice

4

*9. 做   zuò   V : to do, to make

A：你來做什麼？

B：我來換錢。

A: What did you come for?

B: I've come to exchange money.

10. 今天   jīntiān   N : today

今天一塊美金換多少台幣？

How many New Taiwan Dollars does one US Dollar exchange for today?

天   tiān   N/M : day

你哪天去美國？

What day are you going to America?

*11. 明天   míngtiān   N : tomorrow

*12. 昨天   zuótiān   N : yesterday

13. 晚上   wǎnshàng   N : evening

A：你們昨天晚上吃什麼？

B：我們昨天晚上吃日本菜。

A : What did you all have for dinner last night?

B : We ate Japanese food last night.

*14. 上午   shàngwǔ   N : in the morning
早上   zǎoshàng   N : in the morning

*15. 中午   zhōngwǔ   N : at noon

*16. 下午   xiàwǔ   N : in the afternoon

Notes

1. "小謝" is used to address someone whose last name is "謝", given that he/she is young and familiar to the speaker. In this case, "小" is a prefix added to the surname. It is inappropriate to address someone in this way if he/she is senior in age or social rank to the speaker. Chinese people usually continue to address people in this way, even if they have changed their titles or become older. Therefore, when "小謝" gets old, he/she is still addressed as "小謝" by those who knew him/her when he/she was younger. This kind of address is more often used by people in mainland China than people in Taiwan.

2. "您是哪位？" is used to find out who the other party is. This expression is more polite and milder than "你是誰？"

Grammar

2-1 你是哪位？   May I ask who is calling?   (Who are you?)

Explanation: "哪" is a question word. It must be used with a number and a measure word. If the accompanying number is one, then it may be omitted, and the pronunciation becomes "něi".

a)   Q：哪+Nu+M+(N)+ VP   ？   A：NP   +   VP。

| 哪本書
哪位
哪杯茶
哪個 | 便宜
要換美金
是日本茶
好吃 | ？ | _____ 都不貴。　（這兩本書）
_____ 要換美金。　（那位先生）
_____ 是日本茶。　（這十杯）
_____ 好吃。　　（那個） |

b)   Q：   S   + V +哪+Nu+M+(N)？ A：   S   + V +   NP   。
　　　　你是　　　哪　　位？　　　　　我　是　　謝美宜。

| 張太太
他們
錢小姐
你 | 要
賣
刷
是 | 哪本書
哪國車
哪張卡
哪國人 | ？ | 她
他們
錢小姐
我 | 要
賣
刷
是 | 那三本新書
美國車
這張卡
中國人 | 。 |

2-2 我請他吃飯。　　I invite him to dinner.

Explanation: When a particular sentence carries two verb phrases, 1) the object of the first phrase serves as the subject of the second phrase; 2) the two phrases share the same subject, indicating either the two actions occur in order or successively or the second phrase serves to specify the purpose of the first. Here, it is the most important principle of the Chinese word order—Temporal Sequence Principle, first do, first said.

Q：NP	+ VP₁ +	做什麼？	A：NP + VP₁ + VP₂。
你	請他	做什麼？	我請他＿＿＿＿＿＿。
張先生	約你	做什麼？	張先生約我＿＿＿＿。
小謝	給他太太錢	做什麼？	小謝給他太太錢＿＿＿＿。
你	買包子	做什麼？	我買包子＿＿＿＿＿。
你	打電話	做什麼？	我打電話＿＿＿＿＿。
你	要錢	做什麼？	我要錢＿＿＿＿。

吃飯　買車　請他吃　約張小姐　來看新書　買菜

2-3 我家　my house

Explanation: Nouns or pronouns that modify another noun express a direct relationship between the two words, and in this case must use the character "的", such as in the phrase "你的車". When kinship (including "home base") is involved, "的" may be omitted, as in "我家".

Q：　S + 　qù (去) 哪裡？　　A：　S　+ 來／qù (去) +　　PW　　。

你 小謝 張台生 白老師	qù (去) 哪裡？	我 小謝 張台生 白老師	來／qù (去)	錢太太家 我們xuéxiào 他gōngsī 你家	。

Additional Vocabulary

qù (去) : to leave, to go　　xuéxiào (學校) : school　　gōngsī (公司) : company

2-4 到我家來吃飯　　come to my house to eat

Explanation: "到" is a CV, specifically one that must come before that which it is modifying, and is followed by a PW or the verbs "來／去". A VP may be placed behind "來／去" to indicate a purpose. Here, it is the Temporal Sequence Principle again—first do, first said—to be at a place first, then do something.

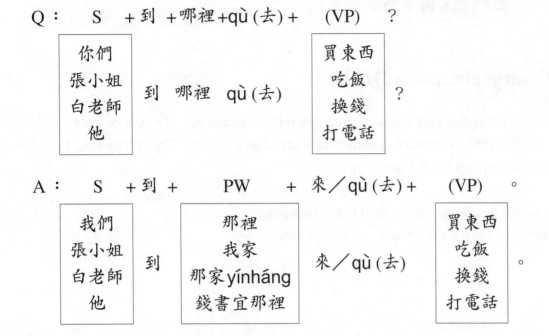

2-5 我想請他到我家來吃飯。　　I'd like to invite him to my house to eat.

Explanation: A VP may follow the verb "想" as the object. By doing so this expresses a feeling of hope or calculation. If a clause is used as the object, it will indicate an opinion of the subject of the sentence.

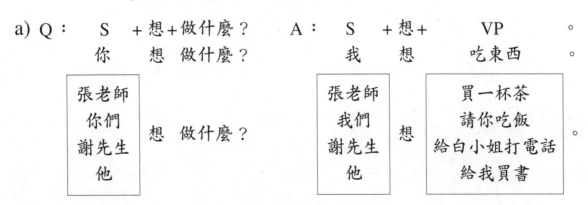

Additional Vocabulary

　　qù(去) : to leave, to go　　yínháng(銀行) : bank

b)　　Q：S ＋ VP？　　　　　　　　A：我想＋a clause。

那本書貴嗎？

他有幾 liàng(輛)車？

誰要付錢？

他是日本人嗎？

他們賣美國車嗎？

我想＿＿＿＿＿＿＿（不便宜）。

我想＿＿＿＿＿＿＿（沒有）。

我想＿＿＿＿＿＿＿（他）。

我想＿＿＿＿＿＿＿（不是）。

我想＿＿＿＿＿＿＿（賣）。

4 Aural Comprehension Drill

The following dialogues may contain some unfamiliar vocabulary. Do not be concerned if you have not yet learned the vocabulary or do not understand its meaning. Try to figure out the meaning from the context, then answer the question.

(　) Where would this conversation most likely take place?

a) doorway　　　b) over the phone　　　c) in a shop

Additional Vocabulary

　　liàng(輛)：M for vehicle

Dialogue III Making an Appointment over the Phone

小張：喂，請問，錢 太太在不在？
Wéi,　qǐngwèn,　Qián tài·tài zài búzài?

錢太太：我就是[1]。你是哪位？
Wǒ jiù shì.　　Nǐ shì něiwèi?

小張：我是 張　台生。我 想　明天下午三　點去看你。
Wǒ shì Zhāng Táishēng.　Wǒ xiǎng míngtiān xiàwǔ sān diǎn qù kàn nǐ.

可以嗎？
Kěyǐ ·ma?

錢太太：對不起。我 有 事。
Duì·bùqǐ.　　Wǒ yǒu shì.

小張：星期四呢？
Xīngqī sì ·ne?

錢太太：這個星期四、星期五我 都 很 忙。
Zhèi·ge xīngqī sì,　xīngqī wǔ wǒ dōu hěn máng.

小張：那麼，你 什麼 時候 有空？
Nà·me, nǐ shén·me shíhòu yǒukòng?

錢太太：下 個 星期一 可以 嗎？
Xià ·ge xīngqī yī kěyǐ ·ma?

小張：好 啊。幾 點？
Hǎo ·a. Jǐ diǎn?

錢太太：兩 點 半。
Liǎng diǎn bàn.

小張：好。下 星期一 見。
Hǎo. Xià xīngqī yī jiàn.

錢太太：再見。
Zàijiàn.

Vocabulary

1. 就   jiù   Adv : (used in the sense of "just" or "exactly")

   A：哪位是謝老師？

   B：我就是。

   A: Which one is Teacher Xie?

   B: I am.

2. 去   qù   V : to go

   1) 你去不去白先生家？

   2) 我要去買一本書。

   1) Are you going to Mr. Bai's house?

   2) I want to go buy a book.

3. 看　　　kàn　　V : to look, to see, to watch, to visit; to read

　　1) 你看，誰來了？

　　2) 我想明天下午去看老師。

　　3) 你要不要看這本書？

　　1) Look, who is here?

　　2) I want to go see the teacher tomorrow afternoon.

　　3) Do you want to read this book?

4. 什麼時候　shén·me shíhòu　　Adv : when

　　你要什麼時候去換錢？

　　When do you want to go exchange money?

　時候　　shíhòu　　N : time

5. 星期四　xīngqī sì　　N : Thursday
　星期² 　xīngqī　　N : week　　(M：個)

　　一個星期有七天。

　　A week has seven days.

　*星期天　xīngqī tiān　　N : Sunday
　　星期一　xīngqī yī　　N : Monday
　*星期二　xīngqī èr　　N : Tuesday
　*星期三　xīngqī sān　　N : Wednesday
　　星期五　xīngqī wǔ　　N : Friday
　*星期六　xīngqī liù　　N : Saturday

6. 有空　　yǒu//kòng　　VO : to have time

　　A：我想請你吃飯。你什麼時候有空？

　　B：我星期六有空。

　　A: I would like to invite you to dinner. When do you have time?

　　B: I have time on Saturday.

7. 事　　shì　　N : thing, matter, affair, business　　(M：jiàn 件)

　　A：你明天有什麼事？

　　B：我去看老師。

　　A: Do you have anything to do tomorrow?

　　B: I am going to see the teacher.

8. 呢　　　　·ne　　P : (used at the end of a sentence as an interrogative)

A：我沒有信用卡。你呢？

B：我有一張。

A: I do not have a credit card. Do you?

B: I have one.

9. 忙　　　　máng　　SV : be busy

她昨天很忙，早上買菜，下午去看老師，晚上請張小姐吃飯。

She was busy yesterday. In the morning she bought food, in the afternoon she went to see her teacher, and in the evening she invited Miss. Zhang to eat.

10. 下(個)　　xià (·ge)　　SP +M : next

她想下(個)星期三去日本。

She plans to go to Japan next Wednesday.

*11. 上(個)　　shàng (·ge)　　SP +M : last

12. 兩點半　　liǎng diǎn bàn　　TW : 2:30

點　　　　diǎn　　N : o'clock

半　　　　bàn　　N : half

*13. 分　　　　fēn　　N : minute

我的車兩點十五分到。

My bus will arrive at 2:15.

14. 再見　　　zàijiàn　　IE : Good-bye.

再　　　　zài　　Adv : again

包子好吃。我要再吃一個。

The steamed buns taste good. I want to eat another one.

見　　　　jiàn　　V : to see

1) 老師，明天兩點見。

2) 老師要我去見他。

1) Teacher, see you tomorrow at two o'clock.

2) The teacher wants me to go see him.

Notes

1. "我就是。" means "Speaking", or "I am the person (whom you want to speak to.)" When a Chinese person answers a phone call and he/she is the person being asked for, he/she will say "我就是。", not "這是他。"

2. "星期" means the same as "禮拜" (lǐbài). Therefore "星期一" is the same as "禮拜一", "星期天" is the same as "禮拜天", etc. However, "星期" is now more commonly used. It can be pronounced as "xīngqī" or "xīngqí."

Grammar

3-1 xiànzài （現在）幾點幾分？　　(Now) What time is it?

1:00 = 一點
1:05 = 一點零五(分)
1:10 = 一點十分
1:15 = 一點十五(分)
　　　 一點一kè (刻)

1:30 = 一點三十(分)
　　　 一點半
1:45 = 一點四十五(分)
　　　 一點三kè (刻)
　　　 chà (差)一kè (刻)兩點

Exercises

Look at the picture to tell the times.

Additional Vocabulary

xiànzài(現在) : now, at this time　　　kè(刻) : a quarter of an hour　　　chà(差) : to be short of

3-2 什麼時候？　　When?

Explanation: "Time-When" time words usually come after the subject and before the verb. If the speaker wishes to add emphasis, then it may be moved to precede the subject. When several "Time-When" time words are used simultaneously, their order should be from the largest to the smallest. This is another principle of word order — from whole to part principle. Questions may use the phrases "什麼時候" and "幾點幾分".

Q：S＋ 什麼時候／ ＋ VP ？　　A：S ＋Time-When＋ VP 。
　　　　 幾點幾分

| 張先生
小謝
他們
錢小姐 | 什麼時候／
幾點幾分 | 來
去看老師
吃晚飯
去買書 | ？ | 張先生
小謝
他們
錢小姐 | 下星期天
明天下午
六點半
早上十點 | 來
去看老師
吃晚飯
去買書 | 。 |

3-3 那麼，星期四呢？　　In that case, how about Thursday?

Explanation: In questions which serve to clarify and follow up the already stated information, the predicate may be omitted and a "呢" added following the noun or pronoun to make a "how about..." question.

a)　A：NP₁ ＋ VP 。　　　　　　　　　B：那麼　NP₂　呢？

A：NP₁ ＋ VP 。

星期三我有事。	那麼 星期四 呢？
小錢、小謝都要來。	那麼 _____ 呢？
明天下午我沒有空。	那麼 _____ 呢？
錢書宜不想去老師家。	那麼 _____ 呢？
三百塊太貴，我不買。	那麼 _____ 呢？

晚上　小張　打九折　張台生　你　兩百五　hòutiān（後天）

Additional Vocabulary

hòutiān(後天)：the day after tomorrow

b)

NP₁	+	VP	,	NP₂	呢？

我	要吃包子
張小姐	想吃飯
白老師	要買書
他們那裡	不可以刷卡

，_____ 呢？
，_____ 呢？
，_____ 呢？
，_____ 呢？

張先生　你們　我們這裡　謝老師　錢太太　你們這裡

4

Aural Comprehension Drill

The following dialogues may contain some unfamiliar vocabulary. Do not be concerned if you have not yet learned the vocabulary or do not understand its meaning. Try to figure out the meaning from the context, then answer the question.

(　) What time is best to meet with 小白？

　　a) Monday morning　　b) Monday afternoon　　c) Tuesday morning

Variety Exercises

I. Do as I Say

xxx, 請你到 xxx 那裡／這裡去／來。

II. Answer the Following Questions

1. 現在幾點？／現在幾點幾分？／現在是幾點幾分？
2. 你幾點吃早飯？
3. 你幾點吃午飯？
4. 你幾點吃晚飯？
5. 你昨天幾點吃早飯？
6. 你昨天幾點吃午飯？
7. 你昨天幾點吃晚飯？
8. 你買菜嗎？
9. 你星期幾去買菜？
10. 你明天早上幾點去買菜？
11. 你什麼時候給老師打電話？
12. 明天下午你什麼時候有空？

III. Game

Can you guess who I am? (all classmates should cover their eyes)

你是誰？

你想我是誰？(disguise your voice)

你是_____。(guess your classmate's name)

對，我就是_____。／不對，我不是_____。

   If you answer incorrectly, continue asking questions. For example, "Do you have a husband or wife?" "Is your surname 謝?" "Is your phone number 3952865?" "Are you Japanese?"... until you correctly identify the speaker. To increase the difficulty of the game, change people at random.

IV. Sentence Building

人	時候	到（地方）	來／去	做	事情

Example

老師 (Teacher)：我去。

A：我明天去。

B：我明天到老師家去。

C：我明天到老師家去吃飯。

V. Activity

Students should first make their own blank schedules, then begin by filling in their own list of appointments for the upcoming week. Upon completion, students should then work in pairs, coordinating their plans in the time remaining.

Example

Student A

星期一	去換錢
星期二	
星期三	去買東西
星期四	請謝小姐吃飯
星期五	
星期六	去看錢老師
星期日	

Student B

星期一	
星期二	買車、等電話
星期三	
星期四	去付車錢
星期五	去買書
星期六	去旅行
星期日	

A：你下個星期來我家，好不好？

B：好啊！下個星期一我有空。

A：對不起，下個星期一不行。我要去換錢。星期二可以嗎？

B：我想買一輛日本車。他們現在沒有。他們說下星期二打電話給我。
　　我要等他們的電話。

A：那麼，星期五呢？

B：星期五書打折，我想去買書。星期天好不好？

A：好，星期天我沒事。那麼我們下個星期天見。

IV. Role Play

打電話約時間去

1. 看老師

2. 吃飯

3. 買東西

4. 換錢

5. 請吃飯

Situation 1: 打錯了。

Situation 2: 他不在。

Situation 3: 我就是。

Try to Guess

1. (　) What do you think "做飯" means?

   a) to cook rice　　b) to cook a meal　　c) to make breakfast

2. (　) What do you think "看來" means?

   a) to have seen someone is coming　　b) to take a look from here　　c) looks likely

3. (　) What do you think "忙什麼" means?

   a) What (are you) busy doing?　　b) Why (are you) so busy?　　c) What is wrong?

4. (　) What do you think "天書" means?

   a) diary　　b) a book for daily use

   c) a book from heaven — hard to read, difficult to understand

Authentic Material

Carefully study and then explain this schedule, or form groups of two and inquire about each other's schedule.

```
五月十三日（星期三）
 7:00  吃飯
 8:30  打電話給老師
 9:00  買菜
12:00  吃飯
 1:00  買旅行支票
 5:45  張家請吃飯
```

1. 白先生什麼時候吃早飯？
2. 他什麼時候打電話給老師？
3. 他什麼時候去買菜？
4. 他中午幾點吃飯？
5. 他下午有什麼事？
6. 他晚上到誰家吃飯？

Translation of the Dialogues

Dialogue I

A : Hello, could you please tell me, is Teacher Xie there?

B : Who?

A : Teacher Xie Meiyi.

B : Sorry, there's no one by that name here.

A : Isn't this 3956825?

B : No, it is not. You have dialed the wrong number.

A : Sorry.

Dialogue II

Little Xie : Hello, excuse me, is Mr. Zhang Taisheng there?

        B : He's not in. May I ask who is calling?

Little Xie : I am Xie Meiyi. I would like to invite him to dinner in my house. Please ask him to give me a call tonight.

        B : Okay. Does he have your number?

Little Xie : I think he does. Thank you.

Dialogue III

Little Zhang : Hello. May I ask, is Mrs. Qian there?

  Mrs. Qian : Speaking. May I ask who's calling?

Little Zhang : This is Zhang Taisheng, I'd like to go to see you around three o'clock tomorrow afternoon. Would that be all right?

  Mrs. Qian : I'm sorry I have some other appointment.

Little Zhang : What about Thursday?

  Mrs. Qian : I'm pretty busy both this Thursday and Friday.

Little Zhang : Well, when will you have some free time?

  Mrs. Qian : How about next Monday?

Little Zhang : Great, what time?

  Mrs. Qian : Two-thirty.

Little Zhang : Okay. See you Monday.

  Mrs. Qian : Good-bye.

第五課　在哪裡？

LESSON 5　WHERE IS IT?

Key Study Points

inquiring about locations (right, across from)／using ordinal numbers／asking directions (inside, up, down)／riding a bus／changing buses

Vocabulary	Grammar
Dialogue I	**Dialogue I**
哪裡，洗手間(洗，手，間)，樓上(樓)，樓下，右邊，左邊，第，公用電話，對面	S＋在＋PW QW哪裡
Dialogue II	**Dialogue II**
拿，筆，知道，沒／沒有，書包，裡面，外面，桌子，椅子，上面，下面，有，也，字典(字)	S＋V了(O)＋嗎／沒有？ 沒V(O) NP₁＋在＋NP₂＋Localizer NP₁＋Localizer＋有＋NP₂ 也
Dialogue III	**Dialogue III**
老陳(陳)，去，萬美百貨公司(百貨公司，公司)，皮鞋，雙，應該，坐，公車，前面，後面，台灣銀行(台灣，銀行)，站，路(bus number)，就，下車(下)，上車(上)，信一路，路口(路)	去＋(PW)＋VO 在＋PW＋VO 要

Dialogue ┃ Finding out Locations

A： 請問 洗手間[1] 在 哪裡？
　　Qǐngwèn xǐshǒujiān zài nǎlǐ?

B： 在 樓 上， 右邊 第一 間。
　　Zài lóu shàng, yòubiān dì yī jiān.

A： 公用　電話 呢？
　　Gōngyòng diànhuà ·ne?

B： 在 對面。
　　Zài duìmiàn.

Vocabulary

1. 哪裡[2]　　nǎlǐ　QW : where
　　　　A：你今天晚上在哪裡吃飯？
　　　　B：我今天晚上在小張家吃飯。
　　　　A: Where will you eat tonight?
　　　　B: I will eat at Little Zhang's house tonight.

2. 洗手間　　xǐshǒujiān　　N : restroom　　（M：間）

洗　　　　xǐ　　V : to wash

手　　　　shǒu　　N : hand　　（M：zhī 隻）

我去洗一下手。請你等一下。

I am going to wash my hands. Please wait a moment.

間　　　　jiān　　BF/M : room/ (for rooms)

3. 樓上　　lóu shàng　　PW : upstairs

樓　　　　lóu　　N/M : floor　　（M：céng 層）

我家在二樓。白先生家在我家樓上。

My house is on the second floor. Mr. Bai's house is upstairs.

*4. 樓下　　lóu xià　　PW : downstairs

5. 右邊　　yòubiān　　PW : right side

*6. 左邊　　zuǒbiān　　PW : left side

7. 第　　　　dì　　SP : (the ordinal prefix)

8. 公用電話　gōngyòng diànhuà　　N : public telephone

在美國，打公用電話貴不貴？

In America, is it expensive to call from a public phone?

9. 對面　　duìmiàn　　PW : the opposite side

Notes

1. "洗手間" is washroom, rest room, or bathroom. Another commonly used word for toilet is "廁所" (cèsuǒ). The correct Chinese for "I need to use the rest room." is "我要上 (shàng, to go to) 廁所。" or "我要去洗手間。"

2. "哪裡" means the same as "哪兒". People in northern China usually say "哪兒", whereas "哪裡" is more common in the south.

Grammar

1-1 洗手間在哪裡？ Where is the rest room?

Explanation: This pattern indicates the location of a particular person or thing.

Q： S ＋ 在哪裡？ A： S ＋ 在 ＋ PW 。

你家 在哪裡？ 我家 在 小張家對面 。

| 我的書
電話
謝先生 | 在哪裡？ | 你的書
電話
謝先生 | 在 | 我這裡
樓下
白小姐右邊 | 。 |

Aural Comprehension Drill

The following dialogues may contain some unfamiliar vocabulary. Do not be concerned if you have not yet learned the vocabulary or do not understand its meaning. Try to figure out the meaning from the context, then answer the questions.

Listen to the following dialogues and choose the most appropriate answer.

1. (   ) Where is Miss Xie?

   a) upstairs, second room on the left   b) downstairs, second room on the left

   c) on the second floor, second room on the right

2. (   ) Which floor does not have a public phone?

   a) 4th floor   b) 10th floor   c) 14th floor

Dialogue II The Case of the Missing Pen

A：誰 拿了我的 筆？
Shéi ná·le wǒ·de bǐ?

B：不知道。我 沒 拿。你¹書 包 裡面²有 沒有？
Bù zhīdào.   Wǒ méi ná.   Nǐ shūbāo lǐmiàn yǒu méiyǒu?

A：沒有。
Méiyǒu.

B：桌子 上面³ 呢？
Zhuō·zi shàngmiàn ·ne?

A：也不在桌子 上。……噢，在這裡，在字典下面。
Yě bú zài zhuō·zi shàng.   Òu, zài zhèlǐ, zài zìdiǎn xiàmiàn.

Vocabulary

1. 拿　　　　ná　V : to take

　　　　　A：你要拿什麼？

　　　　　B：我要拿那本書。

　　　　　A: What do you want to take?

　　　　　B: I want to take that book.

2. 筆　　　　bǐ　N : pen　　(M：zhī 枝)

3. 知道　　　zhīdào　V : to know

　　　　　1) 我不知道他是誰。

　　　　　2) 你知道他的新車多少錢嗎？

　　　　　1) I do not know who he is.

　　　　　2) Do you know how much his new car costs?

4. 沒／沒有　méi/méiyǒu　Adv : did not, have not

　　　　　我沒有買包子。

　　　　　I did not buy steamed buns.

5. 書包　　　shūbāo　N : school bag, book bag　　(M：個)

6. 裡面　　　lǐmiàn　PW : inside

*7. 外面　　　wàimiàn　PW : outside

8. 桌子　　　zhuō·zi　N : table, desk　　(M：張)

*9. 椅子　　　yǐ·zi　N : chair　　(M：bǎ 把)

10. 上面　　　shàngmiàn　PW : above, top

11. 下面　　　xiàmiàn　PW : under, beneath, bottom

12. 有　　　　yǒu　V : there is/are

　　　　　書包裡面，書、筆都有。

　　　　　Inside the book bag there are both a book and a pen.

13. 也　　　　yě　Adv：also

你可以刷卡，也可以給旅行支票。

You can use a credit card or traveler's checks.

14. 字典　　zìdiǎn　N：dictionary　（M：本）

字　　　zì　N：character　（M：個）

Notes

1. "你書包裡面有沒有？" is equivalent to "你的書包裡面有沒有？". The particle "的" has been omitted, which is common in rapid, informal conversation.

2. "裡面" means the same as "裡邊" or "裡頭" (lǐ·tou). "外面" means the same as "外邊" or "外頭" (wài·tou). "上面" means the same as "上邊" or "上頭" (shàng·tou). "下面" means the same as "下邊" or "下頭" (xià·tou).

3. "桌子上面" can be shortened to "桌子上" or "桌上".

Grammar

2-1 誰拿了我的筆？　Who took my pen?

Explanation: (1) Adding the particle "了" to the end of action verbs indicates completion of a certain action. However, not all completed actions require the addition of "了". For example, a sentence describing a certain situation does not need "了"; only sentences or phrases emphasizing the completion of action require the use of "了". (2) Habitual actions or manners, due to their frequency of occurrence, do not require "了". (3) The object following "V了" most often has a numeric modifier (the quantity), or some other modifier. (4) When the object of a verb does not carry with it a modifier, "了" usually appears after the verb-object structure. (5) In sentences that negate a particular question, the "沒有" should be placed in front of either the main verb or a coverb. (6) "了" indicating completion cannot appear with "沒有" in the same sentence.

a)　Q：S ＋V了＋ O？　　A：S ＋V了＋ 　　(O)。

你	約了	誰？	我	約了	張小姐。
誰	拿了	我的筆？	___	拿了___	(你的筆)。(我)
誰	吃了	那個包子？	___	吃了___	(那個包子)。(小張)
你	買了	什麼？	我	買了___	(一本書)
錢小姐	賣了	哪國車？	她	賣了___	(美國車)

b) Q：S ＋ V了＋幾／多少＋ M+N？ A： S ＋V了＋Nu+M+N。

你	看了	幾本	書？	我	<u>看了　　兩本</u>。
張小姐	填了	幾張	表？	張小姐	＿＿＿＿＿＿＿。
小謝	拿了	幾杯	茶？	小謝	＿＿＿＿＿＿＿。
陳老師	買了	多少	書？	陳老師	＿＿＿＿＿＿＿。
白太太	換了	多少	錢？	白太太	＿＿＿＿＿＿＿。

c) Q：S ＋ V(O)了 ＋嗎／沒有？ A：S+V(O)了／沒有V(O)。

你	買車了	沒有？	我	<u>買</u>了。
你	吃飯了	嗎？	我	＿＿＿＿＿＿。
張先生	換錢了	沒有？	他	＿＿＿＿＿＿。
陳小姐	昨天來了	嗎？	他	＿＿＿＿＿＿。
他	給你打電話了	沒有？	他	＿＿＿＿＿＿。

d) Q：O，(S) ＋ 都＋V了 ＋嗎／沒有？ A：都V了／沒有(V)。

小陳、小張，你	都	請了	嗎？	<u>都請了</u>。
你們的車，	都	賣了	嗎？	＿＿＿＿＿＿。
這兩張表，老陳	都	填了	沒有？	＿＿＿＿＿＿。
他的書，	都	拿了	嗎？	＿＿＿＿＿＿。
三位老師家，小張	都	去了	沒有？	＿＿＿＿＿＿。

2-2 你書包裡面　inside your book bag

Explanation: Localizers may take the form of place words in many instances, where they are often placed immediately after nouns. Some common nouns with locational reference may not need a localizer, e.g. a school or a company.

Q： NP₁ ＋ 在哪裡？　A： NP₁ ＋ 在 ＋ NP₂+L。

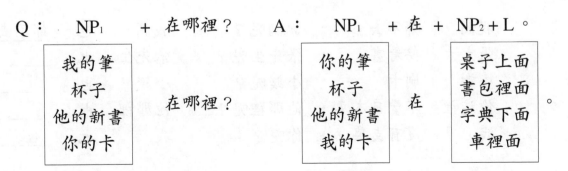

我的筆 杯子 他的新書 你的卡	在哪裡？	你的筆 杯子 他的新書 我的卡	在	桌子上面 書包裡面 字典下面 車裡面

2-3 書包裡面有沒有筆？　　Is there a pen in your book bag?

Explanation: When a sentence begins with a place word or a localizer, the verb "有" expresses its existence. Exactly what exists is indicated immediately after "有", which is non-specific.

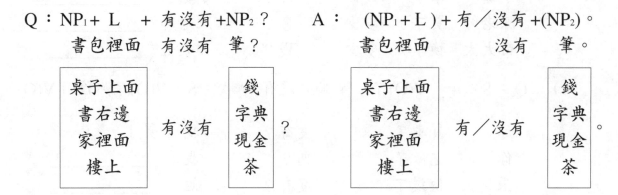

Q：NP₁＋ L　＋ 有沒有＋NP₂？　　　A：　(NP₁＋L)＋ 有／沒有 ＋(NP₂)。

書包裡面　　有沒有　筆？　　　　　書包裡面　　　　沒有　　筆。

| 桌子上面 書右邊 家裡面 樓上 | 有沒有 | 錢 字典 現金 茶 | ？ | 桌子上面 書右邊 家裡面 樓上 | 有／沒有 | 錢 字典 現金 茶 | 。 |

Exercises

Game: 你那裡有什麼？

(Every student is given one card. Then the teacher asks "你那裡有什麼？" or "xxx在誰那裡？". Whereupon every student should say what he has (the object that his/her card shows). Students and teacher may turn this into a competition, first by forming two teams and then watching which team can best identify the objects on their cards. Once the students have finished answering the questions, the teacher may ask "誰那裡有xxx？")

2-4 也不在桌子上　　(it's) not on the table either

Explanation: If the subject is different and the predicate is the same, or if the subject and verb are the same but the object is not, then a "也" should be added before the predicate of the second clause. If several adverbs are in use at the same time, then "也" should be the first.

a)　　Q：NP₁ ＋ VP　　　, NP₂呢？　　A：NP₂ ＋ 也 ＋ VP 。

我們	都不去	，	你們呢？	我們	也	都不去。
張太太	要看書	，	張先生呢？	張先生	也	＿＿＿。
小謝	刷卡	，	小錢呢？	小錢	也	＿＿＿。
你這裡	不賣日本車，		他那裡呢？	他那裡	也	＿＿＿。
我	沒有支票	，	你呢？	我	也	＿＿＿。

b)　S　＋　　Adv　＋　　V　＋　NP₁　，　也 ＋ Adv ＋ V ＋　NP₂ 。

筆	不	在	書包裡，	也	<u>不　　在　桌子上</u>。
我		買了	書，	也	_____。
他們	不	收	信用卡，	也	_____。
白老師	沒	去	小錢家，	也	_____。
我	沒	給他打	電話，	也	_____。

字典　那裡　現金　支票　小謝家　你　筆　老陳

Aural Comprehension Drill

The following dialogues may contain some unfamiliar vocabulary. Do not be concerned if you have not yet learned the vocabulary or do not understand its meaning. Try to figure out the meaning from the context, then answer the questions.

1. (　) What is this lady looking for?
    a) a book
    b) a pen
    c) a book bag

2. (　) Altogether, how many forms did he fill in?
    a) one
    b) two
    c) three

3. (　) Which currency do they accept?
    a) US Dollars
    b) Japanese Yen
    c) New Taiwan Dollars

Dialogue III   Bus Directions

小錢：老[1]陳，我 明天要去萬美 百貨 公司 買皮鞋。
Lǎo Chén,   wǒ míngtiān yào qù Wànměi Bǎihuò Gōngsī mǎi píxié.

應該 坐 什麼 公車？
Yīnggāi zuò shén·me gōngchē?

老陳：你在 我們 公司 前面[2] 坐 二七八[3]，到 台灣 銀行
Nǐ zài wǒ·men gōngsī qiánmiàn zuò èr qī bā,   dào Táiwān Yínháng

那一站，換 十五路 就可以了[4]。
nà yí zhàn,   huàn shíwǔ lù   jiù kěyǐ ·le.

小錢：在 哪裡下車？
Zài   nǎlǐ xiàchē?

老陳：在 信一路路口下車。萬美 百貨公司 就在 對面。
Zài   Xìnyī Lù lùkǒu xiàchē.   Wànměi Bǎihuò Gōngsī jiù zài duìmiàn.

Vocabulary

1. 老陳　　Lǎo Chén　　Prefix+ Proper N : familiar address for a man surnamed Chen
   (see note₁)

   陳　　Chén　　Proper N : a Chinese family name

2. 去　　qù　　V : to go

   請你去謝先生那裡拿書。

   Please go to Mr. Xie's and get the book.

3. 萬美百貨公司

   Wànměi Bǎihuò Gōngsī　　Proper N : Wanmei Department Store

   百貨公司　bǎihuò gōngsī　　N : department store　　(M：家)

   公司　　gōngsī　　N : company　　(M：家、個)

   張先生有兩、三家公司。

   Mr. Zhang has two or three companies.

4. 皮鞋　　píxié　　N : leather shoes　　(M：shuāng 雙 pair、zhī 隻 piece)

*5. 雙　　shuāng　　M : a pair of

6. 應該　　yīnggāi　　Aux : should, ought to

   你要去看他應該先給他打電話。

   If you want to go see him, you should first give him a call.

7. 坐　　zuò　　V : to take (bus, taxi, etc.) ; to sit

   1) 你坐什麼車去老師家？

   2) 請坐一下。我去請陳先生來。

   1) What bus do you take to go to the teacher's house?

   2) Please sit a moment. I will go ask Mr. Chen to come.

8. 公車　　gōngchē　　N : public bus (the short name for 公共汽車 gōnggòng qìchē)

   (M：liàng 輛)

9. 前面　　qiánmiàn　　PW : front, in front of

   我家前面有一家百貨公司。

   There is a department store in front of my house.

*10. 後面　　hòumiàn　　PW : back, behind

萬美百貨公司在我家後面。

Wanmei Department Store is behind my house.

11. 台灣銀行　Táiwān Yínháng　　Proper N : Bank of Taiwan

台灣　　Táiwān　　Proper N : Taiwan

銀行　　yínháng　　N : bank　　(M：家)

12. 站　　zhàn　　N/V : bus stop/to stand　　(M：個)

13. 路　　lù　　N : bus number

14. 就　　jiù　　Adv : then

包子不好吃，我就不吃。

The steamed buns do not taste good, so I will not eat.

15. 下車　　xià//chē　　VO : to get off

下　　xià　　V : to go down

電話在樓下。我下樓去打個電話。

The telephone is downstairs. I will go down and make a call.

*16. 上車　　shàng//chē　　VO : to get on

車來了。我們可以上車了。

The bus is here. We can get on now.

上　　shàng　　V : to go up

17. 信一路　　Xìnyī Lù　　Proper N : Xinyi Road

18. 路口　　lùkǒu　　N : crossing; intersection　　(M：個)

路　　lù　　N : road　　(M：tiáo 條)

Notes

1. "老" is used to address someone who is familiar to the speaker. This "老" is a prefix. It does not necessarily mean old, like its original meaning. This kind of address, similar to "小謝", is used among acquaintances. As it is informal, it is better not to use it to address someone who is one's senior.

2. "前面" means the same as "前邊", and its opposite "後面" means the same as "後邊".

3. "二七八" is the bus (route) number. For the sake of balance, when the bus number is one or two digital, "路" is added to the end of the number, e.g. "3路", "15路". When the bus number is three digital, only the number is spoken, such as "278" is read as "two-seven-eight", there is no need to add "路".

4. "就可以了" means "Then you'll be okay. (Here, you can make it to the place you want to go.)" This "了" is at the end of the sentence, indicating the change of status. (after you change to the right bus, you'll be fine.)

Grammar

3-1 去萬美百貨公司買皮鞋 going to the Wanmei Department store to buy leather shoes

Explanation: When the verb "去" is used directly with place words, a VO may be added to indicate the speaker's motive in going to the indicated place. The word order of this sentence pattern follows Temporal Sequence Principle — to be at a place first, then do something.

a)　Q：NP ＋ 去哪裡 ＋ VP？　　　　A：NP ＋ 去 PW ＋ VP。

你	去哪裡	吃飯？	我	去	小張家吃飯。
你們	去哪裡	買鞋？	我們	去	_____。
他們	去哪裡	洗手？	他們	去	_____。
白小姐	去哪裡	付錢？	白小姐	去	_____。
老張	去哪裡	打電話？	老張	去	_____。

樓上　洗手間　百貨公司　錢小姐那裡　外面　老師家

b) Q：NP ＋ 去 PW　　　　＋做什麼？ A：NP ＋ 去(PW) ＋　　　　VO。

你	去	萬美百貨公司	做什麼？	我	去(萬美百貨公司) 買皮鞋。
老陳	去	你們公司	做什麼？	他	去_____。
他們	去	老師家	做什麼？	他們	去_____。
白小姐	去	銀行	做什麼？	他	去_____。
你們	去	那裡	做什麼？	我們	去_____。

拿支票、買東西、吃飯、換錢、坐車

3-2 在我們公司前面坐二七八。 Take number 278 in front of our office.

Explanation: Placing the preposition "在" in front of the desired place word indicates exactly where the action is taking place. The word order of this sentence pattern follows Temporal Sequence Principle — to be at a place first, then do something.

Q：NP ＋ 在哪裡 ＋ VO ？　　　　A：NP＋ 在 ＋PW ＋ VO。
　　我　　在哪裡　下車？　　　　　　你　　在 我們公司前面　下車。

陳小姐 你們 小張 他	在哪裡	看書 吃飯 打電話 等你	？

陳小姐 我們 小張 他	在	我們公司 家裡 樓下 外面	看書 吃飯 打電話 等我	。

3-3 我明天要去買鞋。 I am going to buy shoes tomorrow.

Explanation: "要" placed immediately after a time word indicates action about to be taken.

Q：NP ＋ TW ＋ 要＋做什麼？　　　A：NP＋ TW ＋ 要＋ VP。
　　你　　明天　要 做什麼？　　　　　我　　明天　　要 去買鞋。

小張 錢書宜 謝老師 他們	下午 晚上七點半 下星期一 明天早上	要 做什麼？

小張 錢書宜 謝老師 他們	下午 晚上七點半 下星期一 明天早上	要	看書 去吃飯 來我家 去看你	。

3-4a 換十五路就可以了。 Change to number 15 bus will be OK.

Explanation: "就" indicates the consequence of the previous statements.

Q：你家坐公車可以到嗎？　　　A：坐三路，在東一街口下，就到了。
　　你要我在哪裡等你？　　　　　＿＿＿＿＿＿＿＿＿＿，就好了。
　　這張表應該給誰？　　　　　　＿＿＿＿＿＿＿＿＿＿就可以了。
　　換錢，要不要填表？　　　　　＿＿＿＿＿＿＿＿＿＿就知道了。

給我　 你在外面等我　 你去銀行問一下　 他請我

- 102 -

3-4b 萬美百貨就在對面。 Wanmei Department Store is right across (the street).

Explanation: "就" is indicative of added affirmation.

Q：請問，誰是謝小姐？　　　A：我是。→ 我就是。

洗手間在哪裡？　　　　　在你後面。→＿＿＿＿＿。

哪裡有銀行？　　　　　　萬美百貨公司樓下有。→＿＿＿＿＿。

哪本字典是你的？　　　　這本。→＿＿＿＿＿。

請問哪個是中國白菜？　　這個。→＿＿＿＿＿。

Aural Comprehension Drill

The following dialogues may contain some unfamiliar vocabulary. Do not be concerned if you have not yet learned the vocabulary or do not understand its meaning. Try to figure out the meaning from the context, then answer the questions.

Listen to the following dialogues and choose the most appropriate answer.

1. (　) How many people are coming to the man's house?
    a) three
    b) four
    c) five

2. (　) What did Old Zhang have to do yesterday afternoon?
    a) go exchange money
    b) go to study
    c) go see the teacher

3. (　) What did this lady go downstairs for?
    a) buy something
    b) exchange leather shoes
    c) wait for Little Mei

Variety Exercises

I. One person draws what the other says. For example:

我有一張桌子。我的桌子在樓上(二樓)。桌上有一個書包。書包的左邊有一本字典，右邊有兩本書。書上有一枝筆。我的皮鞋在桌子下面……

II. The teacher draws a picture, either of a building or an empty room, along with a list of items, and then distributes a copy to each student. Students should then take this list of decorations and furnishings and place them into the empty room, not necessarily using all of the items. After this is completed, students can form small groups, discussing and comparing the differences and similarities in their own pictures. For example:

A：我的車子在我家的右邊。你的呢？
B：我的在我家的前面。
A：我家對面有一家銀行。你們家對面有什麼？
B：我家對面是車站。車站裡有一個公用電話。

Or ask each other similar questions such as the following:

1. 你家前面有什麼？
2. 在哪裡可以打公用電話？
3. 公車站在哪裡？
4. 你有車子嗎？

list for the building

車子	銀行	公車
公用電話	車站	
路	百貨公司	

list for the empty room

桌子	字典	錢	電話
皮鞋	書	筆
支票	信用卡	

III. Draw a road map, indicating several places, such as school, company, department store, etc. Then ask:

「我要去(你們學校)，應該坐什麼公車？」
Your intended destinations should include several changes of buses.

IV. Role Play

You need to go to a job interview. Telephone the company in question and ask them what bus routes can be taken to reach their office.

Try to Guess

1. ( ) What do you think "七上八下" means?
      a) seven up eight down
      b) almost balance
      c) an unsettled state of mind

2. ( ) What do you think the "左右" in "一個一百塊左右" means?
      a) left and right
      b) about, more or less
      c) both sides

5

Authentic Material

1. What does this number represent? Which is your stop? How many stops from here to the final station?

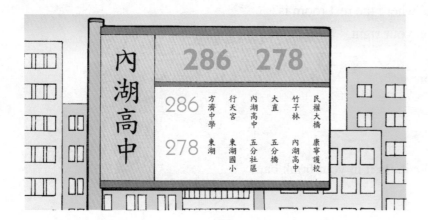

2. What do these signs mean? What is this called besides 「洗手間」?

3. What is the meaning of this sign? Is this a coin operated phone, or does it require a card?

Translation of the Dialogues

Dialogue I

A: Could you please tell me where the rest room is?

B: Upstairs, the first door on your right.

A: And a public phone?

B: Across from the rest room.

Dialogue II

A: Who took my pen?

B: I don't know. I didn't take it. Is it in your book bag?

A: No.

B: What about on the table?

A: It's not on the table either. Oh, here it is, under the dictionary.

Dialogue III

Little Qian : Old Chen, I want to go to the Wanmei Department Store to buy some leather shoes tomorrow. Which bus should I take?

Old Chen : Take bus 278 in front of our office to the Bank of Taiwan bus-stop. Then change to number 15 bus, that will take you there.

Little Qian : Where should I get off?

Old Chen : Get off at the Xinyi intersection. The Wanmei Department Store is right across from the stop.

第六課　找房子[1]

LESSON 6 LOOKING FOR A PLACE TO LIVE

Key Study Points

asking directions (on the street, north, south, east, and west)／discussing time／renting an apartment(rent, utilities, deposit)

Vocabulary	Grammar
Dialogue I	**Dialogue I**
找，房子，公寓，萬，日新百貨公司，怎麼，走，開車(開)，從，東三街(街)，往，南，北，過，紅綠燈(紅，綠，燈)，火車站(火車)，轉，再，分，鐘，小時	Topic - Comment QW 怎麼 Transportation + 來／去 從 + L／PW + 往 + D／PW + VP V (了) + Time duration 再
Dialogue II	**Dialogue II**
王，房間，出租(租)，房東，學生(學)，房租，月，水電費(水費，電費，水)，算，押金，家具，床，還，衣櫃，放，衣服，跟，電視，客廳，廚房，洗澡間(洗澡)	是不是 + 句子？ N₁ 跟 N₂ V (一) V

6 **Dialogue** ┃ Asking for Directions

小萬：老 張，我 要 去 日 新 百 貨 公 司 後面 看 房子。
Lǎo Zhāng, wǒ yào qù Rìxīn Bǎihuò Gōngsī hòumiàn kàn fáng·zi.

日 新 百 貨 公 司 怎 麼 走？
Rìxīn Bǎihuò Gōngsī zěn·me zǒu?

老張：你 開 車 去 嗎？
Nǐ kāichē qù ·ma?

小萬：是 啊。
Shì ·a.

老張：你 從 東 三 街 往 南 開，過 兩 個 紅 綠 燈，
Nǐ cóng Dōngsān Jiē wǎng nán kāi, guò liǎng ·ge hónglǜdēng,

到 了 火 車 站，左 轉，再 開 幾[2] 分 鐘，就 到 了。
dào·le huǒchēzhàn, zuǒ zhuǎn, zài kāi jǐ fēn zhōng, jiù dào ·le.

Vocabulary

1. 找　　　zhǎo　　V : to look for

張老師在哪裡？我們有事找他。

Where is Teacher Zhang? We are looking for him.

2. 房子　　fáng‧zi　　N : house　　(M：dòng 棟)

*3. 公寓　　gōngyù　　N : apartment　　(M：間、dòng 棟)

4. 萬　　　Wàn　　Proper N : a Chinese family name

5. 日新百貨公司

Rìxīn Bǎihuò Gōngsī　　Proper N : Rixin Department Store

6. 怎麼　　zěn‧me　　QW : how

這個菜很好吃，怎麼做？

This food is delicious. How is it cooked?

7. 走　　　zǒu　　V : to walk, to go

到小謝家應該怎麼走？

How do you get to Little Xie's house?

8. 開車　　kāi//chē　　VO : to drive a car

我沒有車，怎麼開車去你家？

I do not have a car. How can I drive to your house?

開　　　kāi　　V : to drive

我們已經開了兩個小時了，怎麼還沒到？

We have been driving for two hours. How come we are not there yet?

9. 從　　　cóng　　CV : from

從星期三到星期五，我都沒有空。

From Wednesday to Friday, I do not have any time.

*10. 東三街　Dōngsān Jiē　　Proper N : Dongsan Street
　　街　　jiē　　N : street　　(M：tiáo 條)

11. 往　　　wǎng　　CV : toward

從日本到美國是不是往東走？

Going from Japan to America, is it heading east?

12. 南　　nán　　N : south

*13. 北　　běi　　N : north

14. 過　　guò　　V : to pass

過了這個路口就到我家了。

My house is just past this intersection.

15. 紅綠燈　　hónglǜdēng　　N : traffic light　　（M：個）

紅　　hóng　　N : red

綠　　lǜ　　N : green

燈　　dēng　　N : light, lamp　　（M：zhǎn 盞）

16. 火車站　　huǒchēzhàn　　N : train station　　（M：個）

火車　　huǒchē　　N : train

17. 轉　　zhuǎn　　V : to turn

你在前面左轉，往前走，到第一個路口右轉，就到了。

Turn left ahead, then go straight, turn right at the first intersection, then you are there.

18. 再　　zài　　Adv : then

你先洗手再吃飯。

Wash your hands first, then eat.

19. 分　　fēn　　M : minute

20. 鐘　　zhōng　　N : clock

請你在這裡等我五分鐘。

Please wait for me here for five minutes.

*21. 小時[3]　　xiǎoshí　　N : hour　　（M：個）

Notes

1. "找房子" means "looking for a place (to live)". This "房子" has a general meaning. It refers to any kind of building in which people can live. It can be a house, an apartment, or even a room within a house.

2. "幾分鐘" means "a couple of minutes." This "幾" is not a question word; it means "several" or "a couple of".

3. "小時" means the same as "鐘頭" (zhōngtóu), hour.

Grammar

1-1 日新百貨公司怎麼走？   How do I get to the Rixin Department Store?

Explanation: Most Chinese sentences consist of the Topic-Comment structure. Topic, quite naturally, refers to the indicated topic of the sentence. This could be in the form of a noun phrase, verb phrase, time phrase, place phrase or even a complete sentence. This topic could exist as the sentence's subject, object, or neither of them.

Q：	Topic	+	Comment	?
1)	這本書	，	誰要	?
2)	在這裡買東西	，	可以刷卡嗎	?
3)	明天下午兩點	，	你們有沒有空	?
4)	公車上	，	可以吃東西嗎	?
5)	我想去看張老師	，	怎麼約時間	?

A：	Topic	+	Comment	。
1)	這本書	，	_____	。
2)	在這裡買東西	，	_____	。
3)	明天下午兩點	，	_____	。
4)	公車上	，	_____	。
5)	你想去看張老師	，	_____	。

我們沒空　可以刷卡　可以先打電話　不可以吃東西　我要

1-2 怎麼去？   How to go (there)?

Explanation: When the question word "怎麼" is placed before the verb, it is used to represent how or by what means the indicated action should be carried out. The word order of this sentence pattern follows Temporal Sequence Principle — first decide the manner of the action, then do the action.

a)   Q：S   +怎麼來／去＋PW／VO？   A：S   + transportation +來／去。

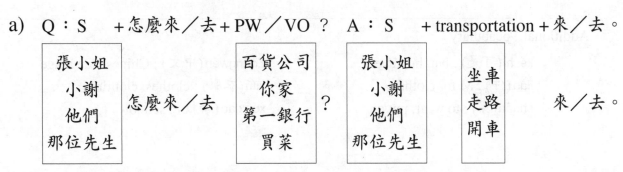

- 111 -

b) Please complete the following sentences. 請完成下面的句子。

他要填表，kěshì（可是）不知道＿＿＿＿＿＿＿＿＿。

我應該去老師家，kěshì（可是）不知道＿＿＿＿＿＿＿＿＿。

老張想找房子，kěshì（可是）不知道＿＿＿＿＿＿＿＿＿。

陳先生要換旅行支票，kěshì（可是）不知道＿＿＿＿＿＿＿＿＿。

1-3 從東三街往南開。　　Go south from Dongsan Street.

Explanation: "從" points to the origin (in place or time) of the verb it precedes, whereas "往" indicates the direction of an action. The word order of this sentence pattern follows Temporal Sequence Principle — from the beginning to the end.

Q：	Topic	+	Comment	？
	Zhōngwén（中文）書		怎麼看	？
	你家		怎麼走	？
	這jiàn（件）yīfú（衣服）		怎麼chuān（穿）	？
	這路公車		往哪裡開	？
	我要到樓上去		應該從哪裡走	？

A：	Topic	+從 +L／PW+ 往+	D／PW + VP	。
	Zhōngwén（中文）書	從　右　往	左	看 。
	我家	要從＿＿＿＿往＿＿＿＿		開 。
	這jiàn（件）yīfú（衣服）	從＿＿＿＿往＿＿＿＿	chuān（穿）	。
	這路公車	從＿＿＿＿往＿＿＿＿		開 。
	你要到樓上去	應該從＿＿＿＿往＿＿＿＿		走 。

東　西　南　北　上　下　裡　外　這裡
那裡　東三街　台灣銀行　火車站
日新百貨公司　xuéxiào（學校）

Additional Vocabulary

kěshì（可是）: but, however	Zhōngwén（中文）: Chinese language
jiàn（件）: M for clothes	yīfú（衣服）: clothes, clothing
chuān（穿）: to wear, put on	xuéxiào（學校）: school

1-4 多少時候　how long

1	min. = 一分鐘		30 min. =	三十分鐘
5	min. = 五分鐘		or	半個小時
7-8	min. = 七、八分鐘		1 hr. =	一個小時
10	min. = 十分鐘		70 min. =	七十分鐘
15	min. = 十五分鐘		or	一個小時零十分鐘
	or 一 kè(刻)鐘		1 day =	一天
10-20	min. = 一、二十分鐘		1 week =	一個星期
	or 十幾分鐘			

1-5 開幾分鐘　drive a few minutes

Explanation: Placing a time-indicating measure word after a verb will automatically indicate the length of time the action takes place.

6

Q：	Topic	，	V(了)+ 多少時候／幾 +M+TW	？
1)	開車去台灣銀行	，	要走　幾分鐘	？
2)	下 bān(班)公車	，	要等　多少時候	？
3)	你們昨天吃飯	，	吃了　幾個小時	？
4)	謝小姐上個 yuè(月)去美國	，	去了　幾天	？

A：	Topic	，	V(了) + T-duration	。
1)	開車去台灣銀行	，	要走	一個下午　半天　二十分鐘
2)	下 bān(班)公車	，	要等	兩個星期　五分鐘　三天
3)	我們昨天吃飯	，	吃了	半個小時　一個半小時
4)	謝小姐上個 yuè(月)去美國	，	去了	一 kè(刻)鐘　半個 yuè(月)

Additional Vocabulary

kè(刻) : a quarter of an hour　　bān(班) : M for scheduled bus, train, or flight, etc.

yuè(月) : month

1-6 左轉，再開幾分鐘就到了。 Turn left, then drive a few minutes and you will get there.

Explanation: a) This "再" indicates that an action will occur during a certain period of time or after something has already occurred.   b) "再" also refers to the repetition or continuation of a certain action or state that has yet to occur.

a) Q：1) 我們什麼時候去？現在嗎？
　　　 2) 你們這個星期要買車嗎？
　　　 3) 我們買了東西，東西沒來。要先給你錢嗎？
　　　 4) 你換旅行支票了沒有？

　　 A：1) 我們現在不去，＿＿＿＿＿＿再去。
　　　 2) 這個星期沒錢，＿＿＿＿＿＿再買。
　　　 3) 不要。＿＿＿＿＿＿再給。
　　　 4) 沒有。早上沒空，＿＿＿＿＿＿再去。

> 下個星期　東西來了　下午　吃了飯
> 有空　拿了東西　有了錢

b) 我家就在前面，再＿＿＿＿＿＿就到了。
　　 這個包子好吃，再＿＿＿＿＿＿。
　　 他拿了我的書，我要再＿＿＿＿＿＿。
　　 那是不是兩千塊的旅行支票？請再＿＿＿＿＿＿。

> 走五分鐘　給我一個　買一本　點一下
> 開幾分鐘　買幾個

Activity

「怎麼從火車站到我家？」 How to get to my house from the train station?

The teacher and students talk according to the map. For example, the teacher asks, "怎麼從火車站到我家？". The teacher intentionally says something wrong and the student must correct the statement; such as the teacher says, "在火車站前面坐三路車。" The student should say, "不對。是在火車站後面。" The teacher correctly says, "在火車站後面坐三路車。過兩個紅綠燈右轉。" The student says, "不是右轉，是左轉。" The teacher says, "過兩個紅綠燈左轉。再往前走，到大有皮鞋公司下車。" The student says, "不是皮鞋公司，是百貨公司。" The teacher says, "到大有百貨公司下車。我家就在大有百貨公司對面四樓。" The student says, "不是四樓，是十樓。" The teacher says, "我家就在大有百貨公司對面十樓。" This activity can also be done in pairs. Each draws his/her own map and gives directions according to his/her partner's map. The same activity can be done after the second dialogue by using a drawing according to furniture arrangement including desks, bed, wardrobe, telephone, TV, etc.

Aural Comprehension Drill

The following dialogues may contain some unfamiliar vocabulary. Do not be concerned if you have not yet learned the vocabulary or do not understand its meaning. Try to figure out the meaning from the context, then answer the question.

( ) The Rixin Department Store is in what part of this area?

    a) southeast   b) northwest   c) southwest

6 Dialogue II Renting a Room

小王：請問，你們是不是有個房間要出租？
Qǐngwèn,　nǐ·men shì búshì yǒu ·ge fángjiān yào chūzū?

房東：是啊。你是學生嗎？
Shì ·a.　　Nǐ shì xuéshēng ·ma?

小王：對。
Duì.

房東：那麼房租可以便宜一點。一個月五千五百塊，
Nà·me fángzū kěyǐ　piányí yìdiǎn.　Yí ·ge yuè wǔqiān wǔbǎi kuài,

水電費不算。
shuǐdiànfèi bú suàn.

小王：要不要押金？
Yào búyào yājīn?

房東：要，一個月的房租。
Yào,　yí ·ge yuè ·de fángzū.

小王：有 沒有 電話、家具？
Yǒu méiyǒu diànhuà, jiājù?

房東：有。 房間 裡，床、桌子 都 有，還有一個 大衣櫃，
Yǒu. Fángjiān lǐ, chuáng, zhuō·zi dōu yǒu, háiyǒu yí ·ge dà yīguì,

可以 放 很 多 衣服。 電話 跟 電視 在 客廳。
kěyǐ fàng hěn dūo yīfú. Diànhuà gēn diànshì zài kètīng.

小王：我可以看看 房間 嗎？
Wǒ kěyǐ kàn·kàn fángjiān ·ma?

房東：可以啊。
Kěyǐ ·a.

6

Vocabulary

1. 王 　　　　Wáng　　N : a Chinese family name

2. 房間　　　fángjiān　　N : room　　(M：個、間)

3. 出租　　　chūzū　　V : to rent
　　　　王太太有兩個房間要出租。
　　　　Mrs. Wang has two rooms for rent.

　租　　　　zū　　V : to rent
　　　　租一輛車一天要多少錢？
　　　　How much does is cost to rent a car for a day?

4. 房東　　　fángdōng　　N : landlord　　(M：位)

5. 學生　　　xuéshēng　　N : student　　(M：個、位)
　學　　　　xué　　V : to learn
　　　　你要買車，就要先學開車。
　　　　If you want to buy a car, then you must first learn how to drive.

6. 房租　　　fángzū　　N : rent

7. 月　　yuè　　N : month　　(M：個)

我的房租一個月一萬塊。

My rent is $10,000 per month.

8. 水電費　　shuǐdiànfèi　　N : utility fee

水費　　shuǐfèi　　N : water bill

電費　　diànfèi　　N : electricity bill

水　　shuǐ　　N : water　　(M：杯)

9. 算　　suàn　　V : to count

請你算一下一共幾本書。

Please count how many books there are altogether.

10. 押金　　yājīn　　N : deposit

11. 家具　　jiājù　　N : furniture　　(M：jiàn 件)

12. 床　　chuáng　　N : bed　　(M：張)

13. 還　　hái　　Adv : in addition

小張家有一輛美國車，還有兩輛日本車。

Little Zhang's family has an American car. In addition, they have two Japanese cars.

14. 衣櫃　　yīguì　　N : closet, wardrobe　　(M：個)

15. 放　　fàng　　V : to put

A：你的床要放哪裡？

B：衣櫃右邊，好不好？

A: Where do you want to put your bed?

B: How about to the right of the wardrobe?

16. 衣服　　yīfú　　N : clothes, dress　　(M：jiàn 件、tào 套)

17. 跟　　gēn　　CV : and

我跟我太太都開日本車。

My wife and I both drive Japanese cars.

18. 電視　　diànshì　　N : TV set

19. 客廳　　kètīng　　N : living room　　(M：間)

我們在客廳裡看電視。

We watch TV in the living room.

*20. 廚房　　chúfáng　　N：kitchen　　（M：間）

*21. 洗澡間　xǐzǎojiān　N：bathroom　（M：間）
　　　洗澡　　xǐ//zǎo　　VO：to take a bath or shower

Grammar

2-1 是不是有房間要出租？　　Isn't there a room for rent?

Explanation: When a "是不是" phrase is inserted into the sentence, the sentence becomes a question, specifically the kind where the speaker is trying to confirm what he/she has known about a fact or a situation. "是不是" can be placed in the beginning or end of a sentence, as well as before the predicate.

小王<u>有房間要出租</u>。　　→　　小王是不是有房間要出租？

小王有房間要出租。　　→　　小王有房間要出租，是不是？

<u>小王</u>有房間要出租。　　→　　是不是小王有房間要出租？

日本茶很貴。　　　　　　→　　＿＿＿＿＿＿＿＿＿＿＿

張小姐要買車。　　　　　→　　＿＿＿＿＿＿＿＿＿＿＿

那位先生姓陳。　　　　　→　　＿＿＿＿＿＿＿＿＿＿＿

你的筆<u>在我這裡</u>。　　　→　　＿＿＿＿＿＿＿＿＿＿＿

小謝沒來。　　　　　　　→　　＿＿＿＿＿＿＿＿＿＿＿

我今天要買車。　　　　　→　　＿＿＿＿＿＿＿＿＿＿＿

他們昨天<u>到老師家去了</u>。→　　＿＿＿＿＿＿＿＿＿＿＿

6

2-2 電話跟電視在客廳。　　The telephone and television are in the living room.

Explanation: When more than one noun appears in the sentence, a "跟" may be added between the last two as a connector, "都" can be placed after the last noun.

a)　Q：NP　　　＋　　　VP　　？　　A：N_1……跟N_n + VP　。

　　　什麼　　　　　在客廳　　？　　　＿＿＿＿＿＿在客廳　。

　　　誰　　　　　　有空　　　？　　　＿＿＿＿＿＿都有空　。

　　　哪個　　　　　便宜　　　？　　　＿＿＿＿＿＿都便宜　。

　　　誰　　　　　要去老陳家　？　　　＿＿＿＿＿＿都要去　。

小張　白老師　衣服　鞋　電話　電視
書　我　他　我們　他們　這個

- 119 -

b)

Q：	NP	+	VP	？	A：	NP	+	V	+ N_1 ······ 跟 N_n 。
	你		買了什麼	？		我		買了	_____ 。
	客廳裡		有什麼	？		客廳裡		有	_____ 。
	他們		要去哪裡	？		他們		要去	_____ 。
	小錢昨天		去看誰	？		他昨天		去看	_____ 。

小謝　白老師家　衣服　鞋　電話　電視　書
你家　我　他　我們　他們　這個

2-3 我可以看看房間嗎？ May I see the room?

Explanation: The reduplication of verbs indicates either that the time period of the action is short and rushed, or that some action is being attempted. The reduplication of verbs also carries with it a tone of casualness, especially in command sentences. In addition, when a verb is monosyllabic, an "一" can be added.

我可以看房間嗎？	→	我可以看(一)看房間嗎？
他想吃這個菜。	→	_____
請給我找那本書。	→	_____
請在樓下等。	→	_____
去洗手！	→	_____

Aural Comprehension Drill

The following dialogues may contain some unfamiliar vocabulary. Do not be concerned if you have not yet learned the vocabulary or do not understand its meaning. Try to figure out the meaning from the context, then answer the questions.

1. (　) Why is the lady making a phone call?

    a) to invite a friend out to Dongsan street

    b) to find out how to get to Dongsan street

    c) to rent a room

2. (　) Where did the man arrange to meet the lady?

    a) at home

    b) at the room she wants to rent

    c) before the Dongsan intersection

Variety Exercises

I. Activity

Study the picture carefully for one minute, then close your book. Can you remember the things in the picture? Where are they?

II. Role Play

1. You are lost and decide to ask a policeman for directions.
2. You want to rent an apartment. Act out your phone conversation with the landlord.

Try to Guess

1. (　) What do you think "從早到晚" means?

    a) from morning till night   b) from time to time   c) morning and evening

2. (　) What do you think "客房" means?

    a) guest room   b) guest house   c) inn

3. (　) What do you think "打算" means?

    a) to use a calculator   b) to plan   c) to play with an abacus

Authentic Material

1. 租屋廣告

租　雅房出租　鬧中取靜　交通方便

三房兩廳　兩套衛浴　簡單家具、廚具
限單身女性
月租一萬五，不包括水電
押金兩個月
意者請洽王太太　電 3956954（白天）
　　　　　　　　　　　　7387002（晚上）

a. What is the intended purpose of this ad?
b. How many rooms does this apartment have?
c. How much is the rent? Does it include utilities?
d. How much is the deposit?
e. Is there any furniture?
f. What does "衛浴" mean?

2. 交通號誌

a. Please guess the meanings of the following traffic signs.
b. Where have you seen these signs?

Translation of the Dialogues

Dialogue I

Little Wan : Old Zhang, I'd like to go look at a room behind the Rixin Department Store. How do I get there?

Old Zhang : Are you going to drive?

Little Wan : Yes.

Old Zhang : Go south on Dongsan Street. After two lights you'll be at the train station. Make a left turn, keep going for a few minutes and you're there.

Dialogue II

Little Wang : Excuse me, do you have a room for rent?

Landlord : Yes. Are you a student?

Little Wang : Yes.

Landlord : Well, in that case, you can have the room for a little cheaper, $5,500 per month. Water and electricity are not included.

Little Wang : Do you require a deposit?

Landlord : Yes, one month's rent.

Little Wang : Is there a telephone or any furniture?

Landlord : Yes. The room has a bed and a desk. In addition, there is a large wardrobe. You should be able to fit quite a bit of clothing in there. The telephone and television are both in the living room.

Little Wang : Well, may I see the room?

Landlord : Sure.

6

第七課　租房子

LESSON 7　RENTING A PLACE

Key Study Points

asking others'opinions on rooms ／ voicing an opinion ／
signing a contract ／ the weather ／ subjunctive mood

Vocabulary

Dialogue I

喜歡，為什麼，覺得，小，大，
學校，遠，近，方便，可是，
多，少，這樣，好，住，搬

Dialogue II

決定，簽約，最少，最多，年，
Nu年，去年，今年，明年，如
果，要是，只，怎麼辦(辦)，房
客，拿回去(回去)，每，下雨，
朋友，辦法，幫，天氣，現在，
四月十一號(月，號)，一月，二
月，三月，四月，五月，六月，
七月，八月，九月，十月，十一
月，十二月

Grammar

Dialogue I

SV一點
好(容易)＋V
先……再……

Dialogue II

V來／去
V回來／回去
要是……就……
sentence＋了
先……等……再……

Dialogue I | Discussing a Room for Rent with a Friend

小張：你 今天 去看 房子了沒有？
　　　Nǐ　jīntiān　qù kàn　fáng·zi ·le méiyǒu?

小王：看了 一個 公寓。我 不 太 喜歡。
　　　Kàn·le　yí ·ge gōngyù.　Wǒ bú tài xǐhuān.

小張：為什麼？
　　　Wèishén·me?

小王：我 覺得 太 小 了。
　　　Wǒ jué·dé　tài xiǎo ·le.

小張：遠 不遠？
　　　Yuǎn bùyuǎn?

小王：很 近，去學校 很 方便。房租 一 個 月 六千塊，
　　　Hěn jìn,　qù xuéxiào hěn fāngbiàn.　Fángzū yí ·ge yuè liùqiān kuài,

　　　也不貴。可是我的 東西 很 多，房間 大 一點兒 好[1]。
　　　yě bú guì.　Kěshì wǒ·de dōng·xi hěn duō, fángjiān dà　yìdiǎnr　hǎo.

- 125 -

小張：這樣的 房子 不好 找。你 可以 先 在 那裡 住
Zhèyàng·de fáng·zi bù hǎo zhǎo. Nǐ kěyǐ xiān zài nàlǐ zhù

兩、三 個 月，不 喜歡，再 搬。
liǎng, sān ·ge yuè, bù xǐhuān, zài bān.

小王：也 好[2]。
Yě hǎo.

Vocabulary

1. 喜歡   xǐhuān   V : to like

　　A：你喜歡哪國車？

　　B：日本車好，也不貴。我喜歡日本車。

　　A: Which country's cars do you like?

　　B: Japanese cars are good. They are not expensive, either. I like Japanese cars.

2. 為什麼   wèishén·me   QW : why

　　這個房子很好。你為什麼不喜歡？

　　This room is really good. Why don't you like it?

3. 覺得   jué·dé   V : to feel

　　一百萬的車，你覺得貴不貴？

　　Do you think a million dollar car is expensive?

4. 小   xiǎo   SV : to be small

5. 大   dà   SV : to be big, large

　　我覺得大房子好，小房子不好。我喜歡大房子。

　　I think big rooms are good, small rooms are not good. I like big rooms.

6. 學校   xuéxiào   N : school   (M：suǒ 所)

7. 遠   yuǎn   SV : to be far

　　那個百貨公司很遠。開車要一個小時。

　　That department store is far away. It takes an hour to drive there.

8. 近　　jìn　　SV : to be near

從我家到學校很近。走十分鐘就到了。

My house is near the school. It just takes ten minutes to walk there.

9. 方便　　fāngbiàn　　SV : to be convenient

在那家百貨公司買東西很方便。付現金、刷卡都可以。

It is really convenient to buy things at that department store. Cash or credit cards are both okay.

10. 可是　　kěshì　　Conj : but

這本字典很好，可是太貴。我現在沒有錢買。

This dictionary is really good, but it is too expensive. I don't have the money to buy it now.

11. 多　　duō　　SV : much, many

我們學校很大，學生很多。

Our school is really big. There are many students.

*12. 少　　shǎo　　SV : little, few

這裡書店很少。買書很不方便。

There are few bookstores here. It's really inconvenient to buy books.

13. 這樣　　zhèyàng　　PN : such, this kind

A：王先生的新車很好，也很便宜。

B：這樣的車子不多。

A: Mr. Wang's new car is really good. It's also cheap.

B: Such cars are rare.

14. 好　　hǎo　　Adv : to be easy to

這個菜很好吃，可是不好做。

This food is delicious, but it is not easy to prepare.

15. 住　　zhù　　V : to live, to stay

A：你要在張老師家住幾天？

B：我想住三天。

A: How many days do you want to stay at Teacher Zhang's house?

B: I think three days.

7

16. 搬　　　bān　　　V : to move

我的房租太貴。我要搬家。

My room is too expensive. I want to move.

Notes

1. "房間大一點兒好" means "It is better if the room is bigger." "房間大一點兒" is the topic of the sentence, and "好" is the comment.

2. "也好" means "(That option) is also good." This "也" indicates a tone of concession or resignation. 小王 doesn't like the place at first because the room is too small, but then he chooses to agree with his friend 小張 because 小張 has a good point.

Grammar

1-1 大一點　　a little bigger

Explanation: "SV 一點" indicates the stated condition a little more or a little less.

1) 我喜歡<u>大一點</u>的客廳。太小不好。

2) 這個 bīngxiāng (冰箱) 太舊了。我要換個＿＿＿＿＿＿的。

3) 這裡太遠不方便。我想找＿＿＿＿＿＿的房子。

4) 太 wǎn (晚) 給人打電話不好。應該＿＿＿＿＿＿打。

5) 這個衣櫃太貴了。有沒有＿＿＿＿＿＿的？

新一點　好一點　便宜一點　早一點　忙一點　近一點

1-2 這樣的房子不好找。　　This kind of apartment is hard to find.

Explanation: Adding a "好" before an action verb indicates that the indicated action is easy to do.

王：我想找近一點，也不太貴的房子。

錢：這樣的房子不好找。

王：小謝做這個菜做了三個小時。

錢：這個菜 zhēn (真) 不＿＿＿＿＿。

Additional Vocabulary

　　bīngxiāng (冰箱) : refrigerator　　wǎn (晚) : to be late　　zhēn (真) : really

王：我昨天、今天要約張小姐，她都沒空。

錢：她太忙，不_____。

王：我打電話找張小姐，打了一個下午都打不tōng(通)。

錢：你晚上再打。那個時候電話_____一點。

王：小陳不喜歡開日本車。

錢：我也覺得日本車不_____。

王：我昨天去買鞋，可是看了幾雙，都太大。

錢：你的jiǎo(腳)太小。鞋不_____。

1-3 先住兩、三個月，不喜歡，再搬。

First stay two or three months, if you don't like it, then move out.

Explanation: In the case of more than one action, "再" may be added before the final one to show that the relative actions are done according to a certain sequence.

Q：NP + VP ？　　　　　　A：先……，再……

你要搬家嗎？　　　　　　　　我先住兩、三個月，不喜歡，再搬。

我們是不是現在去老師家？　　我們先_____再_____。

這個菜怎麼做？　　　　　　　做這個菜先_____再_____。

洗手間在哪裡？　　　　　　　你先_____再_____。

你什麼時候買房子？　　　　　我先_____再_____。

去買菜　回家　去老師家　打電話　上樓　下樓　買房子
右轉　左轉　放一點水　放白菜　洗一洗　等一下　買車

Aural Comprehension Drill

The following dialogues may contain some unfamiliar vocabulary. Do not be concerned if you have not yet learned the vocabulary or do not understand its meaning. Try to figure out the meaning from the context, then answer the question.

(　) Why does this person not like that type of car?

　　a) too expensive　　b) too big　　c) not easy to drive

Additional Vocabulary

　　打不tōng(通)：can't get through　　　jiǎo(腳)：foot

- 129 -

Dialogue II Talking with the Landlord about Leasing and Moving in

7

小王：我 決定 租了。要不要 簽約？
Wǒ juédìng zū ·le.　Yào búyào qiānyuē?

房東：要。最少 租 半年。
Yào.　Zuì shǎo zū bàn nián.

小王：如果 我 只住 五個 月，押金 怎麼 辦？
Rúguǒ wǒ zhǐ zhù wǔ ·ge yuè,　yājīn zěn·me bàn?

房東：要是 有 新 房客，就 可以 拿回去。你 什麼 時候 搬來？
Yàoshì yǒu xīn fángkè,　jiù kěyǐ náhuíqù.　Nǐ shén·me shíhòu bān lái?

小王：這 兩天¹ 每天 下雨，不 太 方便。我 朋友 也 都
Zhè liǎng tiān měitiān xiàyǔ,　bú tài fāngbiàn.　Wǒ péngyǒu yě dōu

　　　有事，沒辦法 幫 我。
　　　yǒu shì,　méi bànfǎ bāng wǒ.

房東：我們 可以 先 簽約。等 天氣 好了，你 再 搬。
Wǒ·men kěyǐ xiān qiānyuē.　Děng tiānqì hǎo ·le,　nǐ zài bān.

小王：好。那 我們 現在 簽約。今天 是 四月 十一 號[2]。
Hǎo.　Nà wǒ·men xiànzài qiānyuē.　Jīntiān shì sì yuè shíyī hào.

簽 半 年，到 十月 十號。
Qiān bàn nián,　dào shí yuè shí hào.

Vocabulary

1. 決定　　juédìng　　V : to decide
你什麼時候去美國？決定了沒有？
When are you going to America? Have you decided yet?

2. 簽約　　qiān//yuē　　VO : to sign a lease, to sign a contract
我們簽約了。他一個月要付五千塊給我。
We have signed a contract.　He will pay me $5,000 per month.

3. 最少　　zuì shǎo　　Adv : at least

*4. 最多　　zuì duō　　Adv : at most
A：今天晚上有多少人要來？
B：最多二十個人，最少十五個人。
A: How many people will come tonight?
B: At most, 20.　At least, 15.

5. 年　　nián　　N/M : year
一年有五十二個星期，三百六十五天。
There are 52 weeks or 365 days in a year.

*6. Nu 年　　nián　　N : the year of Nu
一九九六年的二月有二十九天。
There were twenty nine days in February 1996.

*7. 去年　　qùnián　　N : last year

*8. 今年　　jīnnián　　N : this year

*9. 明年　　míngnián　　N : next year
去年是一九九八年。明年是二〇〇〇年。
Last year was 1998.　Next year is 2000.

7

10. 如果　　　rúguǒ　　Conj : if

如果你要來我家，請先給我打電話。

If you want to come to my house, please give me a call first.

11. 要是　　　yàoshì　　Conj : if

要是你有一百萬，你要做什麼？

If you had a million, what would you do?

12. 只　　　　zhǐ　　Adv : only

A：你昨天買了什麼？

B：我只買了一本書。

A: What did you buy yesterday?

B: I only bought a book.

13. 怎麼辦　　zěn·me bàn　　IE : What can be done about it?

這個月我沒有錢付房租。怎麼辦？

I do not have the money to pay the rent this month. What should I do?

辦　　　　bàn　　V : to handle, to manage

跟萬美公司簽約的事，我想請王小姐辦一下。

About signing the contract with Wanmei Company, I'd like Miss Wang to handle it.

14. 房客　　　fángkè　　N : tenant, lodger　　(M：位)

15. 拿回去　　náhuíqù　　V : to take back

我不要你的錢。你拿回去。

I do not want your money. Take it back.

回去　　　huí qù　　V : to return, to go back

家裡沒有人。我不想回去。

There is no one at home. I do not want to go back.

16. 每　　　　měi　　SP : each, every

老師要每個學生每天看一本書。

The teacher wants each student to read a book a day.

17. 下雨　　　xià//yǔ　　VO : to rain

這幾天每天下雨，去學校很不方便。

It has rained everyday these few days; it is inconvenient to go to school.

18. 朋友　　péngyǒu　　N : friend　　(M：位、個)

19. 辦法　　bànfǎ　　N : method, way　　(M：個)

20. 幫　　bāng　　V : to help

你沒有錢，我也沒有錢，沒有辦法幫你。

You do not have any money. I do not have any money either. There is no way to help you.

21. 天氣　　tiānqì　　N : weather

22. 現在　　xiànzài　　Adv : now

我現在很忙。請你明天再來。

I am busy now. Please come again tomorrow.

23. 四月十一號

sì yuè shíyī hào　　N : April 11

月　　yuè　　N : month

號　　hào　　N : date

今天是六月六號。

Today is June 6.

*24. 一月　　yī yuè　　N : January

*25. 二月　　èr yuè　　N : February

*26. 三月　　sān yuè　　N : March

*27. 四月　　sì yuè　　N : April

*28. 五月　　wǔ yuè　　N : May

*29. 六月　　liù yuè　　N : June

*30. 七月　　qī yuè　　N : July

*31. 八月　　bā yuè　　N : August

*32. 九月　　jiǔ yuè　　N : September

*33. 十月　　shí yuè　　N : October

*34. 十一月　　shíyī yuè　　N : November

*35. 十二月　　shíèr yuè　　N : December

Notes

1. "這兩天" doesn't mean exactly two days. It refers to the last few days recently.
2. "四月十一號" is the eleventh of April. "號" is used to refer to the days of the month in spoken Chinese. In written Chinese, "日" is used. Therefore, spoken "四月十一號" will be "四月十一日" in written Chinese.

Grammar

2-1 你什麼時候搬來？　　When will you move in?

Explanation: The addition of "來" to the verb indicates the direction of the action performed is towards the speaker. Conversely, the addition of "去" shows that the direction of this action is away from the speaker.

王：這個房子，我決定租了。

錢：你什麼時候<u>搬來</u>？

王：小張要給你打電話。

錢：他要什麼時候_____？

王：到小陳家沒有公車。

錢：那麼，我們_____。

王：他在家等你。

錢：我現在就_____。

王：下雨了。你的車呢？

錢：在那邊。我去_____。

開來	拿來	回來	走來	開去	拿去
回去	走去	打來	打去	過來	過去

2-2 拿回去　　to take it back

Explanation: In addition to the directional word of "來" or "去" to express direction of a particular action, some other directional verbs may be added to fit the situation more appropriately and more clearly to describe the circumstances. These words may be added before "來" and "去", such as "回"、"上"、"下"、"過" ("進jìn"、"出chū").

王：我這本書，你今天看不看？
錢：不看。你可以先<u>拿回去</u>。

王：你的車呢？
錢：我開到學校去了，沒 _____ 。

王：小張不喜歡住樓下。
錢：樓上的人搬了，他就可以 _____ 。

王：老錢，我要十張五十塊的美金。你那裡有沒有？
錢：有。我給你 _____ 。

王：我想坐diàntī(電梯)，可是人太多了。
錢：你可以 _____ 啊。

> 搬上去　搬上來　開回去　開回來　拿過來　拿過去　走上去　走上來

7

2-3 要是有新房客，就可以拿回去。

If there is a new tenant, then you can take it back.

Explanation: The phrase "要是／如果……，就……" indicates supposition (subjunctive mood), the particular terms of this hypothetical situation should follow "要是／如果".

Q：押金可以拿回來嗎？　　　　　　A：<u>要是有新房客</u>就可以拿回去。
　　你們明天搬家嗎？　　　　　　　　要是 _____ 就搬。
　　下星期一zǎo(早)一點來，好不好？　要是 _____ 我就早一點來。
　　這jiàn(件)衣服，你要不要買？　　要是 _____ 我就買。

Additional Vocabulary

jìn(進)：to enter　　　　　chū(出)：to go out　　　　　diàntī(電梯)：elevator
zǎo(早)：to be early　　　jiàn(件)：M for clothing, article

你買了新 kǎoxiāng(烤箱)， 要是 ＿＿＿＿＿＿ 就拿去。
舊的給我，好不好？

沒事　你喜歡　不下雨　可以打折

2-4 天氣好了。　The weather becomes good.

Explanation: All "了" in "SV 了"、"不 V 了"、"沒 N 了" indicate a change in the present situation.

王：你們那裡上星期每天下雨。這星期呢？

錢：這星期天氣好了。

王：去年八月很多人去旅行。今年呢？

錢：今年 jīpiào(機票)＿＿＿＿＿＿，人就 ＿＿＿＿＿＿。

王：陳老師昨天下午有事。今天呢？

錢：今天下午 ＿＿＿＿＿＿。

王：現在房子好不好找？

錢：上個月不好找。這個月 ＿＿＿＿＿＿。

王：你明天來不來？

錢：事情今天都做了。要是沒事明天就 ＿＿＿＿＿＿。

沒有事了　好找了　貴了　少了　不來了

2-5 先簽約，等天氣好了，再搬。

First sign the contract, wait until the weather is good, then move in.

Explanation: If the clause "等……，" is added to a set of connected actions, it specifically indicates that the following event must only take place under certain conditions or after something has been completed. The word order of this sentence pattern follows Temporal Sequence Principle.

王：你什麼時候搬？

錢：先簽約，等天氣好了，再搬。

Additional Vocabulary

kǎoxiāng(烤箱) : oven, stove　　　　jīpiào(機票) : airplane ticket

王：我們現在走嗎？

錢：你先坐一下，等 _____ ，再走。

王：你要不要租那個房子？

錢：我先跟房東約時間，等 _____ ，再決定。

王：我們什麼時候可以換車？

錢：我們先開舊的，等 _____ ，再換。

王：我要買那本書，可是書diàn(店)沒有了。

錢：你可以先看我的，等 _____ ，再買。

書來了　他們來了　看了房子　有錢了

Aural Comprehension Drill

The following dialogues may contain some unfamiliar vocabulary. Do not be concerned if you have not yet learned the vocabulary or do not understand its meaning. Try to figure out the meaning from the context, then answer the questions.

7

1. (　) Are we going on vacation tomorrow?

　　a) Yes, we will go.　　b) No, we will not go.　　c) It depends on the weather.

2. (　) What is this gentleman saying?

　　a) The room has already been rented out.

　　b) The room has not yet been rented out.

　　c) He has some money to take this girl out to dinner.

Additional Vocabulary

　　diàn(店) : store, shop

Variety Exercises

I. Answer the following questions.

1. 要是你今天要付房租，可是沒錢，怎麼辦？
2. 要是你在公車上想上洗手間，怎麼辦？
3. 要是你要找 shìyǒu(室友)，有人來看房子，可是你都不喜歡，怎麼辦？
4. 要是你的房東要你下星期搬家，可是你沒有時間找房子，怎麼辦？
5. 要是有人早上三點鐘打電話來，可是不 shuōhuà(說話)，你怎麼辦？
6. 要是你有一百萬，你要做什麼？
7. 要是你喜歡一個人，可是他不喜歡你，你怎麼辦？

II. Read the chart and then answer the questions:

6月2日	6月3日	6月4日	6月5日	6月6日	6月7日	6月8日
下雨	下雨	晴天	陰天	陰天	晴天	陰天

1. 昨天下雨，今天 qíngtiān(晴天)，那麼今天應該是幾月幾日？
2. 明天天氣 zěn·meyàng(怎麼樣)？
3. 六月六日天氣怎麼樣？
4. 你今天簽了約，你想這個星期搬家，哪一天好？
5. 這個星期下了幾天雨？

III. Role Play

Carefully read the rental advertisement on the next page, then:

1) call a friend who would like to rent a place
2) call the landlord.

Additional Vocabulary

shìyǒu(室友)：roommate   shuōhuà(說話)：to talk, to speak
qíngtiān(晴天)：sunny day   zěn·meyàng(怎麼樣)：How is it?
yīntiān(陰天)：cloudy day

Try to Guess

1. (　) What do you think "大小" means?
   a) sizes (of dresses, shoes, etc.)
   b) big or small
   c) both big ones and small ones
2. (　) What do you think "拿手" means?
   a) hand in hand
   b) to hold in hand
   c) to be good at
3. (　) What do you think "不知不覺" means?
   a) out of consciousness
   b) without being aware of (it)
   c) without feelings

Authentic Material

一、出租廣告

五層公寓三樓
三房兩廳
租　雙衛浴
房租低廉
請洽：李太太，5457863

十層大樓公寓七樓
兩房　兩廳　兩衛　有家具
交通便利
請洽：張先生，3318457（白天）
7625631（晚上）

頂樓雅房出租
一房一廳一衛
有家具　可做飯
有車位　　租
房租便宜
請洽：錢小姐，9234561

套房出租
限單身女性
住家安全交通方便
近學校、超市　　租
請洽：王小姐，3456690

1. 我要四間房的公寓，應該打幾號電話？
2. 我要兩個洗澡間的房子，應該打幾號電話？
3. 我喜歡做飯。我要廚房，應該打幾號電話？

```
┌─────────────────────────────────────┐
│      十層大樓   公寓六樓              │
│   兩房 兩廳 兩衛 有家具          租   │
│    交通便利 環境優雅                 │
│  月租兩萬五千，押金兩個月            │
│    請洽：張先生，3318457（白天）    │
│              7625361（晚上）        │
└─────────────────────────────────────┘
```

1. 這個公寓房子在幾樓？
2. 房租一個月多少錢？
3. 要不要押金？
4. 如果想看房子，應該給誰打電話？
5. 如果要打電話，應該什麼時候打？

Translation of the Dialogues

Dialogue I

Little Zhang : Did you go to look at rooms today?

Little Wang : I saw one apartment. I didn't like it very much.

Little Zhang : Why not?

Little Wang : I thought it was too small.

Little Zhang : Is it far away?

Little Wang : It's quite close, very convenient to go to school. The rent is 6,000 dollars per month, not too expensive. But I have so much stuff, it would be better if the room was a bit bigger.

Little Zhang : This kind of room isn't that easy to find. You could live there for two or three months first, and if you don't like it, move again.

Little Wang : Yeah, that's fine.

Dialogue II

Little Wang : I've decided to rent the room. Do I need to sign a lease?

Landlord : Yes, for at least half a year.

Little Wang : If I only stay for five months, what will happen to my deposit?

Landlord : If there's a new renter, then you can have it back. When would you like to move in?

Little Wang : It has been raining these days; it is not very convenient. My friends are all busy and can't help me.

Landlord : We can first sign the lease, then once the weather improves, you can move in.

Little Wang : Great, then let's sign the lease now. Today is April 11, so signing for half a year would be until October 10.

第八課　真麻煩！

LESSON 8 HOW TROUBLESOME!

Key Study Points

discussing housing problems ∕ the landlord's demand ∕ not getting through on the phone ∕ a stranger answering the phone ∕ dialing an extension

Vocabulary

Grammar

Dialogue I

真，麻煩，搬家(搬)，地方，些，問題，跟，交朋友，怕，吵，能，玩，因為，睡覺，所以，晚，早，用，做飯，洗衣機，對方付費(對方)，長途(長)，說，嗯，吧

Dialogue I

為什麼
因為……所以……
(relative clause)
<u>S-Adv-AV-V-O</u> 的 + N
能
N₁ 跟 + N₂ + (在 + PW) + V
吧

Dialogue II

李紅，趙奇，奇怪，好幾，次，接(to answer the phone)，辦公室，試，希望，大千公司，轉，稍等，聽，出去，進來，留話(留，話)，還是，下班，上班，以前，以後，吧，回電，自己

Dialogue II

V 了 + Nu - M + (了)
V 到 + PW ∕ TW
還是
V(O) 以前 ∕ 以後
吧

8

Dialogue I Discussing Housing Problems with a Friend

A：我 想 搬家。你知不知道哪裡有 房子出租？
Wǒ xiǎng bānjiā. Nǐ zhī bùzhīdào nǎlǐ yǒu fáng·zi chūzū?

B：你為什麼 要 搬家？你現在 住 的 地方不 好 嗎？
Nǐ wèishén·me yào bānjiā? Nǐ xiànzài zhù ·de dìfāng bù hǎo ·ma?

A：有一些 問題。你知道我喜歡交 朋友，
Yǒu yìxiē wèntí. Nǐ zhīdào wǒ xǐhuān jiāo péngyǒu,

可是 房東 怕吵，我 不 能 請 朋友 來玩。
kěshì fángdōng pà chǎo, wǒ bù néng qǐng péngyǒu lái wán.

B：這 不 是 大 問題。你可以跟 朋友 在 外面 玩 啊！
Zhè bú shì dà wèntí. Nǐ kěyǐ gēn péngyǒu zài wàimiàn wán ·a!

A：對。可是因為 房東 每天 晚上 十一點 睡覺，
Duì. Kěshì yīnwèi fángdōng měitiān wǎnshàng shíyī diǎn shuìjiào,

所以我不 能 太晚 回去。
suǒyǐ wǒ bù néng tài wǎn huí qù.

B：你也¹應該 早一點 回家 啊。
Nǐ yě yīnggāi zǎo yìdiǎn huíjiā ·a.

A：我 可以用 廚房，可是 不能 做飯。我也不 能 用
Wǒ kěyǐ yòng chúfáng, kěshì bù néng zuòfàn. Wǒ yě bù néng yòng

洗衣機。
xǐyījī.

B：那 真不 方便。
Nà zhēn bù fāngbiàn.

A：昨天 晚上 我要打一個 對方付費的 長途 電話，
Zuótiān wǎnshàng wǒ yào dǎ yí ·ge duìfāng fùfèi ·de chángtú diànhuà,

他也 說 不可以。
tā yě shuō bù kěyǐ.

B：嗯²。那你就搬家 吧。
·En. Nà nǐ jiù bānjiā ·ba.

8

Vocabulary

1. 真   zhēn   Adv : very, truly
房租一個月五千塊，真便宜。
Rent at five thousand dollars a month is really cheap.

2. 麻煩   máfán   SV/V/N : to be troublesome; May I trouble you to...; trouble   (M：個)
1) 換錢要填很多表，真麻煩。
2) 麻煩你拿那三本書給我。
3) 麻煩來了！老師要我去見他。
1) To exchange money you need to fill out a lot of forms. It's really a bother.
2) May I trouble you to bring those three books to me?
3) Trouble is here! (I'm in trouble now!) The teacher wants me to go see him.

3. 搬家　　bān//jiā　VO : to move one's residence

我買了新房子，下個星期要搬家。

I bought a new house. I will move next week.

搬　　bān　V : to move

這個桌子是你的。請你搬回去。

This table is yours. Please take it back.

4. 地方　　dìfāng　N : place　　(M：個)

這本書裡面有幾個地方錯了。

There are several errors in this book.

5. 些[3]　　xiē　M : some, several

1) 請你給我一些一塊錢的美金。

2) 這些書我不看了。你可以拿回去了。

3) 我買了些新衣服。你要不要看看？

1) Please give me some one-dollar bills.

2) I will not read these books anymore. You can take them back.

3) I bought some new clothes. Do you want to see (them)?

6. 問題　　wèntí　N : problem, question　　(M：個)

1) 你要買車子，錢不是問題，我可以幫你。

2) 我可以問你一個問題嗎？

1) If you want to buy a car, money is not a problem. I can help you.

2) May I ask you a question?

7. 跟　　gēn　CV : with

你要跟誰去旅行？

Whom do you want to travel with?

8. 交朋友　　jiāo//péngyǒu　VO : to make friends

他在美國住了一年，交了很多朋友。

He lived in America for a year and made a lot of friends.

9. 怕　　pà　V : to be afraid of; to fear

1) 有些先生怕太太買很多東西。

2) 如果你怕他不在家，就先給他打個電話。

1) Some husbands are afraid that their wives will buy a lot of things.

2) If you are afraid he is not at home, then give him a call first.

10. 吵　　　chǎo　　SV/V : to be noisy; to make noise; to annoy

1) 路上車多，人多，很吵。

2) 我現在要看書。請你不要吵我。

1) There are many cars and people on the street. It's really noisy.

2) I want to read now. Please do not bother me.

11. 能　　　néng　　AV : to be able to, can, may

1) 你一個晚上能看幾本書？

2) 我請了他，可是他太忙，不能來。

1) How many books can you read in one night?

2) I invited him, but he was too busy to come.

12. 玩　　　wán　　V : to play, to have fun

有空請你來我家玩。

Please come to my house (to have fun) when you have time.

13. 因為　　yīnwèi　　MA : because (of), for

A：你昨天為什麼沒來？

B：因為我朋友搬家，我去幫他。

A: Why didn't you come yesterday?

B: Because I helped my friend move.

14. 睡覺　　shuì//jiào　　VO : to sleep, to go to bed

他每天中午吃了飯就要睡一覺。

Every afternoon he takes a nap after eating.

15. 所以　　suǒyǐ　　Conj : therefore, so

因為他們不收信用卡，所以我付現金。

Because they did not accept credit cards, I paid in cash.

16. 晚　　　wǎn　　SV : to be late

十一點了。太晚了，我們應該回家了。

It is eleven o'clock, too late. We should go home.

17. 早　　　zǎo　　SV : to be early

A：這個月的房租星期四給你，好不好？

B：星期四太晚了。能不能早兩天？

A: I will pay you this month's rent on Thursday, okay?

B: Thursday is too late. Can you pay a couple of days earlier?

8

18. 用　　　yòng　　V : to use

我可不可以用一下你的電話？

May I use your telephone?

19. 做飯　　zuò//fàn　　VO : to cook

家裡沒菜，所以我沒做飯。我們去外面吃，好不好？

There is no food at home, so I didn't cook. Let's go out to eat, okay?

20. 洗衣機　　xǐyījī　　N : washing machine　　（M：台）

21. 對方付費　duìfāng fùfèi　　IE : the other party pays; collect phone call
    對方　　　duìfāng　　N : the opposite party

22. 長途　　chángtú　　N : long distance
    長　　　cháng　　SV : to be long

這張桌子很長，可以坐二十個人。

This table is really long. It can seat 20 people.

23. 說　　　shuō　　V : to say, to speak

A：他跟你說了些什麼？

B：他說不能說。

A: What did he say to you?

B: He said he could not tell.

24. 嗯　　　·en　　I : (indicates affirmation)

A：這個白菜很好吃。

B：嗯，真好吃。

A: This cabbage is really delicious.

B: Mmm, it's really good.

25. 吧　　　·ba　　P : (indicates suggestion)

時間不早了。我們回家吧。

It is not early. Let's go home.

Notes

1. "你也應該早一點回家啊" means "Still you should go home earlier." or "You should go home earlier anyway." In this dialogue, although speaker B understands why person A does not like going home before eleven o'clock every night, he/she still feels that it is better for A to go home earlier. "也" is used to express this tone.

2. "嗯" is used to affirm something the other party has said. Its tone is low and descending.

3. "些" is classified as a measure word. However, the number placed before it can only be "一". "一些" means "some." "這些" means "these", and "那些" means "those." In both cases "一" is omitted.

Grammar

1-1 你為什麼要搬家？　Why do you want to move?

Explanation: The question word "為什麼" is used to inquire about a reason and can be placed either before or immediately after the subject.

王：我想搬家。

李：你為什麼想搬家？

王：小謝沒來。

李：他 _____ ？

王：陳太太給小張買了一雙鞋。

李：她 _____ ？

王：他們家的洗衣機在客廳裡。

李：洗衣機 _____ ？

1-2 因為房租太貴，所以要搬家。

My house is too expensive, so I want to move.

Explanation: In the pattern "因為⋯⋯，所以⋯⋯", the appropriate reason follows "因為", while the result or conclusion follows "所以". Both parts of this pattern may be used together or on their own to express a cause-effect relationship. When answering a "為什麼" question, "所以⋯⋯" may be omitted.

8

Q：你為什麼要搬家？　　　　A：因為房租太貴 (，所以要搬家)。
　　為什麼他來？　　　　　　　因為_____ (，所以他來)。
　　張小姐今天為什麼沒空？　　因為_____ (，所以沒空)。
　　為什麼開車去？　　　　　　因為_____ (，所以開車去)。
　　我們為什麼不明天請客？　　因為_____ (，所以不明天請客)。
　　小陳為什麼沒買書？　　　　因為_____ (，所以沒買)。

小謝沒空　要搬家　去看房子　不方便　客人都很忙
太遠　他沒事　沒有現金　沒公車　東西很多　太貴

1-3 你現在住的房子　　the house you live in now

Explanation: Aside from N and SV, VP or a separate sentence may be used as a noun modifier as well. The structure of this type of sentence should be S-Adv-AV-V-O
的 + N, but S, Adv, AV, and O will not necessarily appear every time.

a) Q：這個房子有大客廳。那個房子有大廚房。你要租哪個？
　 A：我要租有大客廳的那個房子。

　 Q：王太太給了我一本書。張太太也給了我一本書。你喜歡哪本書？
　 A：我喜歡_____。

　 Q：這個小姐 chuān(穿)中國衣服。那個小姐 chuān(穿)日本衣服。
　　　你覺得哪個小姐 hǎokàn(好看)？
　 A：我覺得_____ 好看。

　 Q：這個銀行可以換美金，那個銀行不可以換美金。哪個銀行近？
　 A：_____ 近。

　 Q：這個房客明天搬來。那個房客下星期一搬來。哪個房客要住樓上？
　 A：_____ 要住樓上。

Additional Vocabulary

chuān(穿): to wear　　hǎokàn(好看): pretty (look good)

8

b) Q：誰是王明？A：<u>在睡覺的那個人</u>是王明。　　誰是小陳？

　　誰是錢書宜？　　　　　　　　　　　　　　　　誰是小謝？

　　誰是張台生？　　　　　　　　　　　　　　　　誰是小萬？

王明
錢書宜
張台生

小陳
小謝
小萬

c) 王：你昨天買的書多少錢？

　李：<u>我昨天買的書</u>兩百塊。

　王：我給你的衣服，你喜歡嗎？

　李：_____，我很喜歡。

　王：小張開的是哪國車？

　李：_____是美國車。

　王：今天的菜是誰做的？

　李：今天的菜是_____。

　王：昨天晚上來找你的那個人是誰？

　李：_____是張老師。

8

d) Activity: Big Wind Blowing

　　Everyone sits in a circle. The teacher stands in the center first where there is no seat. To begin the game the teacher says, "大風吹。". The students ask, "吹什麼？". The teacher answers, "吹有書包的人。". The students with a school bag race with the teacher to the empty seats. The one who misses the empty seat must stand in the center and continue to say the following:

大 fēng chuī (風吹)。
Chuī (吹)什麼？
Chuī (吹)……的人。(At least two people share the same characteristic.)

1-4 我不能請朋友來玩。   I cannot invite any friends over.

Explanation: The auxiliary verb "能" is used to express that the subject possesses the ability or qualifications to perform a certain action. Likewise, used in a negative
sentence, "能" indicates an action or manner is limited due to restrictions of
the environment.

a) 這裡不是車站，不能＿＿＿＿＿＿＿＿。
   我住的地方沒有廚房，不能＿＿＿＿＿＿＿。
   樓上的人太吵了，我不能＿＿＿＿＿＿＿。
   我的車有問題，不能＿＿＿＿＿＿＿。

> 看書　洗衣服　做飯　睡覺　上車　下車　開了

b) 王：今天下雨，我不能出去。在家裡能做什麼？
   李：在家能做的事很多啊。你可以看電視、看書啊。

   王：你一個晚上能看幾本書？
   李：＿＿＿＿＿＿＿＿＿＿＿＿。

   王：今天有客人要來，你能不能早一點回家幫我？
   李：不行，＿＿＿＿＿＿＿＿＿＿＿＿＿＿＿＿。

   王：你要不要 hē (喝)茶？
   李：謝謝，＿＿＿＿＿＿＿＿。hē (喝)了茶，我晚上沒辦法睡覺。

   王：一百塊能買幾斤白菜？
   李：＿＿＿＿＿＿＿＿＿＿。

> 能買五斤　我不能喝茶　我今天不能早回家　我能看三本書

Additional Vocabulary

   fēng (風)：wind　　chuī (吹)：to blow　　hē (喝)：to drink

1-5 你可以跟朋友在外面玩。　　You can have fun with your friends outside.

Explanation: "N₁跟 + N₂ + (在 + PW) + V" indicates two people or groups take part in the same action. The negative is placed before "跟" and is followed by the main verb.

王：我不能請朋友來家裡玩。
李：你可以<u>跟朋友在外面玩</u>。

王：我不想一個人去看老師。
李：我可以_____。

王：小錢明天搬家。你能不能幫他？
李：不行。我要_____。

王：我不知道你的車在哪裡。
李：老張知道。你_____。

王：小萬到哪兒去了？
李：他_____。

跟謝先生去旅行去了　　跟他去拿　　跟小陳到百貨公司去買鞋　　跟你去

8

1-6 那你就搬家吧。　　Then you should move.

Explanation: The modal particle "吧" placed at the end of a sentence indicates suggestion. Without the addition of "吧", a phrase or sentence may often sound like a command.

王：我不喜歡現在住的房子。
李：那就<u>搬家吧</u>。

王：他們這裡不收信用卡，怎麼辦？
李：那就_____。

王：陳老師家的電話打不 tōng (通)。
李：那就_____。

Additional Vocabulary

　　tōng (通) : to connect; through

王：小王星期三沒事。

李：那就 _____。

王：我不想做飯。

李：那就 _____。

等一下再打　星期三去看他　給他們現金　出去吃

Aural Comprehension Drill

The following dialogues may contain some unfamiliar vocabulary. Do not be concerned if you have not yet learned the vocabulary or do not understand the meaning. Try to figure out the meaning from the context, then answer the questions.

Listen to the following dialogues and choose the most appropriate answer.

1. (　) What are they talking about?

   a) the lady has trouble sleeping

   b) the lady has a problem with her landlord

   c) the lady has a problem with the man

2. (　) Which one of the following is correct?

   a) The lady's landlord makes noise every night.

   b) The lady is not afraid of noise.

   c) The man feels the lady should move.

8

Dialogue II Calling a Friend Who Is Never Home

李紅[1]：奇怪，他到哪裡去了？打了好幾次了，都沒人接。
Lǐ Hóng　　Qíguài,　　tā dào nǎlǐ qù ·le? Dǎ ·le hǎo jǐ cì ·le,　dōu méi rén jiē.

　　　　我打到 辦公室 去試試。希望他在。
　　　　Wǒ dǎ dào bàngōngshì qù shì·shì.　Xīwàng tā zài.

李紅：五七一一四三八。
　　　Wǔ qī yī yī sì sān bā.

A：大千公司，你好。
　　Dàqiān Gōngsī,　nǐ hǎo.

李紅：請你 轉二九五四。
　　　Qǐng nǐ zhuǎn èr jiǔ wǔ sì.

A：請稍等[2]。
　　Qǐng shāo děng.

B：喂？
　　Wéi?

李紅：麻煩你請趙奇 先生 聽電話[3]。
　　　Máfán nǐ qǐng Zhào Qí xiān·sheng tīng diànhuà.

B：他 出 去 了。你 要 留話 還是 等一下 再打來⁴？
Tā chū qù ·le.　Nǐ yào liúhuà　háishì děng yíxià zài dǎ lái?

李紅：他 什麼 時候回來？
Tā shén·me shíhòu huí lái?

B：他沒 説。我 想 下班 以前吧。
Tā méi shuō.　Wǒ xiǎng xiàbān yǐqián ·ba.

李紅：我 打到他家，他 都 不在。我留了話，他也沒 回電⁵。
Wǒ dǎ dào tā jiā,　tā dōu bú zài. Wǒ liú ·le huà,　tā yě méi huídiàn.

B：那 怎麼 辦？啊⁶，等一下，他回來了，你 自己跟他 説。
Nà zěn·me bàn?　·A,　děng yíxià,　tā huí lái ·le.　Nǐ zìjǐ gēn tā shuō.

趙奇，你的電話。
Zhào Qí,　nǐ·de diànhuà.

Vocabulary

1. 李紅　Lǐ Hóng　Proper N : a Chinese name

2. 趙奇　Zhào Qí　Proper N : a Chinese name

3. 奇怪　qíguài　SV : to be strange
   奇怪，他有車，為什麼不開？
   Strange, he has a car, why doesn't he drive?

4. 好幾　hǎo jǐ　Adv-Nu : many, several
   我找你找了好幾天了，你到哪裡去了？
   I have been looking for you for several days. Where have you been?

5. 次　cì　M : a time; occasion
   1) 你説什麼？請你再説一次。
   2) 上次可以刷卡，這次為什麼不行？
   1) What did you say? Please say it once again.
   2) Last time credit cards were accepted. Why not this time?

6. 接　jiē　V : to answer (the phone)

小王，麻煩你去接一下電話。

Little Wang, could I bother you to go answer the phone?

7. 辦公室　bàngōngshì　N : office　(M：間)

8. 試　shì　V : to try

這個舊電話你拿去試試能不能用。

Take this old telephone and see if it works.

9. 希望　xīwàng　V : to hope

我希望你喜歡我給你的書。

I hope you like the book I gave you.

10. 大千公司　Dàqiān Gōngsī　Proper N : Daqian Company

11. 轉　zhuǎn　V : to pass on; to transfer

我的電話是三九五四二四八轉四三五七。

My phone number is 3954248, extension 4357.

12. 稍等　shāo děng　IE : Wait a moment.

王：我要找陳小姐。

李：請稍等。

Wang: I am looking for Miss Chen.

Li: Please wait a moment.

13. 聽　tīng　V : to listen, to hear

先聽老師說一次，你們再說。

First listen to the teacher once, then you say it.

14. 出去　chū qù　V : to go out

謝小姐每天晚上吃了飯，就出去走走。

When Miss Xie finishes dinner every evening, she goes out for a walk.

*15. 進來　jìn lái　V : to come in

請你進來坐一下。

Please come in and sit for a while.

8

16. 留話　　liú//huà　　VO : to leave a message

王：張先生不在。你要不要留話？

李：不要了，謝謝。我晚上再打。

Wang:　Mr. Zhang is not here. Would you like to leave a message?

Li:　No, thank you. I will call again this evening.

留　　liú　　V : to leave; to keep, to save, to reserve

小王上個星期搬家了。他留了這幾本書給你。

Little Wang moved last week. He left these books for you.

話　　huà　　N : word　　(M：jù 句)

我要看書。你現在不要跟我說話，好不好？

I want to read. Please don't talk to me now, okay?

17. 還是　　háishì　　Conj : or

那個小姐是日本人還是中國人？

Is that lady Japanese or Chinese?

18. 下班　　xià//bān　　VO : to get off from work, to go off work

*19. 上班　　shàng//bān　　VO : to go to work, to be on duty

我們每天上午九點上班，下午五點下班。

We start work at nine o'clock every morning and get off at five o'clock in the afternoon.

20. 以前　　yǐqián　　MA : before

你來看我以前，先給我打個電話吧。

Before you come to see me, please give me a call.

*21. 以後　　yǐhòu　　MA : after

你下班以後要去哪裡？

Where do you want to go after you get off work?

22. 吧　　·ba　　P : (indicates guess, probability or suggestion)

王：你開日本車吧？

李：不是，我開美國車。

Wang:　Do you drive a Japanese car?

Li:　No, I drive an American car.

23. 回電　　huídiàn　　V : to return a call

王：小張，王小姐打電話來，你不在。她請你回電。

李：好，知道了。

Wang: Little Zhang, Miss Wang called when you were not here. She wants you to return her call.

Li:　Okay, I know.

24. 自己　　zìjǐ　　N : self, oneself

這些菜都是你自己做的嗎？

Did you prepare these dishes all by yourself?

Notes

1. "李紅" is a Chinese female name. "紅" is the first name. Chinese given names usually consist of two syllables, but many people have one-syllable names.

2. "請稍等" means "Just a second, please." or "Wait for a while, please." "請稍候" is another way of saying the same thing. Since both are formal, sometimes people will say "請等一下" instead.

3. "麻煩你請趙奇先生聽電話" means "Could you please ask Mr. Zhao Qi to come to the phone?" "麻煩你請趙奇先生接電話" has the same meaning. A less formal way is to say "請問趙奇先生在不在？".

4. "等一下再打來" means "Call again in a while." "等一下" is a verb phrase, meaning to wait for a moment. But in this sentence it is used as a time word, which is usually placed before a verb, referring to something done at a later time. Another example: "我等一下來" "I will come in a while."

5. "回電" means "to call back", "to return a phone call." It is a shortened phrase, the same as saying "回電話" or "給X回電話".

6. "啊，等一下，他回來了". This "啊" indicates a tone of surprise.

Grammar

2-1 打了好幾次了　　called many times

Explanation: When the object following "V 了" carries a number-measure word modifier, if "了" is added to the end of the sentence, it expresses that the action of the verb is still being carried on at the time the sentence is spoken. Accordingly, no "了" would indicate that the action was already completed by that time.

王：你昨天給她打電話了沒有？

李：打了好幾次了，可是她都不在。

王：我給你的那三本書，你都看了嗎？

李：今天＿＿＿＿＿＿＿＿＿＿＿＿＿＿，還有一本明天再看。

王：小萬想約的朋友都約了嗎？

李：他想約十個，現在＿＿＿＿＿＿＿＿＿＿＿＿。

王：你在這裡住了幾個月了？

李：到下個月就＿＿＿＿＿＿＿＿＿＿＿。

王：房間裡的東西都搬了沒有？

李：＿＿＿＿＿＿＿＿＿＿＿，還有一半。

看了兩本	看了兩本了	約了五個	約了五個了
搬了一半	搬了一半了	住了半年	住了半年了

2-2 打到辦公室去　　call the office

Explanation: The post-verb "到" can connect with a place word or time word to show the precise location of the object in question by the time the action of the verb is completed or the precise place or time the action was completed.

王：家裡沒人接電話。

李：那打到辦公室去試試。

王：請問，公用電話在哪裡？

李：這裡沒有。你要＿＿＿＿＿樓上去。

王：這個房間裡東西太多了。

李：那，電視＿＿＿＿＿＿＿客廳去吧。

王：你昨天在公司做什麼？爲什麼九點 cái (才) 下班？

李：昨天等一 tōng (通) 美國來的電話，＿＿＿＿＿晚上九點。

王：你們想在這裡住幾個月？

李：從五月＿＿＿＿＿＿＿十一月，一共六個月。

走到	開到	拿到	搬到	做到	睡到	看到	住到　等到

Additional Vocabulary

　　　cái (才)：then and only then　　　tōng (通)：M for telephone call

2-3 你要留話還是等一下再打來？

Do you want to leave a message or call back in a few minutes?

Explanation: When options are presented in a question, "還是" is often placed before the last choice.

王：請問，錢書宜老師在不在？
李：他不在。你要<u>留話</u>還是<u>等一下再打來</u>？

王：小姐，一共多少錢？
李：三百六。您要＿＿＿＿＿還是＿＿＿＿＿？

王：我明天可以去看你嗎？
李：可以啊。你要＿＿＿＿＿還是＿＿＿＿＿？

王：張先生很喜歡看書。
李：他看＿＿＿＿＿還是＿＿＿＿＿？

王：我昨天請朋友來吃飯。
李：你請他們吃＿＿＿＿＿、＿＿＿＿＿還是＿＿＿＿＿？

> 刷卡　給支票　付現金　早上來　中午來　下午來　晚上來
> 中 wén（文）書　外 wén（文）書　中國菜　日本菜　美國菜

8

2-4 下班以前　before getting off work

Explanation: A specific time or action modifier may be directly inserted before "以前/以後". It is not necessary to add any particles.

王：他什麼時候回來？
李：<u>下班以前</u>。

王：錢小姐到哪兒去了？
李：不知道。她＿＿＿＿＿＿＿＿在桌上給你留了話。

王：我應該什麼時候給張老師打電話？
李：＿＿＿＿＿＿＿＿吧。太晚他就回家了。

Additional Vocabulary

中 wén（文）: Chinese (language)　　　外 wén（文）: foreign language(s)

王：押金什麼時候可以拿回來？

李：_____。

王：要是我想搬家，應該什麼時候跟你說？

李：_____。

王：小陳什麼時候去買菜？

李：他每天_____去買菜。

王：對不起，小張還沒有回來。

李：請他_____給我打個電話。

王：我要去銀行換錢。

李：明天再去吧。銀行_____就沒有人了。

王：你們什麼時候跟那家公司簽約？

李：_____。

上課以前　一個月以前　搬家以後　回來以前　出去以前

五點以前　三點半以後　下班以後　一個星期以後　回家以後

8

2-5 我想下班以前吧。　　Before getting off work, I suppose.

Explanation: "吧" placed at the end of a sentence has a tone of supposition. Its tone either as a supposition or suggestion is indicated by the context.

王：他什麼時候回來？

李：我想下班以前吧。

王：小陳要怎麼來？

李：我想_____。

王：你們什麼時候搬家？

李：我想_____。

王：租房子簽約，一次要簽幾個月？

李：最少_____。

王：明天誰要去老師家吃飯？

李：我想＿＿＿＿＿＿。

走路　坐公車　明年　下個月　一個月　三個月　半年　小王　小李

Aural Comprehension Drill

The following dialogues may contain some unfamiliar vocabulary. Do not be concerned if you have not yet learned the vocabulary or do not understand the meaning. Try to figure out the meaning from the context, then answer the questions.

Listen to the following dialogues and choose the most appropriate answer.

1. (　) Under what circumstance is the above dialogue being read?

a) You have not met the desired party. Leave a message.

b) The desired party is not in. Leave a message.

c) Leave a message on the answering machine.

2. (　) Under what circumstance would you be most likely to hear the following statement?

a) You call, but no one is there, so you leave a message.

b) Leave a message on the answering machine.

c) You have not run into the desired party, leave a message.

8

Variety Exercises

I.

問：你怕＿＿＿＿＿＿＿＿嗎？

答：怕／不很怕／不怕。

問：你怕什麼？

答：我怕＿＿＿＿＿＿＿。

Additional Vocabulary

māo(貓) : cat   gǒu(狗) : dog   shé(蛇) : snake   guǐ(鬼) : ghost

lǎoshǔ(老鼠) : mouse   zhānglāng(蟑螂) : cockroach   坐 fēijī(飛機) : to travel by airplanes

看 yáyī(牙醫) : to see a dentist   pàng(胖) : to be fat   gāo(高) : to be high

II. Make a questionnaire of the household chores you do and don't like.

	喜歡	不很喜歡	很不喜歡
買菜			
做飯			
to wash dishes			
to wash clothes			
to wash car			
to wash bathroom			
to mop floor			
to vacuum carpet			
to mow			

Students can ask the teacher any words they are not able to say. The teacher can write the words on the board for reference.

When the questionnaire is finished, fill it in yourself first, then interview the teacher and classmates. Then find classmates who like and dislike the same chores as you. Finally, the entire class can make a chart explaining "喜歡／不喜歡……的人有 X 人。"

III. Role Play

1. Make rules for all of your housemates to follow.

2. Make a telephone call.

  1) Ask for the person to come to the phone. (Assume that the person who answers is not the individual to whom you wish to speak.)

  2) The desired party is not there. Ask the person who answers to help you leave a message.

  3) Ask the operator to dial an extension.

Try to Guess

1. (　) What do you think "少見多怪" means?

      a) a few people have seen many strange things

      b) to wonder much because one has seen little

      c) one is so surprised by something weird

2. (　) What do you think "早晚" means?

      a) early in the evening   b) morning or night   c) sooner or later

3. (　) What do you think "睡午覺" means?

      a) to take a nap in the afternoon   b) to daydream   c) to sleep away the noon

4. (　) What do you think "試用" means?

      a) to try to use

      b) to test

      c) to try out something or to hire someone on a probational basis

Authentic Material

1. Listen once to the following dialogue.

   Question 1: Guess what "chá(查)" means.

   Question 2: Why is this person making this phone call?

      a) He wants to know the train schedule.

      b) He would like to know how to get to the train station.

      c) He would like to know the phone number of the train station.

2. If you want to call a number which has already been disconnected, what will you hear after dialing the number? Try to guess what the following recording says.

「對不起，您剛剛撥的是空號。請查明後再撥。」

   Question 1: Guess how to express in Chinese an invalid phone number.

      a) kōnghào (空號)   b) gānggāng (剛剛)   c) chámíng (查明)

   Question 2: What should you do if you encounter the above-mentioned situation?

      a) dial again

      b) wait a moment then dial again

      c) first confirm the number and then dial again

3. You dialed the number many times, and every time you hear the following message:

「現在所有的線路都在忙線中。請稍候再撥。」

Question 1: What does "mángxiànzhōng (忙線中)" mean?

     a) No one answers the phone.   b) The line is busy.   c) The call cannot go through.

Question 2: What does the person on the other line suggest you do?

     a) call again in a moment

     b) confirm the number and then dial again

     c) dial again

4. Listen to the following dialogue.

Question 1: What kind of phone call does B want to make?

     a) station to station   b) person to person   c) local

Question 2: Who will pay for the call?

     a) the person making the call

     b) the person receiving the call

     c) both parties will split the cost of the call

5. You make a call to your friend working at a large trading company and his number is 5558888 extension 7, and after dialing 5558888 you hear the following:

Question 1: What number should you press first?

     a) #1   b) #2   c) #9

Question 2: What is the " fēnjī (分機)" of the number you are calling?

Question 3: If you do not know your friend's extension, what would you do?

Question 4: What does "àn (按)" mean?

Question 5: Please use the words you have already learned to explain the meaning of "shāohòu (稍候)".

Translation of the Dialogues

Dialogue I

A : I want to move. Do you know where there is a room for rent?

B : Why do you want to move? Isn't the place you live now okay?

A : There are a few problems. You know that I like to make friends, but the landlord is afraid it will be too noisy. He won't let me bring my friends over.

B : That's not a problem. You can just go out with your friends.

A : Yes, but since the landlord goes to bed at eleven o'clock every night, I can't get back too late.

B : You should go home earlier anyway.

A : I can use the kitchen, but I'm not allowed to cook. Besides, I can't use the washing machine.

B : That's inconvenient.

A : Last night I wanted to make a long distance collect call, but the landlord wouldn't let me.

B : Eh, then you should move.

Dialogue II

Li Hong : That's strange, where could he have gone? I've called so many times, but no one answers. I'll try his office. I hope he's there.

Li Hong : 5711438

    A : Hello, Daqian Company.

Li Hong : Extension 2954, please.

    A : One moment, please.

    B : Hello?

Li Hong : Could you please ask Mr. Zhao Qi to come to the phone?

    B : He stepped out. Would you like to leave a message or call back in a little while?

Li Hong : When will he be back?

    B : He didn't say, I think before the end of the day.

Li Hong : I've called his home, and he was not there. I've left him messages, but he hasn't returned my call.

    B : Well, what should be done? Ah, hold on. He's back. You can ask him yourself. You have a telephone call, Zhao Qi.

8

第九課 交朋友
LESSON 9 MAKING FRIENDS

Key Study Points

introducing oneself-names／hometown／family background／introducing friends／talking about one's job／talking about one's pastime

Vocabulary

Grammar

Dialogue I

Dialogue I

王家明，貴姓，林金水，台灣大學(大學)，念書，家(M)，爸媽(爸爸，媽媽)，上海(海)，多(麼)，大，久，歲，英文，一定，會，教，台北，台南，還，哥哥，姊姊，妹妹，弟弟，有的，在(Adv)，做事，女孩子(女，孩子)，男孩子(男)，上課

是……V 的

多＋SV？

就／要……了

會

還

在＋V

有的……有的……

Dialogue II

Dialogue II

大概，認識，大有，介紹，王明，謝新雨，喝，可樂，啤酒(酒)，電腦，工程師，名片，難，容易，懂，工作，貿易公司，常常，電影，逛街，愛，爬山(爬，山)，打球(打，球)

大概

一＋M＋(N)＋都／也＋不／沒V

VO 的時候

V V O

Dialogue I   Meeting a New Neighbor

家明：你好。我 叫 王 家明。你貴姓？[1]
Nǐ hǎo.   Wǒ jiào Wáng Jiāmíng.   Nǐ guì xìng?

金水：你好。我 姓 林，我 叫 林 金水。你是 學生 嗎？
Nǐ hǎo.   Wǒ xìng Lín,   wǒ jiào Lín Jīnshuǐ.   Nǐ shì xuéshēng ·ma?

家明：是啊！我 在 台灣 大學 念書。你呢？
Shì ·a!   Wǒ zài Táiwān Dàxué niànshū.   Nǐ ·ne?

金水：我 在 一家 公司 上班。你是 哪裡人？[2]
Wǒ zài yì jiā gōngsī shàngbān.   Nǐ shì nǎlǐ rén?

家明：我 是 從 美國 來的，可是我爸媽 都 是 上海 人。
Wǒ shì cóng Měiguó lái ·de,   kěshì wǒ bà mā dōu shì Shànghǎi rén.

金水：你今年 多大了？[3] 在 美國 住了多久？
Nǐ jīnnián duó dà ·le?   Zài Měiguó zhù·le duó jiǔ?

家明：我 下 個 月 就 二十 歲了。我 在 美國 住了十二 年。
Wǒ xià ·ge yuè jiù èrshí suì ·le.   Wǒ zài Měiguó zhù·le shíèr nián.

金水：那你的 英文 一定 很 好。我 不 太 會 說 英文。
Nà nǐ·de Yīngwén yídìng hěn hǎo. Wǒ bú tài huì shuō Yīngwén.

你 有 空，請 你 教 我，好 不 好？
Nǐ yǒu kòng, qǐng nǐ jiāo wǒ, hǎo bùhǎo?

家明：好。你 是 台北 人 嗎？
Hǎo. Nǐ shì Táiběi rén ·ma?

金水：我 家 在 台南。我 爸爸 媽媽 都 還 住 台南。
Wǒ jiā zài Táinán. Wǒ bà·ba mā·ma dōu hái zhù Táinán.

家明：你 家 有 幾 個 孩子？⁴
Nǐ jiā yǒu jǐ ·ge hái·zi?

金水：我 有 三 個 哥哥、兩 個 妹妹。有 的 在 念書，
Wǒ yǒu sān ·ge gē·ge, liǎng ·ge mèi·mei. Yǒu·de zài niànshū,

有 的 在 做事。
yǒu·de zài zuòshì.

家明：我們 家 有 三 個 女孩子，只有 我 一 個 男孩子。
Wǒ·men jiā yǒu sān ·ge nǚhái·zi, zhǐyǒu wǒ yí ·ge nánhái·zi.

噢，對 不 起，我 要 去 上課 了。再見。
Òu, duì·bùqǐ, wǒ yào qù shàngkè ·le. Zàijiàn.

Vocabulary

1. 王家明　　Wáng Jiāmíng　　Proper N : a Chinese name

2. 貴姓　　guì xìng　　IE : your honorable surname

3. 林金水　　Lín Jīnshuǐ　　Proper N : a Chinese name

4. 台灣大學 Táiwān Dàxué　　Proper N : Taiwan University
   大學　　dàxué　　N : university　　(M：所)

5. 念書　　niàn//shū　　VO : to study

你在哪個大學念書？

In which university do you study?

6. 家　　jiā　　M : for company, bank, etc.

7. 爸媽　　bà mā　　N : father and mother

爸爸　　bà·ba　　N : father　　(M：個)

媽媽　　mā·ma　　N : mother　　(M：個)

8. 上海　　Shànghǎi　　Proper N : Shanghai, China

海　　hǎi　　N : sea, ocean　　(M：piàn 片)

9. 多(麼)　　duō/duó(·me)　　Adv : how SV? to what degree

從日本到美國(有)多遠？

How far is it from Japan to America?

10. 大　　dà　　SV : to be old

你今年多大？

How old are you?

11. 久　　jiǔ　　SV : to be a long time

A：你學開車學了多久了？

B：學了一個月了。

A: How long have you learned how to drive?

B: One month.

12. 歲　　suì　　M : year, age

13. 英文　　Yīngwén　　N : English

14. 一定　　yídìng　　Adv : surely, certainly

1) 你明天一定要來。我等你。

2) 東西貴不一定好。

1) You must come tomorrow. I will wait for you.

2) Expensive things are not necessarily good.

9

15. 會　　　huì　　AV : can, to know how to

你學英文學了一個月了，會說了吧？

You have been studying English for one month. I suppose you can speak it?

16. 教　　　jiāo　　V : to teach

你做的這個菜很好吃。你教我做，好不好？

This food you cooked is delicious. Would you teach me how to cook it?

17. 台北　　Táiběi　　Proper N : Taipei

18. 台南　　Táinán　　Proper N : Tainan

19. 還　　　hái　　Adv : still

學生都回家了，可是老師還在學校。

The students have all gone home, but the teacher is still at school.

20. 哥哥　　gē·ge　　N : elder brother　　(M：個)

*21. 姊姊　　jiě·jie　　N : elder sister　　(M：個)

22. 妹妹　　mèi·mei　　N : younger sister　　(M：個)

*23. 弟弟　　dì·di　　N : younger brother　　(M：個)

24. 有的　　yǒu·de　　N : some, some of

這些書，有的我看了，有的我還沒看。

Of these books, some I have read, others I have not yet read.

25. 在　　　zài　　Adv : (indicating an action in progress)

王：小林，你在做什麼？

林：我在想搬家的事。

Wang : Little Lin, what are you doing?

Lin : I am thinking about the moving.

26. 做事　　zuò//shì　　VO : to do things, to work

1) 我每個星期天都很忙，要做很多事。

2) 我在學校做事。我教英文。

1) I am busy every Sunday. I must do many things.

2) I work at school. I teach English.

27. 女孩子　　nǚhái·zi　　N：girl　　(M：個)
    女　　　　nǚ　　N：female (of persons)
    孩子　　　hái·zi　　N：child　　(M：個)

28. 男孩子　　nánhái·zi　　N：boy　　(M：個)
    男　　　　nán　　N：male (of persons)

29. 上課　　shàng//kè　　VO：to have class, to go to class
    我們每天早上十點十分上英文課。
    Every morning at 10:10 we have English class.

Notes

1. "貴姓？", is the polite form for "你姓什麼？". "你貴姓？", "您貴姓？", "小姐貴姓？" and "先生貴姓？" are common variations. The answer to this question may be one's family name or full name. Usually only the family name is given when answering a stranger. It is considered polite for Chinese people to ask for someone's family name, rather than his/her first name, when they meet for the first time. To ask the name of a person who is about the same age as the speaker or younger, it is acceptable to ask directly "你叫什麼名字(míng·zi)？" (What is your name?). To ask someone who is older or senior; the polite form is "請問您怎麼稱呼？", which means "May I know your name?" (literally: "May I ask you how you should be addressed?" "稱呼" (chēnghū) means to address.

2. "你是哪裡人？" means "Where are you from?" It is used to ask where one's home town is. In this dialogue, 王家明 doesn't answer the question directly. He says that he came from the United States, and that his parents are from 上海. According to Chinese tradition, if one's parents are from 上海, their children are also 上海人. But 王家明 doesn't say that he is a 上海人. It seems that 王家明 doesn't wish to identify himself as a 上海人.

3. "你(今年)多大了？" means "How old are you (this year)?" It is used to ask someone who is about the same age or younger. "你幾歲？" is used to ask young people, especially children. "X 今年多大歲數(suìshù)？" is used to ask the age of an older person.

4. "你家有幾個孩子？" means "How many children are there in your family?" Some people would ask "你有幾個兄弟姊妹？" which means "How many brothers and sisters do you have?" 兄(xiōng) means elder brother. "你家有幾口人？" is also used to ask how many people there are in one's family.

9

Grammar

1-1 我是從美國來的。　　I am from the United States.

Explanation: The sentence pattern "是……的" is used to gain further information or understanding about a past event's time, place, people, reason, method, etc. "是" is placed before the matter about which one wants to inquire and can often be omitted; "的" is placed after the main verb.

王：我去年八月到日本旅行去了。　　李：你是跟誰去的？

我買了一本書。　　你＿＿＿＿＿＿＿＿＿＿＿＿？

張先生到日本去了。　　他＿＿＿＿＿＿＿＿＿＿＿＿？

這個菜是我做的。　　你＿＿＿＿＿＿＿＿＿＿＿＿？

小陳上星期來了好幾次。　　他＿＿＿＿＿＿＿＿＿＿＿＿？

是怎麼做的　是在哪裡買的　是為什麼來的　是什麼時候去的
是怎麼去的　是什麼時候做的　是跟誰來的　是給誰買的

1-2 多久　　how long

Explanation: The interrogative adverb "多" can be placed before the SV, to inquire about the exact degree or level of a particular state.

王：他住的地方很遠。

李：走路來要多久？

王：半個鐘頭吧。

王：我買的車子真便宜。

李：有＿＿＿＿＿＿？

王：只要三十萬。

王：他想租大一點的房子。

李：要＿＿＿＿＿＿？

王：最少要有五個房間。

王：這種guǒzhī(果汁)真好喝。

Additional Vocabulary

guǒzhī(果汁)：fruit juice

李：有＿＿＿＿＿＿＿？
王：喝了還想再喝。

王：去他家太麻煩了。
李：有＿＿＿＿＿＿＿？
王：要換好幾次車。

多好喝　多麻煩　多便宜　多大

1-3 下個月就二十歲了。　Next month I will be 20 years old.
我要去上課了。　I have to go to class now.

Explanation: "就……了", "要……了", and "就要……了" all indicate something is about to occur.

1) 王太太就回來了。你等一下吧。
2) 走吧。走吧。＿＿＿＿＿＿＿＿＿＿＿。
3) 車＿＿＿＿＿＿＿＿。還沒上車的人請上車。
4) 不要走了。我們＿＿＿＿＿＿＿＿。在我們家吃飯吧。
5) 我們＿＿＿＿＿＿＿＿。有什麼事明天再說吧。

就要吃飯了　要下雨了　要下班了　就要開了

1-4 我不太會說英文。　I cannot speak English well.

Explanation: "會" placed before the verb indicates that the speaker either knows how to or is capable of performing the indicated action.

王：你為什麼不去日本念書？
李：我不會說日文。

王：這裡坐公車不方便。
李：我＿＿＿＿＿＿。我們可以租車。

王：要是你沒有時間，可以用 wēibōlú(微波爐)做飯。
李：沒辦法，我＿＿＿＿＿＿啊。

Additional Vocabulary

　wēibōlú(微波爐) : microwave oven

9

王：我能找什麼工作？

李：你_____，可以試試教英文。

王：你教我做中國菜，好不好？

李：我很想教你。可是我也_____，不能教你。

不會做　會說英文　不會用　會開車

1-5 我爸爸媽媽都<u>還</u>住台南。　　Both my father and mother still live in Tainan.

Explanation: The adverb "還" placed before the verb or stative verb, indicates the situation or action remains the same. The stative verb usually follows "很", "太", or other adverbs. The negative "不" or "沒(有)" placed after "還" and before the verb or stative verb indicates the action or situation has not yet occurred.

a) 還 + V

　　王：你爸爸媽媽都搬來台北了嗎？

　　李：沒有，他們都<u>還住台南</u>。

　　王：九點多了。小張應該回家了吧？

　　李：我五分鐘以前給她打電話，她_____辦公室。

　　王：你五年以前很喜歡開車。現在呢？

　　李：我現在_____開車。

b) 還 + Adv + SV

　　王：這雙鞋打八折，你可以買啊。

　　李：不行，打了折_____，我沒有錢買。

　　王：你家的洗衣機用了幾年了，為什麼不換一個？

　　李：那個洗衣機_____，可以再用幾年。

c) 還 + Neg. + V

　　王：張小姐下班了嗎？

　　李：她這個星期很忙，應該_____吧。

　　王：上課十分鐘了。學生都來了吧？

　　李：王家明_____。

9

1-6 在念書、在做事　studying, working

Explanation: When the structural particle "在" is placed before the verb, it indicates that the action is in progress.

王：李紅在房間裡做什麼？

李：她<u>在看書</u>。

王：你在那裡做什麼？

李：我＿＿＿＿＿＿＿＿＿＿＿＿＿＿。

王：你想這時候你男朋友在做什麼？

李：我想＿＿＿＿＿＿＿＿吧。

王：昨天晚上八點你在做什麼？我打電話去都沒人接。

李：我＿＿＿＿＿＿＿＿。

王：你哥哥在客廳做什麼？

李：＿＿＿＿＿＿＿＿＿。

上課　看電視　洗澡　做飯　想請客的事　睡覺

1-7 有的在念書、有的在做事　some are studying, others are working

Explanation: When expressing individual actions or states within a group, it is common to use the pattern "有的……，有的……".

王：他們在做什麼？

李：有的<u>在念書</u>，有的<u>在做事</u>。

王：這些是什麼書？

李：有的是＿＿＿＿＿＿＿，有的是＿＿＿＿＿＿＿。

王：這幾個菜是誰做的？

李：有的是＿＿＿＿＿＿＿，有的是＿＿＿＿＿＿＿。

王：你們幾點下班？

李：有的＿＿＿＿＿＿＿，有的＿＿＿＿＿＿＿。

9

王：你們喜歡吃什麼菜？

李：有的喜歡吃＿＿＿＿＿＿，有的喜歡吃＿＿＿＿＿＿。

中文書　英文書　日文書　我做的　我媽媽做的　買的
下午五點　晚上九點　早上六點　中國菜　日本菜

Aural Comprehension Drill

The following dialogues may contain some unfamiliar vocabulary. Do not be concerned if you have not yet learned the vocabulary or do not understand the meaning. Try to figure out the meaning from the context, then answer the questions.

Listen to the following dialogues and choose the most appropriate answer.

1. (　) What is the difference in age between the woman's oldest and youngest child?

    a) 1 year　　b) 3 years　　c) 5 years

2. (　) How many hours does the woman work a day?

    a) 7 hours　　b) 8 hours　　c) 9 hours

   (　) Why does the woman like her job?

    a) the work is easy　　b) short working hours　　c) high salary

3. (　) How long has the lady been here?

    a) half a year　　b) 1 year　　c) 1-1/2 years

   (　) Where does the lady's family live now?

    a) England　　b) France　　c) both England and France

9

Dialogue II Getting to Know Someone

大有： 你們大概還不 認識吧？來，來，來，我給你們
Nǐ·men dàgài hái bú rènshì ·ba? Lái, lái, lái, wǒ gěi nǐ·men

介紹介紹[1]。這是 王 明。這是謝新雨。
jièshào jièshào.   Zhè shì Wáng Míng. Zhè shì Xiè Xīnyǔ.

王明： 你好[2]。
Nǐ hǎo.

新雨： 你好。
Nǐ hǎo.

大有： 請坐。你們要喝 什麼？
Qǐng zuò. Nǐ·men yào hē shén·me?

新雨： 請 給我一杯茶。
Qǐng gěi wǒ yì bēi chá.

王明： 我要可樂。
Wǒ yào kělè.

9

新雨：這是我的 名片³。
Zhè shì wǒ·de míngpiàn.

王明：噢，你是電腦 工程師。我覺得 電腦 很 難。
Òu, nǐ shì diànnǎo gōngchéngshī. Wǒ jué·dé diànnǎo hěn nán.

我一點 都不 懂。
Wǒ yìdiǎn dōu bù dǒng.

新雨：那你在哪裡 工作？
Nà nǐ zài nǎlǐ gōngzuò?

王明：我在 貿易公司 上班。
Wǒ zài màoyì gōngsī shàngbān.

新雨：沒事的 時候，你喜歡 做 什麼？
Méi shì ·de shíhòu, nǐ xǐhuān zuò shén·me?

王明：我 常 常 去看 電影、逛街。你呢？
Wǒ chángcháng qù kàn diànyǐng, guàngjiē. Nǐ ·ne?

新雨：我 也愛看 電影⁴。有的 時候也去 爬爬山、打打球。
Wǒ yě ài kàn diànyǐng. Yǒu·de shíhòu yě qù pá·páshān, dǎ·dǎqiú.

Vocabulary

1. **大概**　　dàgài　　Adv : maybe, perhaps, probably

   王：你什麼時候可以回家？

   李：大概下午三點吧。

   Wang: When can you come home?

   Li: Probably at 3:00 p.m.

2. **認識**　　rènshì　　V : to know, to recognize

   王先生是誰？我不認識他。

   Who is Mr. Wang? I do not know him.

3. 大有　　Dàyǒu　　Proper N : a Chinese name

4. 介紹　　jièshào　　V : to introduce

我不認識王先生。你可以給我介紹一下嗎？

I do not know Mr. Wang. Can you introduce me?

5. 王明　　Wáng Míng　　Proper N : a Chinese name

6. 謝新雨　　Xiè Xīnyǔ　　Proper N : a Chinese name

7. 喝　　hē　　V : to drink

我晚上不能喝咖啡，喝了就沒辦法睡覺。

I cannot drink coffee at night; if I do, there is no way I can sleep.

8. 可樂　　kělè　　N : cola　　(M：杯、píng 瓶、guàn 罐)

*9. 啤酒　　píjiǔ　　N : beer　　(M：杯、píng 瓶、guàn 罐)

酒　　jiǔ　　N : wine, liquor　　(M：杯、píng 瓶)

10. 電腦　　diànnǎo　　N : computer　　(M：bù 部)

11. 工程師　　gōngchéngshī　　N : engineer　　(M：位)

12. 名片　　míngpiàn　　N : name card, business card　　(M：張)

13. 難　　nán　　SV : to be difficult

我找你找了好幾次，你都不在。找你真難。

I looked for you many times, but you were never there. It is really difficult to find you.

*14. 容易　　róngyì　　SV : to be easy

我覺得做這個菜很容易。每個人都會。

I think it is easy to cook this food. Everybody can do it.

15. 懂　　dǒng　　V : to understand

你說什麼？我不懂。請你再說一次。

What did you say? I do not understand. Please say it again.

16. 工作　　gōngzuò　　N/V : work; to work

張先生在電腦公司工作。

Mr. Zhang works in a computer company.

9

17. 貿易公司　màoyì gōngsī　　N : trade company

18. 常常　　　chángcháng　　Adv : often, frequently
　　我常常去王先生家喝茶，一個星期去五次。
　　I often go to Mr. Wang's house to drink tea, five times a week.

19. 電影　　　diànyǐng　　N : movie　　(M：bù 部)

20. 逛街　　　guàng//jiē　　VO : to go window-shopping
　　我太太很喜歡逛街，看看新鞋、新衣服。
　　My wife really likes to go window-shopping and look at new shoes and new clothes.

21. 愛　　　　ài　　V/AV : to love; to love to
　　1) 張先生很愛他的女朋友。
　　2) 我很愛吃中國菜，一個星期最少吃兩次。
　　1) Mr. Zhang loves his girlfriend.
　　2) I really love to eat Chinese food. I eat it at least twice a week.

22. 爬山　　　pá//shān　　VO : to climb a mountain, to hike on hills
　　爬　　　pá　　V : to climb, to crawl
　　這個孩子會爬了，還不會走。
　　This child can crawl, but still cannot walk.

　　山　　　shān　　N : mountain　　(M：zuò 座 stand)

23. 打球　　　dǎ//qiú　　VO : to play ball
　　打　　　dǎ　　V : to play
　　球　　　qiú　　N : ball　　(M：個)
　　你喜歡打什麼球？
　　What kind of ball-game do you like to play?

Notes

1. "我給你們介紹介紹" means "Let me introduce you to each other." This should be expressed as "給someone介紹". It is not correct to say "我介紹你們".

2. After Chinese people are introduced, they say "你好", and some people will say "幸會，幸會。", which means "It is a pleasure to meet you." Since this is considered very formal, younger generations prefer to say "很高興認識你。", which means "I'm pleased to meet you." "高興" (gāoxìng) means "to be glad."

3. When Chinese business people meet for the first time, they usually exchange name cards, and very polite people will say "這是我的名片。請多指教。". "請多指教。" means "Please give me your advice." or "Feel free to give your suggestions."

4. "我也愛看電影" means "I love to watch movies, too." The object of "愛" can be a noun which denotes people or a verb phrase that denotes hobbies. "I love this table." will be "我很喜歡這個桌子。" not "我愛這個桌子。" Another point is that "愛", "喜歡", "認識", "知道", "懂", and "希望" are state verbs indicating states (of mind). They are not action verbs, therefore they can not be used in "V-了" pattern indicating action completed, and it is not correct to say "沒愛", "沒喜歡", "沒認識", "沒知道", "沒懂", "沒希望(used as a verb)" either.

Grammar

2-1 你們大概還不認識吧？　You probably still don't know each other.

Explanation: "大概" is used to convey imprecise appraisal or inference of a situation and carry with an unconfirmed tone. It can be coupled with a number-measure word, a time word, or a particular situation. It is commonly used together with "吧".

王：他們為什麼不說話？
李：大概還不認識吧。

王：明天請客，有多少人要來？
李：_____吧。

王：陳大千昨天為什麼沒來上課？
李：_____吧。

王：奇怪。小張說要給我打電話，為什麼沒打？
李：_____。

王：你們昨天是幾點去逛街的？

李：_____。

> 沒有空　下午三點　晚上七點半　二十個
> 五、六個　wàng（忘）了　生 bìng（病）了

2-2 一點兒都不懂　　not understand even a little

Explanation: The sentence pattern "一 + M + (N) + 都/也 + 不/沒……" is used to empha-size an exclusive situation, with "都" meaning "even".

a) 王：你會不會用電腦？教我好不好？

李：對不起，我不會用電腦。

王：一點都不會嗎？

李：<u>一點都不會</u>。

王：你媽媽很會做菜，你呢？

李：我不會。

王：一個菜也不會嗎？

李：_____。

王：請你在這裡等我一下。

李：對不起，我有事，不能等你。

王：一分鐘都不能等嗎？

李：對不起，_____。

王：你有沒有日本朋友？

李：我沒有。

王：一個也沒有嗎？

李：_____。

王：你這個月看了幾本書？

李：我沒看書。

王：一本都沒看嗎？

李：對啊，_____。

Additional Vocabulary

wàng（忘）: to forget　　　生 bìng（病）: to get (be) sick

b) 1. 怎麼辦？明天要付房租了，可是我＿＿＿＿＿＿＿＿＿＿＿＿(有)。房東來了，我沒有錢給他。

　　2. 老師要問我那本書裡的問題，可是我＿＿＿＿＿＿＿＿＿＿(看)，我一定每個問題都不會。

　　3. 這本書只要五塊錢，＿＿＿＿＿＿＿＿＿＿＿(貴)，每個人都有錢買。

　　4. 你搬家的事，沒有人跟我說，我＿＿＿＿＿＿＿＿＿＿(知道)。

　　5. 這種電影很奇怪，我＿＿＿＿＿＿＿＿＿＿(想看)。你為什麼說這種電影很好呢？

2-3 沒事的時候　　when there is nothing to do

Explanation: "……的時候" indicates specifically the time a situation or action occurs, which can be in the past, in the future or habitual. This is possibly a period of time or one moment, depending on the nature of the verb.

a) 1) <u>我認識她</u>的時候，她還在念大學。

　　2) ＿＿＿＿＿＿＿＿＿＿的時候，我在吃飯。

　　3) ＿＿＿＿＿＿＿＿＿＿的時候，她還沒買電腦。

　　4) ＿＿＿＿＿＿＿＿＿＿的時候，打幾折？

　　5) ＿＿＿＿＿＿＿＿＿＿的時候，你問誰？

　　　　你有問題　　她打電話來　　我上次去她家　　你買這本書

b) 1) 上課的時候不可以<u>睡覺</u>。

　　2) 你打電話打錯了的時候，應該＿＿＿＿＿＿＿＿＿＿＿＿。

　　3) 想女朋友的時候，我就＿＿＿＿＿＿＿＿＿＿＿＿。

　　4) 下雨的時候，我＿＿＿＿＿＿＿＿＿＿＿＿。

　　5) 你念大學的時候，＿＿＿＿＿＿＿＿＿＿＿＿？

　　　　打電話給她　　不想出去　　在外面租房子嗎　　說對不起

2-4 爬爬山、打打球　　climb a mountain, play ball

Explanation: When the verb is reduplicated to soften the tone, if the verb is part of a VO structure, one must use a VVO pattern. However, if the action performed by the verb is already completed, then a "了" should be added , thereby forming a "V 了 VO" pattern. In the case of a double syllable verb, the entire verb phrase should be repeated, i.e. ABAB (for example, 認識認識).

9

王：沒事的時候你喜歡做什麼？

李：我常跟朋友去<u>爬爬山</u>、<u>打打球</u>。

王：你們昨天在老萬家坐了很久嗎？

李：沒有啊。我們＿＿＿＿＿＿＿＿＿就回家了。

王：你明天要出去嗎？

李：不要。我想在家＿＿＿＿＿＿＿＿＿。

王：你説那個房子太小，為什麼還是租了？

李：我＿＿＿＿＿＿＿＿，就決定租了。

王：下雨的時候你喜歡做什麼？

李：我喜歡＿＿＿＿＿＿＿、＿＿＿＿＿＿＿。

王：小張右邊那個小姐是誰？

李：你不認識啊？來，我給你＿＿＿＿＿＿＿＿。

看了看他的新電腦　看看書　聽聽 yīnyuè（音樂）
睡睡覺　想了想你説的話　介紹介紹

Aural Comprehension Drill

The following dialogues may contain some unfamiliar vocabulary. Do not be concerned if you have not yet learned the vocabulary or do not understand the meaning. Try to figure out the meaning from the context, then answer the questions.

Listen to the following dialogues and choose the most appropriate answer.

1. (　) Can this man operate a computer?

   a) really able

   b) a little able

   c) not at all

2. (　) What doesn't this lady like to do?

   a) stroll in the department store

   b) climb mountains and play in the water

   c) watch TV and movies

Additional Vocabulary

yīnyuè（音樂）: music

Variety Exercises

I. Bingo

Each student is handed a bingo card. The teacher can prepare this according to the students' background, and every card has a different content; or the students receive a blank card, and mark their cards in their own way according to what the teacher dictates. Therefore, the students' content will be in a different place on their cards. Students move about the room freely, bumping into each other and giving a simple self introduction. If the bingo card matches, ask them to sign the card. Each student can only sign one item. Whoever completes one line first, no matter whether it is horizontal, vertical, or slant, he/she should shout "Bingo" to win the game.

Example of a Bingo card

十八歲	有一個哥哥	會做飯	愛看電視	不喜歡逛街
不會打電腦	想學工程	妹妹也是大學生	姊姊出來做事了	愛喝咖啡
喜歡開車	學法文	也學日文	從美國來的	在外面租房子
喜歡紅鞋	家裡有六個人	現在不跟爸媽住	不懂電腦	媽媽上班
有女朋友	喜歡旅行	常去爬山	住在家裡	媽媽不上班

II. Searching for Something in Common

Each student is given an equal amount of cards. Ask students to write their names on the top of each card, and on the back write their ages, personalities, habits, likes, leisure activities, hobbies, educational backgrounds, families, or anything else they want others to know about themselves. Only one item should be written on the back of each card.

The students walk freely around the room introducing themselves to each other and chatting to see if they have anything in common. If they do have something in common, they should exchange that card; if not, continue to look for someone to exchange a card with. The same two students can only exchange cards once. When time is called, students will see if anyone was able to exchange all of their cards, and discuss the contents of the cards that could not be exchanged.

Through this activity, students can find people with similar traits with whom they can establish a good friendship.

III. It's you.

Each student receives a slip of paper and writes an itemized self introduction, but he/she cannot write down his/her name. Then the papers are folded and put into a bag. Then the students take turns drawing the slips out of the bag. (If they draw their own, they should replace it and draw

9

again.) After all the slips have been drawn, the students walk around the room looking for the person introduced on their slip.

IV. Describe the kind of boyfriend/girlfriend you would like to have.

V. Show and Tell

Each student brings a snapshot of a person and introduces the person in the picture. The description should include the student's relationship to the person, the person's age, occupation, hobbies, etc.

VI. Guess who am I?

Listen to the six descriptions first. Match the descriptions with the pictures. Listen again and change your match if necessary. Then tell the class why you made this match.

VII. Role Play

1. At a tea party you fall in love with a man or woman at first sight. You want to get to know him/her better.

2. You feel a man and a woman are suitable for each other and would make a nice couple, so you decide to be a matchmaker and fix them up. You arrange for them to meet in a coffee shop.

Try to Guess

1. (　) What do you think "沒大沒小" means?

   a) not big not little　　b) do not have both big ones and little ones

   c) ill-mannered or rude to one's elders

2. (　) What do you think "大人" means?

   a) big man　　b) elderly people　　c) grown-up

3. (　) What do you think "小人" means?

   a) children　　b) mean person　　c) small person

Authentic Material

兩廳院十周年

舞蹈：身體與音樂的對話

美國紐約芭蕾舞團

Salute to Balanchine

Take It as a New Yorker

台北、紐約共同享受

　　演出時間與地點

　　9/6 (六)19:30　台北國家音樂廳

　　9/7 (日)14:30　台北社教館

　　9/8 (一)19:30　台南文化中心

票價：$600, $800, $1000, $1200

1. What kind of performance is this? What do you think "芭蕾舞" means?

2. Where are they from?

3. What do you think "演出時間" means? What do you think "地點" means?

4. What do you think "票價" means?

Translation of the Dialogues

Dialogue I

Jiaming : Hello, I'm Wang Jiaming. May I know your honorable surname?

Jinshui : Hi, my surname is Lin, I'm called Lin Jinshui. Are you a student?

Jiaming : Yes, I study at Taiwan University. What about you?

Jinshui : I work in a company. Where are you from?

Jiaming : I came from America, but my father and mother are both Shanghainese.

Jinshui : How old are you this year? How long have you lived in the United States?

Jiaming : I'll be twenty next month. I have lived in America for twelve years.

Jinshui : Then your English must be really good. I can't speak English very well. If you have some time, please teach me, okay?

Jiaming : Okay. Are you from Taipei?

Jinshui : My home is in Tainan. Both my mother and father still live there.

Jiaming : How many children are there in your family?

Jinshui : I have three older brothers and two younger sisters. Some are in school and some are working.

Jiaming : My family has three girls. I'm the only boy. Oh, sorry, I have to go to class now. See you later.

Dialogue II

Dayou : You probably do not know each other yet? Come on, I will introduce you. This is Wang Ming, and this is Xie Xinyu.

Wang Ming : Hello.

Xinyu : Hello.

Dayou : Please sit down. What would you like to drink?

Xinyu : Please give me a cup of tea.

Wang Ming : I'd like some cola.

Xinyu : This is my card.

Wang Ming : Oh, you're a computer engineer. I think computers are so difficult. I don't understand them at all.

Xinyu : Where do you work?

Wang Ming : I work in a trade company.

Xinyu : What do you like to do in your free time?

Wang Ming : I often go to see a movie or go window shopping. What about you?

Xinyu : I love to go to the movies, too. Sometimes I also go hiking or play ball.

第十課　寄信

LESSON 10 MAILING

Key Study Points

asking postage rates／mailing letters／picking up a package at the post office／signing／stamping／faxing

Vocabulary	Grammar
Dialogue I	**Dialogue I**
寄，信，航空信，貼，郵票，超重(重)，輕，的話，公克，加，快，就(sooner than expected)，慢，才(later than expected)，封(M)，忘了，寫，地址，名字，告訴，明信片，掛號信，郵簡，信封	……的話 每＋V_1＋$(Nu＋M＋N)_1$，就＋V_2＋$(Nu＋M＋N)_2$ 就＆才
Dialogue II	**Dialogue II**
領，包裹，窗口(窗子)，門口(門)，把，通知單(通知，單子)，身分證，圖章，帶，簽名	S＋把＋DO＋給＋IO V 在
Dialogue III	**Dialogue III**
旅行社，影本，送，傳真，傳真機，哎呀，壞了(壞)，沒關係(關係)，郵局，費用，市區，別的，台中	拿給＋IO S＋把＋DO＋拿給＋IO N_1＋幫＋N_2＋V(O) S＋把＋O＋V來／去 呢

10

Dialogue ┃ Mailing a Letter at the Post Office

A：請問，寄到日本的 航空信 要貼多少錢郵票？

B：不 超重 的話，十三塊。每超重十 公克 加九塊錢。

A：幾天可以到？

B： 快的話，三天就到了。慢的話，大概要五、六天才能到。

A：這 封 信要多少錢？

B：四十塊。噢，你 忘了寫 地址。

A：啊，我寫了 名字，忘了寫地址。謝謝你 告訴 我。

Vocabulary

1. 寄   jì   V : to send by mail, to mail

   你家太遠。這些東西我不能拿給你。寄給你，好不好？

   Your house is too far away. I cannot carry these things to you. I will mail them to you, okay?

2. 信   N : a letter   (M：fēng 封)

3. 航空信   hángkōngxìn   N : airmail   (M：fēng 封)

4. 貼   tiē   V : to paste, to stick

   我在電話右邊貼了幾張朋友的名片。

   I taped some of my friends' name-cards to the right of the telephone.

5. 郵票   yóupiào   N : stamp   (M：張)

6. 超重   chāozhòng   VO : to overweigh

   你要寄的東西超重。你還要再給我一百塊錢。

   The thing you want to mail is overweight. You need to give me an additional $100.

   重   zhòng   SV/Adv : to be heavy

   這個桌子不重。我可以一個人搬到樓上去。

   This table is not heavy. I can carry it upstairs by myself.

*7. 輕   qīng   SV/Adv : to be light/gently

   孩子在睡覺。你走路輕一點。

   The child is sleeping. Please walk quietly.

8. 的話   ·dehuà   P : if (used with or without 要是／如果)

   要是你喜歡王小姐的話，就去跟她說啊。

   If you like Miss Wang, then go and tell her.

9. 公克   gōngkè   M : gram

10. 加   jiā   V : to add

   我們五個人。三個菜太少。再加一個吧。

   There are five of us. Three dishes are not enough. Let's add another one.

11. 快　　kuài　　SV : to be fast

他吃東西很快，五分鐘吃了十個包子。

He eats really fast. In five minutes he eats ten steamed buns.

12. 就　　jiù　　Adv : (sooner than expected)

為什麼還沒下班他就回家了？

Why did he go home before the working hours were over?

13. 慢　　màn　　SV : to be slow

他做事很慢。一天的事他要做三天。

He does things very slowly. It takes him three days to do one day's work.

14. 才　　cái　　Adv : (later than expected)

你應該三點就到了，為什麼五點才來？

You should have arrived by 3:00. Why didn't you come until 5:00?

15. 封　　fēng　　M : (for a letter, a telegram, etc.)

16. 忘了　　wàng·le　　V : to forget

我想我認識你，可是我忘了你姓什麼。

I think I know you, but I've forgotten your name.

17. 寫　　xiě　　V : to write

小李寫了一封中文信給他的中國朋友。

Little Li wrote a letter in Chinese to his Chinese friend.

18. 地址　　dìzhǐ　　N : address　　(M：個)

19. 名字　　míng·zi　　N : name　　(M：個)

20. 告訴　　gào·su　　V : to tell

小王告訴我他昨天因為有事，所以沒來上課。

Little Wang told me that he had something else to do yesterday, so he did not come to class.

*21. 明信片　　míngxìnpiàn　　N : postcard　　(M：張)

*22. 掛號信　　guàhàoxìn　　N : registered letter　　(M：fēng 封)

*23. 郵簡　　yóujiǎn　　N : aerogramme　　(M：張)

*24. 信封　　xìnfēng　　N : envelope　　(M：個)

10

Grammar

1-1 不超重的話　if it is not overweight

Explanation: "……的話" expresses a conditional mood. The supposed condition is placed before "的話". This structure is frequently used simultaneously with "要是／如果……", thereby becoming "要是／如果……的話".

王：寄到日本的航空信要貼多少錢郵票？

李：<u>不超重</u>的話，十三塊。

王：你明天下午要做什麼？

李：還沒決定。要是＿＿＿＿＿＿＿＿的話我想去看電影。

王：要是下雨，怎麼去王老師家？

李：＿＿＿＿＿＿＿＿的話我們就開車去吧。

王：小姐，這種洗衣機不錯。您不喜歡嗎？

李：如果＿＿＿＿＿＿＿＿＿＿的話我就買。

王：你為什麼只看了一個地方，就決定租了？

李：這樣的房子不好找。＿＿＿＿＿＿＿＿＿＿＿的話，biérén (別人)
　　就要了。

不早一點租　下雨　可以便宜一點　沒事

1-2 每超重十公克加九塊錢。　Add nine dollars for every ten grams overweight.

10

Explanation: "每 + V_1 + $(Nu+M+N)_1$，就 + V_2 + $(Nu+M+N)_2$" shows that a certain action is repeated regularly. In this case, the "就" may be omitted.

Additional Vocabulary

biérén (別人) : other people, others

王：信超重的話，要貼多少錢郵票？

李：每<u>超重十公克</u>加九塊。

王：你們現在打折嗎？

李：對，每_____就便宜十塊。

王：租房子要簽約嗎？

李：要，每_____就要簽一次。

王：坐 jìchéngchē (計程車)怎麼算錢？

李：第一 gōnglǐ (公里)六十五塊錢，以後每_____就加五塊錢。

王：打長途電話到日本去要多少錢？

李：每_____付三十五塊。

> 住半年　買一百塊　打一分鐘　走半gōnglǐ（公里）

1-3 快的話，三天就到了。慢的話，要五、六天才到。

If it is fast, it will arrive in three days. If it is slow, it will take five or six days to arrive.

Explanation: When "就" is placed after a number and a measure word, time word, or time phrase, it indicates that the actual amount or time is respectively smaller or shorter than the speaker originally anticipated. Conversely, "才" used in the exact same place shows that the amount or time in question was actually greater or longer than originally expected.

（Please use "就" or "才"）

王：你朋友還沒來嗎？

李：他昨天____來了。

王：你朋友到了吧。

李：還沒。他明天____來。

王：對不起，我來晚了。

李：你怎麼現在____來？

王：你剛剛到嗎？

李：我半個小時以前____到了。

Additional Vocabulary

    jìchéngchē (計程車) : taxi   gōnglǐ (公里) : kilometer

10

王：三點五十分的公車走了嗎？

李：還沒有。奇怪，已經五十五分了。應該五分鐘以前＿＿＿來了。

王：往台南的車來了沒有？

李：五分鐘以前＿＿＿走了。

王：下班了，你還不回家嗎？

李：不行。今天事情多，大概九點＿＿＿能走。

王：你在家啊！今天沒課嗎？

李：有課，可是老師有事，上了一個小時＿＿＿下課了。

王：我們下星期就要到美國去了。旅行支票換了沒有？

李：上星期＿＿＿換了。

王：老師沒說要看這本書。

李：念書是你自己的事，不能等老師說了你＿＿＿看。

Aural Comprehension Drill

The following dialogues may contain some unfamiliar vocabulary. Do not be concerned if you have not yet learned the vocabulary or do not understand its meaning. Try to figure out the meaning from the context, and then answer the questions.

Listen to the following dialogues and choose the most appropriate answer.

1. (　) How much postage does this man's letter require?

   a) $5 worth   b) $10 worth   c) $15 worth

2. (　) What is this young woman saying?

   a) She goes to bed very late.

   b) She goes to bed very early.

   c) She doesn't go to bed particularly early or late.

3. (　) What does this gentleman mean?

   a) He moved to Taipei a long time ago.

   b) He hasn't lived in Taipei very long.

   c) This has nothing to do with the length of time.

4. (　) What does this dialogue mean?

   a) They have decided to go hiking tomorrow.

   b) They have decided not to go hiking tomorrow.

   c) They still haven't decided whether or not they will go hiking.

10

Dialogue II Picking up a Parcel at the Post Office

A：小姐，請問，是不是在這裡 領 包裹？
ˇ ˇ　　ˇ ˋ　　ˋ ˊ ˋ ˋ ˇ　　lǐng　bāoguǒ

B：不是。請到一號 窗口。
ˊ ˋ　　ˇ ˋ ─ ˋ　　chuāngkǒu

(At window number one)

A：先生，我要領包裹。
─ ·　　ˇ ˋ ˋ ─ ˇ

C：請把 通知單 跟 身分證 給我。
ˇ bǎ　tōngzhīdān　─　shēnfènzhèng　ˇ ˇ

(C gets the parcel)

C：這是你的包裹。 圖章[1] 帶來了嗎？
ˋ ˋ ˇ ·　─ ˇ　　Túzhāng　dài ˊ · ·

A：對不起，沒帶圖章。 簽名 可以嗎？
ˋ · ˇ　　ˊ ˋ ˊ ─　　Qiānmíng　ˇ ˇ ·

C：可以。請簽在這裡。
ˇ ˇ　　ˇ ─ ˋ ˋ ˇ

Vocabulary

1. 領　　lǐng　　V : to pick up

　　辦公室有一封你的掛號信。請你去領。

　　The office has a registered letter for you. Please pick it up.

2. 包裹　　bāoguǒ　　N : parcel　　(M：個)

3. 窗口　　chuāngkǒu　　N/PW : window　　(M：個)

　　你去窗口看看外面下雨了沒有。

　　Go to the window and see if it is raining outside.

　　窗子　　chuāng·zi　　N : window　　(M：個)

　　我的房間有兩個窗子。

　　My room has two windows.

*4. 門口　　ménkǒu　　N/PW : doorway　　(M：個)

　　門　　mén　　N : door; gate　　(M：個)

5. 把　　bǎ　　CV : (used to bring the object before the verb)

　　小王要搬到日本去，所以把車賣了。

　　Little Wang wants to move to Japan. So he has sold his car.

6. 通知單　　tōngzhīdān　　N : notice　　(M：張)

　　通知　　tōngzhī　　V : to notify

　　學校通知我們下星期一不上課。

　　The school has notified us that there will be no class next Monday.

　　單子　　dān·zi　　N : pieces of paper with written words on　　(M：張)

7. 身分證　　shēnfènzhèng　　N : ID card　　(M：張)

8. 圖章　　túzhāng　　N : seal; stamp　　(M：個)

9. 帶　　dài　　V : to bring

　　到學校上課，不要忘了帶書跟筆。

　　Do not forget to take your book and pen when you go to school.

10

10. 簽名　　　　qiānmíng　　VO : to sign (your name)

到銀行去領錢，一定要簽名。

When you go to the bank to withdraw money, you must sign your name.

Note

1. "圖章", not a signature, is used by Chinese people when they are receiving money, parcels, and in matters concerning credit. This custom has a long history and might have originated in ancient China when not everyone could write. Nowadays, signatures are sometimes acceptable in Taiwan.

Grammar

2-1 請把通知單給我。　　Please give me the notice.

Explanation: The "把" sentence pattern is "S + Adv/AV + 把 + O + V + C", used to emphasize and to dispose the object. This pattern has following characteristics: 1) The noun object of a "把" sentence must be specifically indicated or already understood by both speaker and listener. 2) The verb cannot be a SV. 3) A complement is necessary to express fully the result of the verb or the location of the object when the action is completed. 4) When the action involved is more important to the sentence than the O, the "把" structure is not used.

王：小姐，我要領包裹。

李：請把通知單給我。

王：奇怪，我買的包子呢？

李：噢，我把_____了。 (吃那個包子)

王：李先生為什麼不開車來？

李：他上星期把_____了。 (賣車)

王：我從明天kāishǐ (開始)就沒有工作了。

李：你不能把_____。 (告訴你太太這jiàn [件]事)

王：可以走了嗎？

李：等我把_____了就可以走了。 (換衣服)

Additional Vocabulary

kāishǐ (開始) : to start; to begin　　　jiàn (件) : M for matters, affairs

2-2 簽在這裡　　to sign here

Explanation: The specific place indicated after the post-verb preposition "在" shows the actual location of the subject or recipient of the action after the action is completed.

王：要簽名嗎？

李：要。請<u>簽在這裡</u>。

王：這本書，張先生要我拿來。

李：謝謝，＿＿＿＿＿＿＿＿＿＿＿＿就可以了。 (放)

王：小王，你有沒有老陳辦公室的電話？

李：有，我＿＿＿＿＿＿＿＿＿＿＿＿了。 (寫)

王：請把身分證給我。

李：對不起，我＿＿＿＿＿＿＿＿＿＿，忘了帶來了。 (留)

王：對不起，我來晚了。還有位子嗎？

李：你可以＿＿＿＿＿＿＿＿＿＿。 (坐)

Aural Comprehension Drill

The following dialogue may contain some unfamiliar vocabulary. Do not be concerned if you have not yet learned the vocabulary or do not understand its meaning. Try to figure out the meaning from the context, and then answer the questions.

Listen to the following dialogue and choose the most appropriate answer.

1. (　) Where does the conversation most likely take place?

　　a) at a police station　　b) at a post office　　c) at a school

2. (　) What did the lady come for?

　　a) pick up a package　　b) mail a letter　　c) see a notice

3. (　) What problem did the lady encounter?

　　a) did not know where to go to pick up package　　b) did not understand the notice

　　c) forgot to bring her identification card

10

Additional Vocabulary

　　jìshìběn (記事本) : notebook　　　位子 : seat　　　pángbiān (旁邊) : side

Dialogue III Sending a Fax at the Post Office

小李：旅行社 要我五點以前把身分證 影本 拿給他們。
Lǚxíngshè

我沒有時間送 去。你可以幫我 傳真 嗎？
sòng   chuánzhēn

小趙：好啊。你把影本拿來……哎呀[1]！傳真機 壞 了。
Āi·ya   Chuánzhēnjī huài ·le

小李：那怎麼 辦？

小趙：沒 關係。郵局也可以傳真。
Méi guān·xi Yóujú

小李：郵局傳真 費用 怎麼算呢？
fèiyòng

小趙：旅行社在哪裡？在市區，還是在別的地方？
　　　　　　　　　　　　　　shìqū　　　　　bié·de

小李：在 台中。
　　　　　Táizhōng

小趙：台中啊？那 傳真 一張 二十五塊。

小李：太好了²。我現在就去³。

Vocabulary

1. 旅行社　　lǚxíngshè　　N：travel agency　　(M：家)

2. 影本　　　yǐngběn　　N：photo copy　　(M：fèn 份)

3. 送　　　　sòng　　V：to send; to deliver; to give something as a gift; to give someone a ride
   1) 老闆，請你把這些菜送到我家去。謝謝。
   2) 老師送了我一本很好的字典。
   3) 太晚了，一個人走不好。我開車送你回去。
   1) Sir, please deliver this food to my house. Thank you.
   2) The teacher gave me a really good dictionary.
   3) It's too late. It is not good to go alone. I will drive you home.

4. 傳真　　　chuánzhēn　　V：to fax
   他現在就要這封信。請你傳真給他。
   He wants this letter now. Please fax it to him.

5. 傳真機　　chuánzhēnjī　　N：fax machine　　(M：bù 部)

6. 哎呀　　　āi·ya　　I：oh, no (expression of exclamation, surprise or dismay)
   哎呀，我忘了帶錢。
   Oh, no! I've forgotten to bring money.

10

7. 壞了　　huài·le　　IE : It's broken.

電視機壞了。我們今天不能看電視了。

The TV is broken. We cannot watch it today.

壞　　huài　　SV : to be bad; to be broken

這個學生很壞，常常不來上課。

This student is really bad. He often misses classes.

8. 沒關係　　méi guān·xi　　IE : It doesn't matter.

你沒有錢吃飯，沒關係。我可以給你錢。

It doesn't matter if you don't have the money for meals. I can give you some money.

關係　　guān·xi　　N : relationship　　(M：種)

9. 郵局　　yóujú　　N : post office　　(M：家)

10. 費用　　fèiyòng　　N : fee

11. 市區　　shìqū　　N : urban district; city proper

12. 別的　　bié·de　　N : the others

我們家只有我喜歡打球。別的人都不喜歡。

I am the only one in my family who likes to play ball. The others do not like to.

13. 台中　　Táizhōng　　Proper N : Taichung, a city name

Notes

10

1. "哎呀" is an interjection used at the beginning of a sentence indicating surprise mixed with regret. Therefore, "哎呀！傳真機壞了。" means "What a pity! (Oh, I'm sorry.) The fax machine is broken."

2. "太好了" means "Wonderful!". It doesn't mean "too good". When "太" is followed by an adjective denoting positive judgment, it means extremely, not excessively.

3. "我現在就去" means "I will go right now." "就" emphasizes "right now."

Grammar

3-1 拿給我   to hand it to me

Explanation: "給" can act as a post-verb, while the noun following it is the recipient of the designated action. When the speaker refers to the recipient of this action, he/she must use the "V 給" pattern. Never use "V" or "給" alone.

1) 他從日本回來，帶給我一本書。
2) 東三街的房子你_____誰了？
3) 老王的舊車要_____李小姐。
4) 小張一定還沒吃飯。這個包子_____他吧。
5) 買書的錢，應該_____你還是王小姐？

賣給　留給　送給　付給　租給　寄給　帶給

3-2 把身分證影本拿給他們。   to give a photocopy of the ID card to them

Explanation: The pattern "V 給 IO" is often used together with "把" due to the fact that "V 給" also conveys the meaning of disposal.

王：你為什麼要 yǐngyìn (影印) 身分證？
李：因為旅行社要我把身分證影本拿給他們。

王：謝小姐來信說什麼？
李：她要我們把_____給她。　(寄支票)

王：李小姐有沒有男朋友？
李：沒有吧。我們把_____給張先生，好不好？　(介紹她)

王：大新百貨公司為什麼不 kāi (開) 了？
李：他們 lǎobǎn (老闆) 把_____給第一銀行了。　(賣公司)

王：錢書宜搬家了。你找他有什麼事？
李：那能不能麻煩你把_____給他？　(轉這封信)

Additional Vocabulary

yǐngyìn (影印) : to photocopy　　　kāi (開) : to open
lǎobǎn (老闆) : boss, owner

10

- 203 -

3-3 你可以幫我傳真嗎？　Can you help me send a fax?

Explanation: In the pattern "N₁＋幫＋N₂＋V(O)", "幫", acting as a CV, expresses that N₁ helps N₂ to perform an action. N₁ may either complete the action together with N₂, or performs this task alone.

王：哎呀！太晚了！我沒有時間把通知單送去，怎麼辦？
李：沒關係。我有傳真機，可以<u>幫你傳真</u>。

王：我的電腦壞了，可是我不知道哪裡有問題。
李：我懂一點電腦，可以＿＿＿＿＿＿。

王：我今天的事情太多了，大概要很晚才能回家。
李：我沒有事了。我＿＿＿＿＿＿吧。

王：我忘了帶辦公室的 yào·shi (鑰匙)，怎麼辦？
李：沒關係。可以打電話請小陳＿＿＿＿＿＿。

王：我要到郵局去。
李：我有一張包裹的通知單，你能不能＿＿＿＿＿＿？

幫你做一點　幫你看看　幫我領　幫你拿來

3-4 把影本拿來　to bring over the photocopy

Explanation: The pattern "(DV)來／去" can also act as the complement of a "把" sentence. In this case it indicates the direction of the action.

王：我應該拿什麼東西來？
李：請把<u>身分證影本拿來</u>。

王：我明天要送東西到王先生家去。
李：不要忘了把＿＿＿＿＿＿。(帶錢)

Additional Vocabulary

　yào·shi (鑰匙) : key(s)

王：我的車有一點問題。

李：你明天把_____。我幫你看看。(開車)

王：我要到美國去念書，要帶的東西很多。

李：你可以先把_____。自己帶太重了。(寄書)

王：我現在住的地方沒有電腦，真不方便。

李：那我明天先把_____。(搬家裡那個電腦)

3-5 費用怎麼算呢？ How much is the fee?

Explanation: "呢" cannot be used at the end of a yes-no question. Placed at the end of a QW sentence, however, it conveys a sense of wonder or confusion on the part of the speaker. Used in an "A-not-A" or choice-type question, the "呢" takes on an inquisitive meaning, and the tone of the sentence is softened.

1) 你不買日本車，也不買美國車，那_____？

2) 你那通電話不是打給錢書宜，也不是打給張台生，那是_____？

3) 這個燈放在桌上不好，放在地上也不好，那_____？

4) 王老師的電話小李不知道，小張也不知道，_____？

5) 趙奇明天是你妹妹的生日。我們送她_____，還是_____？

6) 王明我們兩個人星期天去台南。你_____，還是_____？

Aural Comprehension Drill

The following dialogue may contain some unfamiliar vocabulary. Do not be concerned if you have not yet learned the vocabulary or do not understand its meaning. Try to figure out the meaning from the context, then answer the questions.

Listen to the following dialogue and choose the most appropriate answer.

1. (   ) Where would this dialogue most likely be spoken?

   a) at a travel agency   b) in a fax   c) over the phone

2. (   ) What does the woman want the man to do?

   a) Give her a call to tell her the time and cost

   b) Fax the time and cost to her

   c) Write a letter explaining the cost and time involved

Variety Exercises

I. The teacher gives every student an apartment floor-plan and tells them that he/she has bought a new apartment. He/She wants their help in moving. The teacher then points out where he/she wants everything placed. The teacher can appoint someone to draw on the board. The other students can use numbers to indicate where everything should go, instead of drawing the object.

For example, the teacher points and says:

請把書桌搬到書房去。Please move the desk into the study.

請把大床搬到我的房間。Please move the big bed into my bedroom.

請把電腦也搬到書房，放在書桌上。

請把小床搬到我孩子的房間。

請把杯子拿到廚房去。

請把衣服放在 wòshì (臥室) 的衣櫃裡。

請把洗衣機搬到洗澡間去。

請把 shāfā (沙發) 搬到客廳，放在窗子前面。

請把電視也搬到客廳，放在 shāfā (沙發) 對面。

請把書拿到書房裡，先放在桌子 pángbiān (旁邊)的地上。

After everything has been moved, the students can take turns to talk about where they moved the furniture. For example:

我(們)把書桌搬到書房去了。We moved the desk into the study.

Finally the students can make sure if they moved the furniture to the right place.

Additional Vocabulary

      wòshì (臥室) : bedroom   shāfā (沙發) : sofa   pángbiān (旁邊) : side

II. First, draw a lot of different articles, and let the students decide how to arrange them. This can be done in pairs with one person speaking and the other performing the actions.

III. Simon says

The teacher appoints a leader and the other students move according to his/her commands. However, the students should only move if the command includes the phrase "老師說", otherwise the students lose. The game ends when all but one of the students have been fooled.

（老師說）把你的錢拿給我。

（老師說）把筆拿起來。

（老師說）把筆放下。

（老師說）坐下。

（老師說）站起來。

（老師說）把書放進書包裡。

（老師說）把你的書從書包裡拿出來，放在桌子上。

（老師說）……

Try to Guess

1. (　) What do you think "超人" means?
   - a) to be outstanding
   - b) superman
   - c) to be faster than other people

2. (　) What do you think "航空公司" means?
   - a) airlines
   - b) aircraft company
   - c) companies which deliver express mail

3. (　) What do you think "簽證" means?
   - a) to sign a document
   - b) to get an ID card
   - c) visa

4. (　) What do you think "傳單" means?
   - a) leaflet
   - b) summons
   - c) a list of faxes

Authentic Material

The teacher prepares two written envelopes, one in Chinese style, the other in English. He/she asks the students to look at the English style and then the Chinese style. Then he/she asks his/her students to guess the following.

1. Which is the receiver? Which is the sender?
2. What does "啟" mean?
3. What are the numbers in the small squares?

10

Translation of the Dialogues

Dialogue I

A : Excuse me, how much postage is needed to send a letter to Japan by air mail?

B : If it's not overweight, thirteen dollars. For every ten grams overweight, add another nine dollars.

A : How long will it take for a letter to get there?

B : It may take three days. If it's slow, it will probably take as many as five or six days.

A : How much for this letter?

B : Forty dollars. Oh, you forgot to write the address.

A : Ah, I wrote the person's name, but I forgot to write the address. Thanks for telling me that.

Dialogue II

A : Excuse me, Miss. Can I pick up a parcel here?

B : No, please go to window number one.

   (At window number 1)

A : Sir, I'd like to pick up a parcel.

C : Please show me your notice and identification card.

   (C gets the parcel)

C : Here is your parcel. Did you bring your seal?

A : Sorry, I didn't bring my seal. Is a signature all right?

C : Sure, please sign here.

Dialogue III

Little Li : The travel agency wants me to give them a photocopy of my ID card before five o'clock, but I don't have the time to deliver it. Could you help me fax it?

Little Zhao : Sure, bring over your photocopy. Oh no, the fax machine is broken.

Little Li : Then, what can we do?

Little Zhao : It's all right. The post office also faxes.

Little Li : How much does the post office charge for faxing?

Little Zhao : Where's the travel agency, in town or somewhere else?

Little Li : It's in Taichung.

Little Zhao : Taichung? Then it will be twenty-five dollars a page.

Little Li : Wonderful. I'll go right now.

第十一課　吃什麼好？

LESSON 11　WHAT SHALL WE EAT?

Key Study Points

polite conversation ／ asking others' opinions on food ／ dining in a restaurant ／ making reservations ／ selecting a table ／ summoning customers ／ reading a menu ／ names of dishes ／ preparation ／ flavors and taste ／ discussing the dishes

Vocabulary	Grammar
Dialogue I	**Dialogue I**
生日，不好意思，中餐(餐)，西餐，法國菜(法國)，怎麼樣，附近，有名，餐廳，飯館，得(·de)，不錯，服務生(服務)，歡迎光臨，訂位，位子，非吸煙區(吸煙，煙)，已經，得(děi)，一會兒，願意	太SV了 怎麼樣？ V得(adv)＋SV, 已經……了 得(děi) 願意 吧
Dialogue II	**Dialogue II**
菜單，比較，宮保雞丁，麻婆豆腐，開洋白菜，蝦米(蝦，米)，一起，燒，味道，鹹，平常，一樣，會，辣，點(to order)，糖醋魚(糖，醋，魚)，叫，青椒牛肉(青椒，牛，肉)，夠，湯，玉米(玉)，青菜	比較 V在一起 S＋把＋O＋放在…… 會……的 跟……一樣

11

Dialogue | Dining with a Friend after Work

王先生：今天是你二十五歲 生日。我請你吃飯。
　　　　　　　　　　　　　　shēngrì

李小姐：你太客氣了。不好意思[1]。
　　　　　　　　　　　　Bùhǎoyì·si

王先生：你想吃什麼？ 中餐 還是西餐？
　　　　　　　　　　　Zhōngcān　　Xīcān

李小姐：西餐好不好？

 王先生：那我們去吃 法國菜，怎麼樣？這兒附近有一家很
　　　　　　　　　　　Fǎguó cài　　zěn·meyàng　　fùjìn

　　　　有名 的法國 餐廳。他們的菜做得不錯。
　　　　yǒumíng　　　cāntīng　　　　　　　búcuò

李小姐：好啊，我們就去那裡吧。[2]

(Getting a table at the restaurant)

服務生：歡迎 光臨。³ 幾位？
fúwùshēng　Huānyíng guānglín

王先生：兩個人。

服務生：訂位 了沒有？
　　　　Dìngwèi

李小姐：沒有。非吸煙區還有位子嗎？⁴
　　　　　　 Fēixīyānqū

服務生：對不起，已經沒有了。得等一會兒。你們願意等嗎？
　　　　　　　　　 yǐjīng　　　　 Děi　 yìhuǐr　　　　 yuànyì

王先生：要等多久？

服務生：大概二十幾分鐘。

李小姐：太久了。那就 吸煙區 吧。⁵

服務生：好，請跟我來。

Vocabulary

1. 生日　　　 shēngrì　　 N : birthday

2. 不好意思 bùhǎoyì·si　　 IE : to feel embarrassed; to be ill at ease
　　　　　 真不好意思，我忘了帶錢。請你先幫我付，好不好？
　　　　　 How embarrassing, I forgot to bring any money. Please pay for me now, okay?

3. 中餐　　Zhōngcān　　N : Chinese food/meal　　(M：dùn 頓)
　　餐　　　cān　　M : meal

4. 西餐　　Xīcān　　N : western food/meal　　(M：dùn 頓)

5. 法國菜　　Fǎguó cài　　N : French food　　(M：dùn 頓)
　　法國　　　Fǎguó　　Proper N : France

6. 怎麼樣　　zěn·meyàng　　IE : How about...?
　　你的工作怎麼樣？忙不忙？
　　How is your work? Is it busy?

7. 附近　　fùjìn　　PW : nearby, around, vicinity
　　他家在我家附近。走路五分鐘就到了。
　　His house is near mine. It just takes five minutes to walk there.

8. 有名　　yǒumíng　　SV : to be famous
　　張台生在我們學校很有名。每個人都認識他。
　　Zhang Taisheng is famous in our school; everyone knows him.

9. 餐廳　　cāntīng　　N : restaurant　　(M：家)

*10. 飯館　　fànguǎn　　N : restaurant　　(M：家)

11. 得　　·de　　P : (used after verbs indicating the degree of the action)
　　我爸爸開車開得很慢。
　　My father drives really slowly.

12. 不錯　　búcuò　　SV : to be not bad, to be good
　　這個孩子不錯，常常幫我們洗車子。
　　This child is good. He often helps us wash the car.

13. 服務生　　fúwùshēng　　N : waiter/waitress　　(M：個)
　　服務　　　fúwù　　N/V : service; to serve
　　1) 這家銀行的服務很好，所以我喜歡去那裡換錢。
　　2) 麻煩你服務一下，送這位老先生上車。
　　1) This bank's service is really good, so I like to go there to exchange money.
　　2) Could I trouble you to help this old man into the car?

11

14. 歡迎光臨 huānyíng guānglín   IE : Welcome.

服務生對來這兒吃飯的人說：「歡迎光臨。」

The waiters here always greet the customers by saying: "Welcome".

15. 訂位   dìng//wèi   VO : to make a reservation

16. 位子   wèi·zi   N : seat   (M：個)

先生，我要訂位。五個人，明天晚上。請給我樓上的位子。

Sir, I want to reserve a table. Five people for tomorrow night. Please give me an upstairs table.

17. 非吸煙區 feīxīyānqū   N : non-smoking area

吸煙   xī//yān   VO : to smoke

你吸什麼煙？

What do you smoke?

煙   yān   N : cigarette   (M：gēn 根、zhī 支、包)

18. 已經   yǐjīng   Adv : already

從昨天晚上到現在，他已經念了十二個小時的書了。

He has studied for 20 hours since last night.

19. 得   děi   AV : must, have to

吃了東西就得付錢。

If you eat, you have to pay.

20. 一會兒   yìhuǐr   N : a moment

我睡覺以前常看一會兒書，大概看十幾分鐘。

I often read for a while before going to bed, probably about 20 or 30 minutes.

21. 願意   yuànyì   AV : to be willing to

我不喜歡他，所以我不願意跟他去看電影。

I do not like him, so I am not willing to go see a movie with him.

11

Notes

1. "不好意思" means "to feel bashful about something" or "find it embarrassing to do something". Whether something is "不好意思" or not depends on one's own values. That means that many things that would make a Chinese feel bad/embarrassed may not make a person from a different culture/value system share the same feeling. For example, if the food is all finished by the guests at a dinner party, the Chinese host will feel "不好意思" because he/she thinks that more food should have been prepared and that he/she didn't treat the guests well enough. If the same thing happens to an American, he/she may not feel "不好意思" because it is good that the food is all gone and nothing is wasted or that the guests have enjoyed it. Sometimes, as in this dialogue, "不好意思" is only a polite remark. It is used when one feels embarrassed to receive someone else's kind offerings or help when the other party has no obligation to do so.

2. "好啊，我們就去那裡吧。" means "Okay. Let's go there." "就" means "then, in this case", and "吧" indicates a mild suggestion.

3. "歡迎光臨。" means "Welcome to this place." Literally: Welcome your presence to grace our place. It is commonly used in a variety of places of business in Taiwan, such as convenience stores, restaurants, etc.

4. "非吸煙區還有位子嗎？" means "Are there still seats in the non-smoking area?" In Taiwan, only bigger restaurants and fast food places have non-smoking areas.

5. "那就吸煙區吧。" means "Well, (since I don't have the choice) then I'll take (a seat in) the smoking area." "吧" indicates a tone of compromise.

Grammar

1-1 你太客氣了。　　You are too polite.

Explanation: "太 SV 了" indicates 1) a prescribed level has been exceeded, often not a welcome occurrence, or 2) a high level, as in praising someone or something. In this case, the SV is most often positive.

a) 王：這個電腦五萬五千塊。你要不要？
　　李：<u>太貴了</u>。我不要。

　　王：要是你不喜歡住在這裡的話，就搬家吧。
　　李：搬家＿＿＿＿＿＿＿＿。我再住幾個月再想辦法。

　　王：這個書櫃放五百本書沒問題。送給你吧。
　　李：謝謝了。可是我的房間很小，這個書櫃＿＿＿＿＿＿＿。

　　王：我們去大千百貨公司逛逛，好不好？
　　李：去那裡要半個小時，＿＿＿＿＿＿。我們在附近看個電影吧。

b) 王：通知單，你不要拿去寄了。我可以幫你傳真。

李：謝謝。有傳真機_____。

王：你還要再去那家飯館啊？我們不是上星期才去的嗎？

李：那裡的菜_____，所以我還想再去。

王：小張昨天買了很多東西，問他錢是從哪裡來的，他都不說。

李：這件事_____。我們應該去告訴他媽媽。

好吃　麻煩　方便　大　奇怪　遠

1-2 去吃法國菜，怎麼樣？　　How about going to eat French food?

Explanation: "怎麼樣" is used to solicit a person's opinion and should always be placed at the end of the sentence.

王：我們今天晚上吃什麼呢？

李：<u>去吃法國菜，怎麼樣</u>？

王：今日百貨公司現在打八折。

李：_____？

王：我明天下午沒事。

李：_____？

王：老陳要搬家了，我們送他什麼好呢？

李：_____？

王：我昨天買了一本書。

李：_____？

王：小姐，我要買一雙爬山穿的鞋，你們有沒有？

李：有，_____？

你看了以後給我看，怎麼樣　我們下午去逛逛，怎麼樣
去看電影，怎麼樣　你試試這雙，怎麼樣　送他一個 wēibōlú(微波爐)，怎麼樣

11

Additional Vocabulary

　wēibōlú(微波爐)：microwave oven

1-3 他們的菜做得不錯。 Their food is pretty good (well cooked).

Explanation: "S + VO，V 得 + Adv + SV" and "S 的 O，V 得 + Adv + SV" are both used to express the degree or conclusion of a certain action which has been performed. In the case of a comparison, an adverb is not necessary.

王：小陳說要開車送我們去老師家。他開車開得怎麼樣？

李：他開得很好。

王：哪種信走得快？

李：航空信＿＿＿＿＿＿＿＿＿＿。

王：你的字，寫得怎麼樣？

李：＿＿＿＿＿＿＿＿＿＿＿＿＿＿＿＿＿。

王：那家飯館的菜怎麼樣？

李：那裡的菜＿＿＿＿＿＿＿＿(做)。

王：我給你們半個小時吃飯，gòu (夠)不 gòu(夠)？

李：半個小時不 gòu (夠)，因為＿＿＿＿＿＿＿＿＿＿。

王：陳老師說的話，你都懂嗎？

李：＿＿＿＿＿＿＿＿＿＿，所以我都懂。

> 我吃得很慢　他說得很慢　做得不錯
> 走得快　我寫得不好

Exercises

Describe the following pictures:

1. How do they move?

2. How are these writings?

Additional Vocabulary

　　gòu(夠) : to be enough

3. Do they come on time?　　4. Do they eat a lot?　　5. Do they live close?

1-4 非吸煙區已經沒位子了。　　There are no seats in the non-smoking area.

Explanation: "已經……了" shows that a certain action or change has either been completed or reached a certain level. This action or situation is placed behind "已經".

王　　　：麻煩你給我們非吸煙區的位子。

服務生：對不起，非吸煙區<u>已經沒有位子了</u>。

王：還沒下班，老陳為什麼不在辦公室呢？

李：他有事，＿＿＿＿＿＿＿＿。

王：我跟朋友約三點在學校門口見。現在幾點了？

李：＿＿＿＿＿＿＿＿。他還沒來嗎？

王：桌上有一封小錢的信，她知道嗎？

李：我＿＿＿＿＿＿＿。

王：要給王小姐的信，你寄了沒有？

李：我＿＿＿＿＿＿＿。

1-5 得等一會兒。　　(You) have to wait a moment.

Explanation: The auxiliary verb "得" is used to indicate that because of a rational, practical, or personal need or desire, the action after "得" must or should be carried out. The negative form is "不必(bì)" or "不用". "不得" cannot be used in this sense.

王：有沒有非吸煙區的位子？

李：對不起，現在沒有。<u>得等一會兒</u>。

王：星期六下午我們去逛街，怎麼樣？

李：不行，我還有很多衣服沒洗。我得＿＿＿＿＿＿。

11

王：這封信，寄kuàidì (快遞) 嗎？

李：不行，王先生今天下午就要。Kuàidì (快遞) 太慢，得_____。

王：我今天要晚一點回來。

李：不行，小林晚上要來看你，你得_____。

王：你今天晚上要做什麼？

李：我明天要kǎoshì (考試)，我得_____。

王：換美金得帶圖章跟身分證嗎？

李：_____帶圖章，可是得帶身分證。

1-6 你們願意等嗎？　　Are you willing to wait?

Explanation: When the auxiliary verb "願意" appears before the verb, it indicates that the particular event or action is in accordance with the wishes of the subject. An adverb such as "很", "不太", or "非常", may precede "願意" to further express to what degree the action is performed.

王：要等多久？

服務生：十分鐘。你們願意等嗎？

妹妹：我喜歡跟小張住在這裡。你為什麼一定要我搬家？

哥哥：我已經告訴你他不是好人。你還是_____，我也沒辦法。

王：下星期天你能來幫我搬家嗎？

李：我很_____，可是我那天要去老師家。真對不起。

王：小萬要你幫他寄這封信。

李：每次我幫他寄東西，他都不給我錢。這次我真_____了。

王：你為什麼不找小錢跟你去看電影？他也很喜歡看電影啊。

李：小錢愛吸煙，我怕煙，所以我_____。

不願意幫他寄　　願意跟他住　　不願意找他　　願意幫你

Additional Vocabulary

kuàidì (快遞) : express delivery　　　kǎoshì (考試) : test, to take a test

11

1-7 那就吸煙區吧。 Then (I'll take) the smoking section.

Explanation: The "吧" used here denotes that a concession has been made.

服務生：非吸煙區要等十分鐘。

　　李：太久了，那我們<u>坐吸煙區吧</u>。

　　王：對不起，我要念書。你們說話太吵了。

　　李：那我們_____。

　　王：太晚了，已經沒有公車了。

　　李：那我們就_____。

　　王：現在打長途電話太貴，晚上便宜一點。

　　李：那我就_____。

　　王：對不起，我們沒有你要的 guǒzhī (果汁)。我們只有 píngguǒzhī
　　　　(蘋果汁)，還有茶跟可樂。

　　李：那就給我_____。

> 坐 jìchéngchē(計程車)吧　　茶吧　　晚上打吧　　到外面去吧

Aural Comprehension Drill

The following dialogue may contain some unfamiliar vocabulary. Do not be concerned if you have not yet learned the vocabulary or do not understand its meaning. Try to figure out the meaning from the context, then answer the questions.

Listen to the following dialogue and choose the most appropriate answer.
1. (　) Why are they going to eat?

a) There is a western restaurant which cooks good food.

b) They do not have to work tomorrow, so they can stay out a bit late.

c) The last time the Japanese restaurant was really good, they want to go again.

2. (　) What do they most want to eat?

a) Chinese food　　b) western food　　c) Japanese food

3. (　) What problem are they worried about encountering?

a) no table　　b) bad food　　c) going home too late

11

Additional Vocabulary

guǒzhī(果汁) : fruit juice　　píngguǒzhī(蘋果汁) : apple juice　　jìchéngchē(計程車) : taxi

Dialogue II   Ordering from the Menu

服務生(拿水來)：兩位好。這是我們的菜單。請看一下。
　　　　　　　　　　　　　　　　　　càidān

陳先生：謝謝。你們餐廳哪些菜比較有名？
　　　　　　　　　　　　　　bǐjiào

服務生：宮保雞丁、麻婆豆腐、開洋白菜都不錯。
　　　　Gōngbǎo jīdīng　　mápó dòufǔ　　kāiyáng báicài

李小姐：開洋白菜是什麼啊？

服務生：就是把蝦米跟白菜放在一起燒。
　　　　　　　xiāmǐ　　　　　　　　yìqǐ　shāo

李小姐：味道怎麼樣？很鹹嗎？
　　　　Wèidào　　　　　　xián

服務生：不鹹，跟平常的菜一樣。我想你們會喜歡的。
　　　　　　　　píngcháng　　　yíyàng

-220-

陳先生：好。謝謝。我們先看一下菜單。(對李小姐說) 你

想吃什麼？

李小姐：我想試試開洋白菜。你呢？

陳先生：宮保雞丁太辣了。你也喜歡吃魚。我們點 一個

糖醋魚，再叫一個青椒 牛肉吧。
tángcù yú　　　　　　　qīngjiāo niúròu

李小姐：好啊。

陳先生：三個菜 夠不夠？
　　　　　　　　gòu

李小姐：夠了[1]，夠了。不夠再點。

陳先生：要不要喝 湯？玉米湯，好不好？
　　　　　　　　tāng　Yùmǐ

李小姐：好。就這樣吧[2]。

11

Vocabulary

1. 菜單　　càidān　　N：menu　　(M：fèn 份)

2. 比較　　bǐjiào　　Adv：comparatively
這個電視兩萬塊，那個電視五萬塊。五萬塊的比較好。
This TV is $20,000; that one is $50,000. The $50,000 one is better.

3. 宮保雞丁　gōngbǎo jīdīng　　N : gongbao chicken

4. 麻婆豆腐　mápó dòufǔ　　N : mapo tofu

5. 開洋白菜　kāiyáng báicài　　N : kaiyang cabbage

6. 蝦米　　xiāmǐ　　N : dried and/or shelled shrimp　　（M：zhī 隻）

   蝦　　xiā　　N : shrimp　　（M：zhī 隻 piece）

   米　　mǐ　　N : rice

7. 一起　　yìqǐ　　PW/Adv : together

   1) 我念大學的時候，跟小張住在一起。

   2) 我喜歡跟朋友一起去看電影，不喜歡自己一個人去。

   1) When I was a university student, I lived with Little Zhang.

   2) I like going to the movies with my friends. I don't like going alone.

8. 燒　　shāo　　V : to cook; to burn

   1) 我們喜歡去王先生家吃飯，因為他燒的菜很好吃。

   2) 我不想再見我的男朋友了。我把他給我的信都燒了。

   1) We like to go to Mr. Wang's house to eat, because he can really cook good food.

   2) I don't want to see my boyfriend any more. I burnt all the letters he gave me.

9. 味道　　wèidào　　N : taste; flavor

10. 鹹　　xián　　SV : to be salty

    海水是鹹的。

    Sea water is salty.

11. 平常　　píngcháng　　Adv : usually

    我平常都是晚上十一點以前就去睡覺，可是昨天晚上十二點才睡。

    I usually go to bed before 11:00 p.m. But last night I didn't get to bed until 12:00.

12. 一樣　　yíyàng　　SV : to be the same, alike

    這兩個包裹一樣重，都是一千五百公克。

    These two packages weigh the same; both are 1500 grams.

13. 會　　huì　　AV : will, would

    明天會不會下雨？

    Will it rain tomorrow?

11

14. 辣　　　là　　SV : to be hot, spicy

這個東西是辣的。

This thing is spicy.

15. 點　　　diǎn　　V : to order food

我不懂法文，在法國餐廳不會點菜。

I do not understand French. I cannot order food in a French restaurant.

16. 糖醋魚　tángcù yú　　N : tangcu fish (sweet and sour fish)

糖　　　táng　　N : sugar　　(M：塊、kē 顆)

醋　　　cù　　N : vinegar　　(M：píng 瓶)

魚　　　yú　　N : fish　　(M：tiáo 條)

17. 叫　　　jiào　　V : to order; to call, to shout, to scream

1) 你要的書，我們已經打電話去叫了。下星期一就送來。

2) 我在辦公室裡面。王先生來了，請你叫我。

1) We have already ordered the book you want. It will arrive next Monday.

2) I will be in the office. Please call me when Mr. Wang comes.

18. 青椒牛肉　qīngjiāo niúròu　　N : green pepper beef

青椒　　qīngjiāo　　N : green pepper　　(M：個)

牛　　　niú　　N : cow, cattle　　(M：tóu 頭)

肉　　　ròu　　N : meat　　(M：塊)

19. 夠　　　gòu　　SV : to be enough

這本字典一千兩百塊錢。我只有一千塊錢，不夠。

This dictionary is $1200. I have only $1000. It's not enough.

20. 湯　　　tāng　　N : soup　　(M：wǎn 碗)

21. 玉米　　yùmǐ　　N : corn

玉　　　yù　　N : jade　　(M：塊)

*22. 青菜　qīngcài　　N : vegetable

11

Notes

1. "夠了" means "That's enough." "了" indicates a change has taken place, as perceived by the speaker: It was not enough before, but now it is.

2. "就這樣吧"。means "Let it be in this way." or "That will be it." "吧" indicates a mild suggestion.

Grammar

2-1 比較有名　　better-known

Explanation: "比較" placed before a SV or "AV + V" indicates the subject has reached a certain level.

王：這兩家飯館，哪家好？
李：<u>大一點的那家比較有名</u>。

王：我們去大新百貨逛逛，怎麼樣？
李：那裡的東西不錯，可是＿＿＿＿＿＿＿＿＿＿。

王：小李，你到哪裡去了？我給你打了好幾次電話你都不在。
李：我這個星期＿＿＿＿＿＿＿，所以常常很晚下班。

王：錢小姐要這些zīliào (資料)。你能不能幫我寄給她？
李：寄給她太慢，＿＿＿＿＿＿＿＿＿＿＿＿＿。

王：你喜歡吃糖醋魚，還是青椒牛肉？
李：我＿＿＿＿＿＿＿＿＿＿＿＿＿＿＿。

王：你跟小錢，誰的菜做得好？
李：我想＿＿＿＿＿＿＿。

王：我應該找小陳幫忙呢？還是找小張？
李：找小張吧，他＿＿＿＿＿＿＿。

比較有空　傳真比較快　比較貴　比較忙
比較喜歡吃青椒牛肉　她做得比較好

Additional Vocabulary

　　zīliào(資料) : information, data

2-2 跟白菜 放在一起燒　(put and) cooked together with cabbage

Explanation: "一起 V" indicates two or more subjects are joined for the completion of the action of the verb. "在一起" indicates several things or people are together in the same location. "在一起 V" is used to emphasize that two or more subjects are together in a single place or location, but they are not necessarily performing the same action jointly. Finally, "V 在一起" indicates that the person(s), thing(s), or affair(s) preceding the verb will be in the same place after the action of the verb has been performed.

a) 跟……一起 V

　　王：我跟小張、小陳明天要去看電影。你呢？

　　李：我沒事，我可以＿＿＿＿＿＿＿＿＿＿＿＿＿＿＿＿＿＿＿嗎？

　　王：哎呀！我忘了把 kèběn (課本) 帶來，怎麼辦？

　　李：沒關係，你可以＿＿＿＿＿＿＿＿＿＿＿＿＿。

b) 跟……在一起

　　王：小李，你哥哥常常不在家，都是去找朋友嗎？

　　李：對啊，他喜歡＿＿＿＿＿＿＿＿＿＿＿＿＿＿＿＿＿＿。

　　王：昨天晚上你在哪裡？一個人嗎？

　　李：不是，我＿＿＿＿＿＿＿＿＿＿＿＿＿＿＿＿＿＿。

c) 在一起 V (O)

　　王：你跟小張每天一起 shàngxué (上學)，你們 tóngbān (同班) 嗎？

　　李：不是，我們不同班，我們不＿＿＿＿＿＿＿＿＿＿＿＿。

　　王：你為什麼不跟哥哥在房間裡玩？

　　李：因為我們喜歡的東西不一樣，所以我們不

　　　＿＿＿＿＿＿＿＿＿＿＿＿＿＿＿＿＿＿。

d) V 在一起

　　王：你要坐在哪裡？

　　李：我要跟你＿＿＿＿＿＿＿＿。

11

Additional Vocabulary

　　kèběn (課本) : textbook　　　　　　　shàngxué (上學) : to attend school
　　tóngbān (同班) : to be in the same class

王：你沒買青椒嗎？

李：買了。大概跟白菜＿＿＿＿＿＿＿，你找一找。

跟女朋友在一起　在一起上課　跟我一起看　跟你們一起去
跟朋友在一起　跟他在一起看書　坐在一起　放在一起

2-3 把蝦米跟白菜放在一起燒　cook the shrimp and cabbage together

Explanation: "V + 在 + PW (+ V)" may act as the complement for "把". The "一起" in "放在一起燒" functions as a PW. The word order of this sentence pattern follows Temporal Sequence Principle.

王：開洋白菜怎麼做？

李：把蝦米跟白菜<u>放在一起</u>燒就可以了。

王：你今天為什麼沒帶孩子來？

李：我把孩子＿＿＿＿＿＿。他爸爸在家。

王：你搬家以後我怎麼找你？

李：這是我的名片。我已經把新地址＿＿＿＿＿＿＿了。

王：這是我的 shēnqǐng（申請）表。身分證影本也要給你嗎？

李：shēnqǐng（申請）表先不要給我。你把身分證影本＿＿＿＿＿＿，再拿
　　給我。

王：你手裡拿的是什麼？

李：我的車 yào·shi（鑰匙）。我怕忘了帶，所以把鑰匙＿＿＿＿＿。

留在家裡　貼在表上　拿在手裡　寫在名片上

11

Additional Vocabulary

　　shēnqǐng（申請）表：application form　　yào·shi（鑰匙）：key(s)

2-4 我想你們<u>會喜歡</u>的。   I think you will like it.

Explanation: The auxiliary verb "會" indicates possibility, often referring to some future event. The "的" at the end of the sentence adds a tone of certainty.

王：這個菜鹹不鹹？

李：不鹹。我想你們<u>會喜歡的</u>。

王：你想張小姐會跟我一起去看電影嗎？

李：要是她喜歡你，她＿＿＿＿＿＿＿＿。

王：小張為什麼還沒來？是不是忘了？

李：再等一下吧。他一定＿＿＿＿＿＿。簽約這種事，他不＿＿＿＿＿＿。

王：你不要告訴我媽媽我吸煙，好不好？

李：我不說，她也＿＿＿＿＿＿＿＿。

王：不要等了。你女朋友不會打電話來了。

李：我要等。她說要打來就一定＿＿＿＿＿＿＿＿。

2-5 跟平常的菜一樣   the same as most dishes

Explanation: "NP₁ 跟 NP₂ 一樣 (+ SV)" is a way of expressing relativity or comparison. NP₂ is used as the standard in this comparison. The negative form is "NP₁ 跟 NP₂ 不一樣 (+ SV)". When the context is clear, NP₁ can be omitted.

王：這個菜鹹嗎？

李：不會，<u>跟平常的菜一樣</u>。

王：謝老師教英文。他太太教什麼？

李：＿＿＿＿＿＿＿＿＿＿＿＿，也教英文。

王：明天天氣怎麼樣？

李：＿＿＿＿＿＿＿＿＿＿＿＿，也會下雨。

王：我的房租很貴，一個月一萬塊。你的呢？

李：＿＿＿＿＿＿＿＿＿＿＿，也是一萬塊。

王：你爸爸喜歡吃辣的，你一定也喜歡吃辣的，對不對？

李：不對。＿＿＿＿＿＿＿＿＿＿＿＿，我不能吃辣的。

11

Aural Comprehension Drill

The following dialogues may contain some unfamiliar vocabulary. Do not be concerned if you have not yet learned the vocabulary or do not understand its meaning. Try to figure out the meaning from the context, then answer the questions.

Listen to the following dialogues and choose the most appropriate answer.

1. (   ) What is this conversation about?

    a) ordering food at a fast food shop

    b) discussing a menu for a party

    c) comparing the dishes

2. (   ) Where does this woman want to eat?

    a) in a restaurant

    b) at home

    c) somewhere outside the home

   (   ) What does this man not like to eat?

    a) meat

    b) fish

    c) vegetables

   (   ) Where do they finally decide to have dinner?

    a) at a French restaurant

    b) at a Chinese restaurant

    c) at home

   (   ) Do you think this man is willing to go out to eat?

    a) yes

    b) no

    c) not certain

11

Variety Exercises

I. Scenarios

Draw five pictures, but do not put the pictures in order. At the start of the activity divide the students into teams. Give each team a copy of the pictures. Then each team will arrange the pictures according to the story. Finally each team explains to (or discusses with) the class the story the pictures tell.

II. Role Play

a) call a friend to invite him/her to go to a Chinese restaurant to eat; b) after you decide the time and place c) you call to reserve a table; at the restaurant d) you order food from the menu. (Refer to Authentic Material)

11

Try to Guess

1. (   ) What do you think "吃醋" means?
     a) to eat vinegar
     b) to be sour
     c) to be jealous about rivalry in love
2. (   ) What do you think "非常" means?
     a) unusual, extremely
     b) not often
     c) abnormal
3. (   ) What do you think "紅燒" means?
     a) to cook at high heat
     b) to cook something red
     c) to braise in soy sauce

Authentic Material

Menu

今日特餐	
魚排飯	80元
雞腿飯	80元
黑胡椒牛柳	100元
蝦仁蛋炒飯	75元
附餐：湯、青菜、紅茶／咖啡	

1. What do you think "今日特餐" means?
2. If you order "雞腿飯", what will you eat?

11

Translation of the Dialogues

Dialogue I

Mr. Wang : Today is your twenty-fifth birthday, so I want to take you out to eat.

Ms. Li : That's very nice. Thank you.

Mr. Wang : What would you like to have, Chinese food or western food?

Ms. Li : How about western food?

Mr. Wang : Well, then, let's go eat French food, how about that? There's a famous French restaurant near here. Their food is pretty good.

Ms. Li : Great, let's go there.

(Getting a table at the restaurant)

Waiter : Welcome. How many (in your party)?

Mr. Wang : Two people.

Waiter : Did you make a reservation?

Ms. Li : No. Are there any seats available in the non-smoking section?

Waiter : I'm sorry, not any more. You will have to wait. Are you willing to wait?

Mr. Wang : How long will it be?

Waiter : Probably about twenty minutes or so.

Ms. Li : That's too long. Well, then I'll take the smoking area.

Waiter : Okay, please come with me.

Dialogue II

Waiter : (Bringing the water) How are you? Here is our menu. Please take a look at it.

Mr. Chen : Thank you. What are your restaurant's more famous dishes?

Waiter : Our gongbao chicken, mapo tofu, and kaiyang cabbage are all quite good.

Ms. Li : What is kaiyang cabbage?

Waiter : It is dried shrimp cooked together with cabbage.

Ms. Li : How is the flavor, very salty?

Waiter : It is not salty; it's about the same as most dishes. I'm sure you will like it.

Mr. Chen : Fine, thank you. We'll take a look at the menu first. (turns to Ms. Li) What would you like to eat?

Ms. Li : I'd like to try the kaiyang cabbage. What about you?

Mr. Chen : Gongbao chicken is too spicy. You like to eat fish too, so let's order a tangcu (sweet and sour) fish, and how about beef with green peppers.

Ms. Li : All right.

Mr. Chen : Three dishes, is that enough?

Ms. Li : It is enough. If it's not, then we'll order more later.

Mr. Chen : Would you like some soup? Is corn soup okay?

Ms. Li : Sure, that will be fine.

11

第十二課　在餐廳吃飯

LESSON 12 DINING AT A RESTAURANT

Key Study Points

expressing opinions on food (polite critique)／debating／polite mealtime
conversation／guessing／paying the bill／doggie bags／tipping

Vocabulary

Dialogue I

好久不見，最近，欸，剛剛，
件，襯衫，顏色，漂亮，樣子，
穿，身上，非常，好看，難看，
上菜，刀叉(刀子，叉子)，筷
子，味精，下次，上次，壺
(M)，熱，冷，盤子(盤)，髒，
乾淨，碗，馬上，慢用

Dialogue II

飽，餓，特別，高興，算帳，買
單，分開(開)，請客，帳單，櫃
台，結帳，包起來，打包，好
像，弄，抱歉，開，小費，不
必，啦，一成

Grammar

Dialogue I

你看

SV 了一點兒

……都＋VP／SV，

就是……

SP＋Nu‑次

多／少＋V（了）＋Nu＋

M(+N)

Dialogue II

吃飽

分開

包起來

把＋O＋RC

弄＋SV

好像

不必

12

Dialogue | Making Small Talk at the Table

Philip：我們 好久 不見 了。[1] 最近 怎麼樣 啊？
　　　　 ˇ ˙ hǎo jiǔ bú jiàn ˙　 Zuìjìn ˇ ˙ ˋ ˙

趙小姐：還不錯。欸[2]，你看我 剛剛 買的這件 襯衫
　　　　 ˊ ˊ ˋ Èi　 ˇ ˋ ˇ gānggāng ˇ ˙ ˋ jiàn chènshān

　　　　 怎麼樣？
　　　　 ˇ ˙ ˋ

Philip：顏色很 漂亮，樣子也不錯，穿 在你 身上
　　　　Yánsè ˇ piàoliàng yàng‧zi ˇ ˊ ˋ　 chuān ˋ ˇ shēnshàng

　　　　 非常 好看。
　　　　 fēicháng hǎokàn

趙小姐：真的啊？謝謝。[3]
　　　　 ー ˙ ˙ ˙ ˙

服務生：對不起，上菜。[4]
　　　　 ˋ ˙ ˇ shàngcài

- 233 -

Philip：先生，麻煩你給我刀叉。我不太會用筷子。
　　　　　　　　　　　　dāochā　　　　　　kuài·zi

(過了一會兒)

服務生：菜都來了嗎？

趙小姐：都來了。

服務生：喜歡我們的菜嗎？

趙小姐：每個菜都做得不錯，就是味精多了一點兒。[5]
　　　　　　　　　　　　　　　　wèijīng

服務生：不會吧？[6]一點兒都不放也不好吃。[7]下次你先告訴
　　　　　　　　　　　　　　　　　　　　　Xià cì

　　　　我，我就叫廚房少放一點兒。還要不要加菜？

趙小姐：我想夠了。[8]麻煩你給我們一壺熱茶。還有，這個
　　　　　　　　　　　　　　　　　　hú rè

　　　　盤子髒了，也麻煩你換一個。
　　　　pán·zi zāng

Philip：請再給我一碗飯。
　　　　　　　　　　wǎn

服務生：好，馬上來。請慢用。[9]
　　　　　　mǎshàng　　　mànyòng

Vocabulary

1. 好久不見 hǎo jiǔ bú jiàn   IE : Long time no see.

   好久不見。我們已經十年沒見了。你好嗎？

   Long time no see. It's already been ten years since we saw each other. How are you?

2. 最近   zuìjìn   Adv : lately, recently

   王小姐最近有什麼事？好幾天沒來上課了。

   What has Ms. Wang been doing lately? She hasn't been to class for a long time.

3. 欸   èi   I : (exclamation) Hey! (used to call someone)

   欸，已經很晚了。我們應該回家了。

   Hey, it's already late. We should go home.

4. 剛剛   gānggāng   Adv : just a moment

   她是五分鐘以前走的，剛剛還在。

   She left five minutes ago; she was just here.

5. 件   jiàn   M : for a shirt, a pair of pants,...

6. 襯衫   chènshān   N : shirt   (M：件)

7. 顏色   yánsè   N : color   (M：種)

8. 漂亮   piàoliàng   SV : to be pretty, beautiful

   王小姐很漂亮，所以有很多男孩子想跟她交朋友。

   Ms. Wang is beautiful, so there are many boys who want to make friends with her.

9. 樣子   yàng·zi   N : style, appearance   (M：種)

   那個人的樣子很奇怪，大概不是住在這裡的人。

   That person looks so strange. He is probably not from around here.

10. 穿   chuān   V : to wear, to put on

    謝小姐今天穿的紅鞋樣子很漂亮。

    The red shoes Ms. Xie is wearing today are beautiful.

11. 身上   shēnshàng   N : on one's body

    你知道嗎？張太太身上穿的那件衣服要三萬塊錢！

    Do you know? The clothes Mrs. Zhang is wearing cost $30,000!

12

12. 非常　fēicháng　Adv : very, pretty

李先生做菜做得非常好。我們吃了還想再吃。

Mr. Li cooks very well. After we eat, we still want more.

13. 好看　hǎokàn　SV : good-looking; interesting

1) 這個菜有紅、白、綠三個顏色，真好看。

2) 這個電影非常好看。一個星期已經有十萬個人去看了。

1) This dish has three colors, red, white, and green; it's really pretty.

2) This movie is really good. In one week 100,000 people went to see it.

*14. 難看　nánkàn　SV : bad-looking; uninteresting

15. 上菜　shàng//cài　VO : to serve the dishes

你點的菜不好做，所以上菜上得慢。

The dish you ordered is not easy to make, so the food is slow to arrive.

16. 刀叉　dāochā　N : set knife and fork　(M：fù 副)

刀子　dāo·zi　N : knife　(M：把)

叉子　chā·zi　N : fork　(M：把)

17. 筷子　kuài·zi　N : chopsticks　(M：雙)

18. 味精　wèijīng　N : MSG (monosodium glutamate)

19. 下次　xià cì　SP-M : next time

我們這次吃中餐，下次吃西餐，好不好？

We will eat Chinese food this time. Next time we will eat western food, okay?

*20. 上次　shàng cì　SP-M : last time; the previous occasion

錢先生上次旅行去日本，這次要去美國。

Mr. Qian went to Japan for his vacation last time; this time he wants to go to America.

21. 壺　hú　M : a pot of

22. 熱　rè　SV : to be hot

今天真熱啊！

Today is really hot!

*23. 冷   lěng   SV : to be cold

今天比較冷，穿一件衣服不夠。你再加一件吧。

It is cooler today. Wearing one layer of clothes is not enough. Add another layer.

24. 盤子   pán·zi   N : plate, dish   (M：個)

    盤   pán   M : a plate of

25. 髒   zāng   SV : to be dirty

要是衣服穿了好幾次都沒洗，一定很髒。

If clothes are worn several times without washing, they will definitely be very dirty.

*26. 乾淨   gānjìng   SV : to be clean

小陳的房間真乾淨，一點兒髒東西也沒有。

Little Chen's house is really clean. There is not one dirty thing there.

27. 碗   wǎn   N/M : bowl; a bowl of   (M：個)

28. 馬上   mǎshàng   Adv : at once, immediately

小李，請你馬上來一下。我一分鐘也不能等了。

Little Li, come here quickly for a moment, I cannot wait even a minute.

29. 慢用   mànyòng   IE : Enjoy your meal.

菜都來了。請慢用。

The food is all here. Enjoy your meal.

Notes

1. "好久不見了。" means "Long time no see." or "I haven't seen you for a long time." "了"indicates "up to now".

2. "欸", here, is used to call someone and get his/her attention. It is very informal and should only be used in casual settings. It is not polite to use this interjection when talking to one's senior.

3. "真的啊？謝謝。" means "Really? Thanks." Traditionally, Chinese people are taught to be modest, therefore they usually do not easily accept praises from other people. Most people will say "哪裡，哪裡。", which means "No, no, I am not as good as you have just said." Nowadays, young people in Taiwan have been somewhat influenced by other cultures and will sometimes accept praise and say "謝謝".

4. "對不起，上菜。" means "Excuse me, may I serve your dishes?" It is used by a waiter or waitress who brings food to the table. It is meant to get the attention of the people at the table and to make room for him/her to stand and serve the food.

12

5. "每個菜都做得不錯，就是味精多了一點。" means "Every dish was good, only there was a little bit too much MSG." or "It would have been better if there was less MSG." 趙小姐 is criticizing the food in a mild way so that she will not offend other people. She praises first, and then mentions only one thing which is not satisfactory.

6. "不會吧？" means "It should not be like this." "吧" denotes a tone of doubt. The waiter is trying to defend against 趙小姐's criticism in a mild way.

7. "一點都不放也不好吃。" means "It will not be delicious if there is no MSG at all." The waiter agrees that it is not good to have too much MSG, but it won't be good if there is no MSG, either. This "也" means "also".

8. "我想夠了。" means "I think it will be enough." This "了" indicates that the situation has reached a certain point or level.

9. "請慢用。" literally means: "Please take your time to have your food." Therefore it can be translated as "Enjoy your meal." It is very polite, and is often used by someone who serves food.

Grammar

1-1 你看我剛剛買的這件襯衫怎麼樣？

Look at this shirt I just bought. What do you think?

Explanation: This "看" means "to think, to consider". "S 看" may be used to bring up a personal suggestion or to inquire about another person's opinion. Subjects which can be used in this case are "我", "你", or "你們".

王：你今天去逛街，買了不少漂亮的衣服吧？
李：對啊。<u>你看我剛剛買的這件衣服怎麼樣？</u>

王：小錢幫了我很多忙。我不知道怎麼謝謝他。
李：他喜歡看電影。＿＿＿＿＿＿＿＿＿＿＿＿吧。

王：我們今天有三個人，應該點幾個菜？
李：＿＿＿＿＿＿＿＿＿＿，夠不夠？

王：白小姐的生日要到了。我們送她什麼好呢？
李：她常逛書店。＿＿＿＿＿＿＿＿＿，怎麼樣？

王：你跟你女朋友下個月要去哪裡旅行？
李：還沒決定。＿＿＿＿＿＿＿＿＿呢？

你看送她一本書　你們看兩個菜、一個湯
你看去哪裡好　我看你請他去看電影

1-2 味精多了一點　　a bit too much MSG

Explanation: "SV 了一點" denotes that the actual situation differs slightly from what the speaker originally expected.

王：你叫的菜怎麼樣？
李：味精<u>多了一點</u>。

王：昨天看的那個房子，你喜不喜歡？
李：還不錯，可是房租_____。

王：我們星期天早上十點去逛街，好不好？
李：我覺得十點_____，百貨公司十一點才開門。

王：今天的青椒牛肉做得怎麼樣？
李：味道不錯，可是_____。

王：小陳說他的車要賣給我。你看怎麼樣？
李：我覺得他的車_____，他賣得太貴了。

牛肉少了一點　舊了一點　早了一點　貴了一點

1-3 每個菜都做得不錯，就是味精多了一點。

Each dish is well prepared, only there is a bit too much MSG.

Explanation: In the "……都 + VP/SV，就是……" sentence pattern, "就是" means "only" and is used to affirm the range of what is being discussed. What follows "就是" is usually fundamentally different from the rest of the situation as a whole.

王：喜歡我們的菜嗎？
李：每個菜都不錯，就是<u>味精多了一點</u>。

王：這本書怎麼樣？
李：每一課都很有用，就是_____。

王：你喜歡你的新公司嗎？
李：喜歡。每個人都很客氣，就是_____。

12

Additional Vocabulary

　　開門：to open the door

王：你昨天為什麼沒買那件襯衫？

李：顏色、樣子都不錯，就是＿＿＿＿＿＿＿＿＿＿。

王：你剛搬家，要買的東西都買了嗎？

李：家具都買了，就是＿＿＿＿＿＿＿＿＿＿。

> 坐車比較麻煩　還沒送來　難了一點　太貴了

1-4 下次你先告訴我。　　Next time tell me first.

Explanation: "SP + Nu-次" should be placed before or after the subject. Possible SP that may be used include: "這", "那", and "第", as well as "前" and "後". In addition, "上", "下", and "每" can all be used in this way as well, however, the number following can only be "一", even though this "一" may be omitted.

王：我不能吃味精。這個菜裡放了嗎？

李：對不起。已經放了。<u>下次你先告訴我</u>，我就不放。

王：我們為什麼不去吃日本菜？

李：我已經訂了位子了。我們今天先吃法國菜，＿＿＿＿＿＿＿＿＿＿＿＿＿吧。

王：小張說他沒帶錢，要我們先付錢。

李：他 yòu (又) 說沒帶錢，＿＿＿＿＿＿＿＿＿＿＿。以後不要跟他一起出來了。

王：這是你第幾次來台灣？

李：這是我＿＿＿＿＿＿＿＿＿＿＿＿＿。

王：你每年八月都去旅行，今年要去哪裡？

李：上次我去英國，＿＿＿＿＿＿＿＿＿＿＿＿＿。

王：今天我請客。

李：不行，＿＿＿＿＿＿＿＿＿＿＿＿＿，我今天一定要請你。

> 這次要去法國　每次都說沒帶錢　第三次來
> 前兩次都是你請我　下次再吃日本菜

12

Additional Vocabulary

　　yòu (又) : again

1-5 我叫廚房少放一點。　　I will tell the cook to add a little less.

Explanation: "多／少 V(了)+ Nu + M + (N)" indicates that an addition or subtraction has been made to a certain action because the original amount was viewed as inadequate or too much.

王：菜裡不要放太多味精。

李：那我叫廚房<u>少放一點</u>。

王：你要做幾個菜？五個嗎？

李：今天有十個人要來，所以得＿＿＿＿＿＿＿。

王：我今天晚上只吃了半碗飯，現在覺得很餓。

李：飯、菜都很多，你為什麼不＿＿＿＿＿＿＿呢？

王：你要買的書都拿了嗎？

李：我看看。哎呀！＿＿＿＿＿＿＿＿＿。那本中文的忘了拿。

王：我貼的郵票夠不夠？

李：不夠。這封信超重。你＿＿＿＿＿＿＿＿。

少拿了一本　　多吃一點　　少貼了三塊錢　　多做幾個

Aural Comprehension Drill

The following dialogues may contain some unfamiliar vocabulary. Do not be concerned if you have not yet learned the vocabulary or do not understand its meaning. Try to figure out the meaning from the context, then answer the questions.

Listen to the following dialogues and choose the most appropriate answer.

1. (　) What is this man saying?

a) He doesn't know where to eat.

b) He wants to know how to get to some place where he can eat.

c) He wants to take this lady out to eat.

2. (　) What is this lady doing?

a) ordering in a coffee shop

b) buying cake in a bakery

c) serving in a coffee shop

12

Dialogue II Settling the Bill

小錢：吃 飽 了 嗎 ？
　　　　　 bǎo

小林：飽 了。今天吃得特別 高興。
　　　　　　　　　　　 tèbié gāoxìng

小錢：我們 算帳 吧。
　　　　　 suànzhàng

小林：好。

小錢：先生，我們要買單。
　　　　　　　　　　　 mǎidān

12

服務生：要不要分開算[1]？
　　　　　　　　 fēnkāi

小林：一起算。

服務生：好，馬上來。

小林：今天我 請客。
　　　ˉ ˉ ˇ qǐngkè

小錢：那太不好意思了。
　　　ˋ ˋ ˋ ˇ ˋ˙ ˙

小林：沒關係啦。
　　　ˊ ˉ ˙ ˙

小錢：好吧[2]，那下次我請你。
　　　ˇ˙

服務生：這是你們的 帳單。 請到門口櫃台 結帳。
　　　　ˋ ˋ ˇ˙ ˙ zhàngdān　ˇ ˋ ˊ ˇ guìtái jiézhàng

　　　　要不要把這個菜包起來[3]？
　　　　ˋ ˇ ˋ ˇ ˙ ˋ bāoqǐlái

小錢：好，麻煩你打包。噢，對不起，帳 好像 算錯了。
　　　ˇ　ˊ ˊ ˇ dǎbāo　ˋ ˋ˙ ˇ　ˋ hǎoxiàng ˋ ˋ˙

　　　我們沒點這個菜。
　　　ˇ˙ ˊ ˇ ˋ˙ ˋ

服務生：是嗎？我再看看。噢，對，是我 弄錯了。真
　　　　ˋ˙　ˇ ˋ ˋ˙　ˋ　ˋ ˇ nòng ˋ˙　 ˉ

　　　　抱歉。我再開一張給你。(服務生走開)
　　　　bàoqiàn　ˇ ˋ kāi ˋ ˉ ˇ ˇ

小林：要不要給小費？
　　　ˋ ˋ ˇ ˇ xiǎofèi

小錢：不必啦[4]。已經加了一成 服務費了。[5]
　　　Bú bì ·la　ˇ ˉ ˉ˙ ˋ yì chéng ˊ ˋ ˋ˙

小林：那就走吧。[6]
　　　ˋ ˋ ˇ˙

- 243 -

Vocabulary

1. 飽   bǎo   SV : to be full (after eating)

我吃了很多東西，已經飽了，不能再吃了。

I ate a lot of things and am already full. I could not eat any more.

*2. 餓   è   SV : to be hungry

我餓了。你有沒有東西給我吃？

I'm hungry. Do you have anything for me to eat?

3. 特別   tèbié   Adv/SV : specially, particularly; to be special

1) 媽媽平常十二點睡覺，今天特別早，八點就去睡了。

2) 她穿得很特別，跟別人都不一樣。

1) Mother often goes to bed at 12:00. But she is unusually early today; at 8:00 she already went to bed.

2) She dresses very special, completely different than other people.

4. 高興   gāoxìng   SV : to be happy

爸爸送我一部最新的電腦。真高興！

Father gave me the latest computer. How happy (I am)!

5. 算帳   suàn//zhàng   VO : to compute or settle the bill

要買的東西都拿了。我們可以去算帳了。

I've got all the things I want to buy. So we can go pay.

6. 買單   mǎi//dān   VO : to pay the bill

你跟男朋友去吃飯是誰買單？

When you and your boyfriend go out to eat, who pays the bill?

7. 分開   fēnkāi   RC/Adv : to separate; separately

1) 她不要跟男朋友分開，不願意到國外念書。

2) 這張桌子不夠我們十個人坐。我們得分開坐。

1) She does not want to separate with her boyfriend, and is unwilling to go abroad to study.

2) This table is not big enough to seat the ten of us. We have to sit separately.

開   kāi   V : to open

有人來了。我去開門。

Someone is here. I will go open the door.

8. 請客　　qǐng//kè　　VO : to treat, to host, to be my guest

今天的晚飯我請客。你們都不要付錢了。

I want to host tonight's dinner; you all do not have to pay.

9. 帳單　　zhàngdān　　N : bill

10. 櫃台　　guìtái　　N : counter　　(M：個)

11. 結帳　　jiézhàng　　VO : to settle a bill

請你去結帳，看看我們買的東西一共多少錢。

Please go settle the bill, and see how much the things we bought amount to.

12. 包起來　　bāoqǐlái　　RC : to wrap up

這雙鞋請你包起來。我要寄給我的孩子。

Please wrap up this pair of shoes. I want to send them to my son.

13. 打包　　dǎbāo　　VO : to pack

我要搬家了，衣服都還沒打包。

I want to move, but none of my clothes has yet been packed.

14. 好像　　hǎoxiàng　　Adv : It seems..., to look like

他好像很忙，每天都有很多事要做。

It looks like he is very busy. He has many things to do everyday.

15. 弄　　nòng　　V : to make, do, manage, handle

哎呀！這張桌子真髒，是誰弄的？

Yikes! This table is really dirty. Who did this?

16. 抱歉　　bàoqiàn　　SV : to be sorry

真抱歉，我忘了昨天要請你看電影。你一定等了很久吧？

I am really sorry, I forgot that I invited you to a movie yesterday. You must have waited for a long time.

17. 開　　kāi　　V : to write (a check, a bill, a ticket, etc.)

小姐，我要結帳。請你開帳單給我。謝謝。

Miss, I want to settle the bill. Please write out the bill for me. Thank you.

18. 小費　　xiǎofèi　　N : tip

12

19. **不必**　　bú bì　　AV : need not

老師通知我們明天不上課，我們明天就不必去學校了。

The teacher notified us that there is no class tomorrow, so there is no need to go to school tomorrow.

20. **啦**　　·la　　I : a phrase-final particle (denoting a tone of exclamation or interrogation.)

21. **一成**　　yì chéng　　N : ten percent

Notes

1. "分開算" means to calculate separately.　In most cases, Chinese will feel "不好意思" for not paying for other people at the table.　That is why Chinese people are often seen fighting for the bill in a restaurant—whoever ends up with the bill pays. Nowadays, however, younger generations usually pay their own portion of the bill themselves; they do not treat people at the same table that often and easily.　The Chinese term for "Go Dutch" is "各付各的(gè fù gè ·de)".

2. "好吧" means "Well, all right." This "吧" denotes a tone of concession or resignation.　As already mentioned, Chinese people usually feel that it is better to treat others at the table than being treated oneself.　Maybe 小錢 does not want to fight with 小林 for the bill, and so he chooses to say that he will treat 小林 next time (下次我請你).

3. "把這個菜包起來" literally means "wrap this dish up."　In this dialogue, it means "put this dish in a doggy bag."　It is common to take leftovers from a banquet home in Taiwan.

4. "不必啦", here, means "(There is) no need (to give a tip)."　The particle "啦" is placed at the end of the sentence, actually combining the sounds of "了" (·le) and "啊" (·a). "啦" can denote a tone of exclamation or interrogation.

5. "已經加了一成服務費了。" means "10% of the total cost has already been added as a service fee (tip)."　In Taiwan, there is no need to tip on most occasions.　Big restaurants usually add 10% of the total cost onto the bill, so there is no need to add additional tips unless the customer feels the service of the waiter/waitress has been extremely good.

6. "那就走吧。" means "Then, let's go." This "吧" indicates a tone of suggestion.

12

Grammar

2-1 吃飽了嗎？　Are you full?

Explanation: V + RVE is a compound verb expressing the result(s) of a certain completed action. Chinese verbs can only represent a single action, and at the same time do not explain the following result. Therefore, a RVE (resultative verb ending) must be added after the verb to indicate the result, thus making the meaning of the phrase or sentence fully clear. RVE is the result of a certain action, and only V or SV may act as a RVE. Furthermore, every RVE has a set meaning or message and cannot be randomly combined with just any verb. For example, verbs that can be used in conjunction with "飽" include: "吃", "喝", and "睡". The affirmative form is "V + R V E 了", while the negative form should be "沒 V + R V E".

先生：今天老張請客。菜很好，可是人很多。

太太：那你吃飽了嗎？還要不要再吃一點？

　王：要上課了，不要再睡了。

　李：可是我昨天晚上＿＿＿＿＿＿＿，現在還想睡。

　王：這些 diǎnxīn (點心)很好吃，多吃一點。

　李：我剛剛喝了幾杯可樂就＿＿＿＿＿，現在一點東西都不想吃。

孩子：家裡有沒有東西可以吃？

媽媽：你已經吃了三個包子了，還＿＿＿＿＿啊？

孩子：你叫我做什麼？

媽媽：已經七點了，＿＿＿＿沒有？要去上課了。不要再睡了，起來吧。

Additional Vocabulary

　　diǎnxīn(點心) : snack(s), dim sum　　　　起來 : to get up, rise

- 247 -

12

2-2 要不要分開算？ Do you want it added separately?

Explanation: "分開" is a resultative compound verb; the meaning of "開" is to be separate, to be ajar. Verbs that can be used with this character include: "走", "拿", "打", "分", "搬", "帶", etc. "分開" can also act as an adverb, and be placed in front of the verb indicating the manner in which the action is carried out.

a) 王：不知道這個包裹裡有什麼東西？
   李：你＿＿＿＿＿＿看看就知道了。

   王：這裡還有沒有位子？
   李：噢，這是我的東西。我可以＿＿＿＿＿＿。

   王：我的身分證好像diào(掉)在這張桌子下面。
   李：那我幫你＿＿＿＿＿＿找找。

   王：喂，請問林先生在不在？
   李：他剛＿＿＿＿＿＿，馬上就回來。你等一下再打來。

搬開　打開　走開　拿開

b) 服務生：兩位的帳一起算嗎？
   李：<u>分開算</u>。

   王：你還跟父母住在一起嗎？
   李：我們＿＿＿＿＿＿。我住三樓，他們住一樓。

   王：這些書有中文的，也有英文的。要放在一起嗎？
   李：不要，請你＿＿＿＿＿＿＿。

   王：吃飯的時候，你要跟你妹妹坐在一起嗎？
   李：都可以。坐在一起，＿＿＿＿＿＿＿，都可以。

   王：這兩個菜包在一起，可以嗎？
   李：一個是冷的，一個是熱的，你＿＿＿＿＿＿＿吧。

12

Additional Vocabulary

　　diào(掉) : to drop

2-3a 要不要把這個菜包起來？　Do you want to wrap this food up?

Explanation: When "起來" acts as an RVE, it has the following characteristics: 1) Its meaning is "to gather together"; verbs that can be used with it are: "包", "收", "留", "加", etc.; 2) It expresses that the direction of a certain action is upwards; verbs that can be paired with it in this case include: "站", "拿", and "搬".

王：先生，麻煩你把帳單拿給我們。

服務生：好。要不要把這個菜<u>包起來</u>？

王：下午大概會下雨。

李：真的嗎？我剛洗的衣服都在外面，我得快一點_____。

王：還有好多菜，可是人都走了，怎麼辦？

李：_____晚上吃啊。

媽媽：你們昨天去玩，用了多少錢？

兒子：吃飯、坐車_____，一共用了一千兩百塊。

王：欸，欸，新 lǎobǎn (老闆)來了。

李：我們_____歡迎他吧。

王：我剛剛買的這件衣服怎麼樣？

李：你_____，我看看。

王：地上那張身分證是誰的？

李：你_____看看就知道了。

拿起來　站起來　留起來　穿起來　收起來　加起來

2-3b 要不要把這些菜包起來？　Do you want to wrap these dishes up?

Explanation: Both RVE and a directional verb may act as a verb complement for the "把" structure.

王：我們要回家了。

李：還有很多菜，你們要不要<u>把這些菜包起來</u>帶回去？

12

Additional Vocabulary

　　lǎobǎn(老闆) : boss, store owner

王：奇怪，我媽媽寄給我的包裹為什麼還沒到？

李：你媽媽會不會＿＿＿＿＿＿＿＿＿＿＿＿？

王：很晚了，你去睡吧。

李：我要先＿＿＿＿＿＿＿＿＿＿＿＿＿＿，再去睡覺。

王：你什麼時候下班？還要多久？

李：我＿＿＿＿＿＿＿＿＿＿＿＿就可以下班了。

王：我的書包真重。

李：那你先＿＿＿＿＿＿＿＿＿＿＿＿，xiūxī (休息)一下。

王：媽，我剛交了一個女朋友。

媽媽：＿＿＿＿＿＿＿＿＿＿＿＿。我們也想認識認識。

王：你已經搬家了，還去房東那兒做什麼？

李：我去＿＿＿＿＿＿＿＿＿＿＿＿。

把押金拿回來　把地址寫錯了　把書包放下來
把她帶回來　把這封信傳真出去　把這些碗、盤洗乾淨

2-4 好像算錯了。　It seems totaled wrong.

Explanation: "好像" expresses the speaker's uncertain tone and can be placed in front of or behind the subject or before the verb. When used to indicate another person's error or mistake, "好像" makes the tone of the sentence or phrase milder and less direct.

服務生：這是兩位的帳單。請看一下。

李：好像弄錯了。我們沒點這個菜。

王：你知不知道第一銀行在哪裡？

李：＿＿＿＿＿＿＿＿，可是我不一定對。你再問問別人吧。

王：小李，明天下午三點有法文課，不要忘了。

李：是三點嗎？＿＿＿＿＿＿＿吧。

Additional Vocabulary

xiūxī(休息) : to rest, to take a rest

12

王：小陳回來了沒有？

李：＿＿＿＿＿＿＿＿＿，你去他房間看看。

王：我今天做宮保雞丁加了一點醋，你試試味道怎麼樣？

李：宮保雞丁＿＿＿＿＿＿＿＿＿，放了醋味道很奇怪。

2-5 弄錯了　　　to be mistaken

Explanation: "弄" means "to do", and can be used as a substitute when either the action cannot or does not need to be expressed by a more specific verb. As a result, it is considered less formal. "弄" often takes SV or V as a complement.

王：這個帳不對吧？

李：我看看。噢，真對不起，是我<u>弄錯了</u>。

王：電腦壞了不能用，真不方便。

李：你的電腦壞了好久了。還＿＿＿＿＿＿＿＿＿啊？

王：你叫我做什麼？

李：我現在要工作，不能跟 gǒu (狗)玩。你幫我把 gǒu (狗)＿＿＿＿＿＿吧。

王：小李，怎麼用電腦傳真？

李：我也不懂。等我＿＿＿＿＿＿＿＿＿再告訴你。

王：你們什麼時候搬家？

李：上一個房客剛搬走。等房東把房子＿＿＿＿＿＿＿＿，我們就可以搬了。

王：已經八點半了，你為什麼還不回家？

李：今天的帳還＿＿＿＿＿＿＿＿＿，所以還不能走。

弄出去　沒弄好　弄乾淨　沒弄對　弄懂了

12

Additional Vocabulary

　　gǒu(狗) : dog　　　　　帳 : account

2-6 不必給小費   no need to give a tip

Explanation: "不必" indicates the lack of need to complete the action of the verb following "不必", either for rational, practical, or personal reasons.

王：要不要給小費啊？

李：已經加了一成服務費，就<u>不必給小費了</u>。

王：你坐公車為什麼不買票？

李：我已經六十五歲了，_____。

王：你一個月要給多少水、電費？

李：我_____。房東說都算在房租裡了。

王：小林還不知道這件事吧。我們應該通知他。

李：_____了。他已經知道了。

王：我想把張小姐介紹給小萬，你看怎麼樣？

李：_____了。小萬已經有女朋友了。

Aural Comprehension Drill

The following dialogues may contain some unfamiliar vocabulary. Do not be concerned if you have not yet learned the vocabulary or do not understand its meaning. Try to figure out the meaning from the context, then answer the questions.

Listen to the following dialogues and choose the most appropriate answer.

1. (   ) Where does this dialogue take place?

   a) at a restaurant   b) at a market   c) at a bakery

   (   ) What does "找錢" mean?

   a) looking for money   b) asking for money   c) giving back change

   (   ) Who is paying for what they are eating?

   a) the man   b) the woman   c) both of them

2. (   ) What is this customer complaining about?

   a) The wrong dish was served.   b) There is something dirty in his food.

   c) The food doesn't taste good.

   (   ) What is the outcome?

   a) This dish is served for free.

   b) The customer is given a free cup of coffee.

   c) A fresh dish is served.

Variety Exercises

I. Scenarios

今天的天氣怎麼樣？

你昨天去看的房子怎麼樣？

我剛剛買的這雙鞋怎麼樣？

那家百貨公司裡的洗手間怎麼樣？

12

II. Divide the students into pairs, with one student asking and the other answering. Students ask each other's opinions. The answers should be based on the actual situation or personal opinion, such as: What do you think of the clothes I am wearing today? How was the movie you watched yesterday?

III. Divide into teams. Students describe their favorite ethnic food and explain why they like it. What is special about the food? What are the most famous dishes?

IV. Role Play

1. You go shopping in a supermarket. When paying the bill, you discover it has been added up wrong. You ask the cashier to check it.

2. You see an article of clothing you like in a store. You really want to buy it, but there is a dirty spot on it. What will you say to the clerk? Ask if there is another one or ask for a discount?

3. You travel to France. Before you go, you ask the travel agency about tipping. (Do they have this custom? When and how much to give?...)

Try to Guess

1. (   ) What do you think "有樣學樣" means?
   a) to use the same mode
   b) to act like the role model when there is one
   c) to copy the style from others

2. (   ) What do you think "特色" means?
   a) a special color   b) very colorful   c) characteristics

3. (   ) What do you think "不見了" means?
   a) to have disappeared   b) to have not met   c) will not see

4. (   ) What do you think "菜刀" means?
   a) knife used to chop vegetables   b) kitchen knife   c) food processor

Authentic Material

shípǔ (食譜) recipe

開洋白菜

材料：①大白菜一棵約一斤
　　　②蝦米3大匙，蔥、薑末各1/2大匙
　　　③料酒1/2大匙、高湯1/2杯、鹽3/4小匙、味精少許
　　　④太白粉1大匙、水2大匙
　　　⑤油3大匙

做法：1.把白菜洗乾淨，切三刀，切成大塊。蝦米洗乾淨，
　　　　放在水裡幾分鐘。
　　　2.⑤燒熱，先炒②，再放①，炒一會兒。加③燒開以
　　　　後，蓋鍋再煮四分鐘。最後用④勾芡就可以上桌了。

12

1.What do you think "材料" means?

2.What do you think "料酒" means?

3.What do you think "做法" means?

4.What should first be done with the cabbage and dried shrimp?

Translation of the Dialogues

Dialogue I

Philip : It has been a long time since we have seen each other. How have you been recently?

Miss Zhao : Not bad. Hey, take a look at this shirt I just bought. What do you think?

Philip : The color is pretty. It has a nice style, and it looks beautiful on you.

Miss Zhao : Really? Thanks!

Waiter : Excuse me, you're food is ready.

Philip : Sir, could I trouble you for a knife and fork. I can't use chopsticks very well.

(a while later)

Waiter : Is that everything?

Miss Zhao : Yes, the food's all here.

Waiter : Do you like our food?

Miss Zhao : It's all well prepared, but there is just a little too much MSG.

Waiter : Do you really think so? It won't taste good if we don't add any at all. Next time let me know, and I'll tell the kitchen to use less. Would you like anything else?

Miss Zhao : I think this is enough. Could you bring us a pot of hot tea, please. Also, this plate is dirty, could you give me another one?

Philip : Please bring me another bowl of rice.

Waiter : Okay, just one moment. Enjoy your meal.

Dialogue II

Little Qian : Are you full?

Little Lin : Yes, I've eaten especially well today.

Little Qian : Then let's get the bill.

Little Lin : Okay.

Little Qian : Sir, we'd like the check, please.

Waiter : Would you like separate checks?

Little Lin : Add it altogether.

Waiter : Okay, I will bring it right over.

Little Lin : Today is my treat.

Little Qian : Thank you. That's very nice.

Little Lin : That's all right.

12

Little Qian : Okay, then I'll treat you next time.

Waiter : Here is your bill. Please pay at the counter by the door. Would you like this food wrapped in a doggie bag?

Little Qian : Yes, please wrap it up. Oh, sorry, but the bill seems to be incorrect; we didn't order this dish.

Waiter : Really? Let me take another look. Oh, right, that's my fault. I'm really sorry. I'll write another one for you. (The waiter leaves)

Little Lin : Should we leave a tip?

Little Qian : It's not necessary. They've already added a ten percent surcharge.

Little Lin : Then, let's go.

12

APPENDIX I   VOCABULARY INDEX
生詞索引

A

·a	啊	啊	Ah, an exclamation; P : (indicates surprise)	2
āi·ya	哎呀	哎呀	oh, no (expression of exclamation, surprise or dismay)	10
ài	愛	爱	love; to love to	9

B

bā	八	八	eight	1
bā yuè	八月	八月	August	7
bǎ	把	把	CV : (used to bring the object before the verb)	10
bà·ba	爸爸	爸爸	father	9
bà mā	爸媽	爸妈	father and mother	9
·ba	吧	吧	P : (indicates suggestion, guess, probably)	8
bái	白	白	to be white	2
báicài	白菜	白菜	Chinese cabbage	2
bǎi	百	百	hundred	2
bǎihuò gōngsī	百貨公司	百贷公司	department store	5
bān	搬	搬	to move	7
bānjiā	搬家	搬家	to move one's residence	8
bàn	半	半	half	4
bàn	辦	办	to handle, to manage	7
bànfǎ	辦法	办法	method, way	7
bàngōngshì	辦公室	办公室	office	8
bāng	幫	帮	to help	7
bāoguǒ	包裹	包裹	parcel	10
bāoqǐlái	包起來	包起来	to wrap up	12
bāo·zi	包子	包子	steamed bun with meat or vegetable filling	1
bǎo	飽	饱	to be full (after eating)	12
bàoqiàn	抱歉	抱歉	to be sorry	12
bēi	杯	杯	a cup of/cup	1
bēi·zi	杯子	杯子	cup	1
běi	北	北	north	6
běn	本	本	M : for books, magazines, etc.	3
bǐ	筆	笔	pen	5

bǐjiào	比較	比较	comparatively	11
biǎo	表	表	form	3
bié·de	別的	别的	the others	10
bú bì	不必	不必	need not	12
bú kèqì	不客氣	不客气	You are welcome.	3
búcuò	不錯	不错	to be not bad, to be good	11
bù	不	不	not	2
bùhǎoyì·si	不好意思	不好意思	to feel embarrassed; to be ill at ease	11

C

cái	才	才	Adv: (later than expected)	10
cài	菜	菜	vegetable; dish, course	2
càidān	菜單	菜单	menu	11
cān	餐	餐	meal	11
cāntīng	餐廳	餐厅	restaurant	11
chā·zi	叉子	叉子	fork	12
chá	茶	茶	tea	1
cháng	長	长	to be long	8
chángtú	長途	长途	long distance	8
chángcháng	常常	常常	often, frequently	9
chāozhòng	超重	超重	to overweigh	10
chǎo	吵	吵	to be noisy, to make noise, to annoy	8
chē	車	车	car, vehicle	2
chén	陳	陈	a Chinese family name	5
chènshān	襯衫	衬衫	shirt	12
chī	吃	吃	to eat	1
chīfàn	吃飯	吃饭	to have a meal	4
chū qù	出去	出去	to go out	8
chūzū	出租	出租	to rent	6
chúfáng	廚房	厨房	kitchen	6
chuān	穿	穿	to wear, to put on	12
chuánzhēn	傳真	传真	to fax	10
chuánzhēnjī	傳真機	传真机	fax machine	10
chuāngkǒu	窗口	窗口	window	10
chuāng·zi	窗子	窗子	window	10
chuáng	床	床	bed	6
cì	次	次	a time, occasion	8
cóng	從	从	from	6
cù	醋	醋	vinegar	11

| cuò | 錯 | 错 | be wrong | 4 |

D

dǎ	打	打	to hit; to play	3,9
dǎbāo	打包	打包	to pack	12
dǎ cuò ·le	打錯了	打错了	wrong number	4
dǎdiànhuà	打電話	打电话	to make a phone call	3
dǎqiú	打球	打球	to play ball	9
dǎzhé	打折	打折	to discount	3
dà	大	大	to be big, large; to be old	7,9
dàgài	大概	大概	maybe, perhaps, probably	9
Dàqiān Gōngsī	大千公司	大千公司	Daqian Company	8
dàxué	大學	大学	university	9
Dàyǒu	大有	大有	a Chinese name	9
dài	帶	带	to bring	10
dān·zi	單子	单子	pieces of paper with written words on	10
dāochā	刀叉	刀叉	knife and fork	12
dāo·zi	刀子	刀子	knife	12
dào	到	到	to, to arrive	4
·de	的	的	P : (suffix indicating modification)	3
·dehuà	的話	的话	if (used with or without 要是／如果)	10
·de	得	得	P : (used after verbs indicating the degree of the action)	11
děi	得	得	must, have to	11
dēng	燈	灯	light, lamp	6
děng	等	等	to wait	3
dì	第	第	SP: (the ordinal prefix)	5
dì·di	弟弟	弟弟	younger brother	9
dìfāng	地方	地方	place	8
dìzhǐ	地址	地址	address	10
diǎn	點	点	dot, point; point (decimal point); to count; o'clock; to order food	2,3 4,11
diànfèi	電費	电费	electricity bill	6
diànhuà	電話	电话	telephone	3
diànnǎo	電腦	电脑	computer	9
diànshì	電視	电视	TV set	6
diànyǐng	電影	电影	movie	9
dìngwèi	訂位	订位	to make a reservation	11
dōng	東	东	east	2

Dōngsān Jiē	東三街	东三街	Dongsan Street	6
dōng·xi	東西	东西	thing, object	2
dǒng	懂	懂	to understand	9
dōu	都	都	all, both	3
duì	對	对	to be right, correct	3
duì·bùqǐ	對不起	对不起	Excuse me. Sorry	2
duìfāng	對方	对方	the opposite party	8
duìfāng fùfèi	對方付費	对方付费	the other party pays, collect phone call	8
duì·le	對了	对了	by the way (indicating one has just thought of something)	3
duìmiàn	對面	对面	the opposite side	5
duō	多	多	much, many	7
duō(·me)	多(麼)	多(么)	how SV? to what degree	9
duōshǎo	多少	多少	how much/many	1

E

è	餓	饿	to be hungry	12
èi	欸	欸	Hey! (used to call someone)	12
·en	嗯	嗯	I : (indicates affirmation)	8
èr	二	二	two	1
èr yuè	二月	二月	February	7

F

Fǎguó	法國	法国	France	11
Fǎguó cài	法國菜	法国菜	French food	11
fàn	飯	饭	meal, cooked rice	4
fànguǎn	飯館	饭馆	restaurant	11
fāngbiàn	方便	方便	to be convenient	7
fángdōng	房東	房东	landlord	6
fángjiān	房間	房间	room	6
fángkè	房客	房客	tenant, lodger	7
fáng·zi	房子	房子	house	6
fángzū	房租	房租	rent	6
fàng	放	放	to put	6
fēicháng	非常	非常	very, pretty	12
fēixīyānqū	非吸煙區	非吸烟区	non-smoking area	11
fèiyòng	費用	费用	fee	10
fēn	分	分	minute	4
fēnkāi	分開	分开	to separate; separately	12

fēng	封	封	M : (for a letter, a telegram, etc.)	10
fù	付	付	to pay	3
fùjìn	附近	附近	nearby, around, vicinity	11
fúwù	服務	服务	service; to serve	11
fúwùshēng	服務生	服务生	waiter/waitress	11

G

gānjìng	乾淨	干净	to be clean	12
gānggāng	剛剛	刚刚	just a moment	12
gāoxìng	高興	高兴	to be happy	12
gào·su	告訴	告诉	to tell	10
gē·ge	哥哥	哥哥	elder brother	9
·ge	個	个	general measure word	1
gěi	給	给	to give; for	2,3
gēn	跟	跟	and; with	6,8
gōngchē	公車	公车	public bus (the short name for 公共汽車)	5
gōngkè	公克	公克	gram	10
gōngsī	公司	公司	company	5
gōngyòng diànhuà	公用電話	公用电话	public telephone	5
gōngyù	公寓	公寓	apartment	6
gōngchéngshī	工程師	工程师	engineer	9
gōngzuò	工作	工作	work; to work	9
gōngbǎo jīdīng	宮保雞丁	宫保鸡丁	gongbao chicken	11
gòu	夠	够	to be enough	11
guàhàoxìn	掛號信	挂号信	registered letter	10
guān·xi	關係	关系	relationship	10
guàngjiē	逛街	逛街	to go window-shopping	9
guì	貴	贵	to be expensive	2
guì xìng	貴姓	贵姓	Your honorable surname	9
guìtái	櫃台	柜台	counter	12
guó	國	国	country	2
guò	過	过	to pass	6

H

hái	還	还	in addition; still	6,9
háishì	還是	还是	or	8
hái·zi	孩子	孩子	child	9
hǎi	海	海	sea, ocean	9

Appendix I

hángkōngxìn	航空信	航空信	airmail	10
hǎo	好	好	to be good, nice, well, OK; to be easy to	2,7
hǎochī	好吃	好吃	to be delicious	2
hǎo jǐ	好幾	好几	many, several	8
hǎo jiǔ bú jiàn	好久不見	好久不见	Long time no see.	12
hǎokàn	好看	好看	good-looking; interesting	12
hǎoxiàng	好像	好像	It seems..., to look like	12
hào	號	号	number; date	3,7
hē	喝	喝	to drink	9
hěn	很	很	very	2
hóng	紅	红	red	6
hónglǜdēng	紅綠燈	红绿灯	traffic light	6
hòumiàn	後面	后面	back, behind	5
hú	壺	壶	M : a pot of	12
huà	話	话	word	8
huài	壞	坏	to be bad; to be broken	10
huài·le	壞了	坏了	It's broken.	10
huānyíng guānglín	歡迎光臨	欢迎光临	Welcome.	11
huàn	換	换	to exchange	3
huídiàn	回電	回电	to return a call	8
huí qù	回去	回去	to return, to go back	7
huì	會	会	can, to know how to; will, would	9,11
huǒchē	火車	火车	train	6
huǒchēzhàn	火車站	火车站	train station	6

J

jǐ	幾	几	how many	2
jì	寄	寄	to send by mail, to mail	10
jiā	加	加	to add	10
jiā	家	家	home, house; M:for company, bank etc.	4,9
jiājù	家具	家具	furniture	6
jiān	間	间	M:room/ (for rooms)	5
jiàn	見	见	to see	4
jiàn	件	件	M : for a shirt, a pair of pants,...	12
jiāo péngyǒu	交朋友	交朋友	to make friends	8
jiāo	教	教	to teach	9
jiào	叫	叫	to be called, named; to order; to call, to shout,to scream	3,11
jiē	接	接	to answer (the phone)	8

jiē	街	街	street	6
jiézhàng	結帳	结帐	to settle a bill	12
jiě·jie	姊姊	姊姊	elder sister	9
jièshào	介紹	介绍	to introduce	9
jīn	斤	斤	catty, Chinese pound	2
jīnnián	今年	今年	this year	7
jīntiān	今天	今天	today	4
jìn	近	近	to be near	7
jìn lái	進來	进来	to come in	8
jiǔ	九	九	nine	1
jiǔ yuè	九月	九月	September	7
jiǔ	久	久	to be a long time	9
jiǔ	酒	酒	wine, liquor	9
jiù	舊	旧	to be old, used	3
jiù	就	就	Adv : (used in the sense of "just" or "exactly"; sooner than expected); then	4,5, 10
jué·dé	覺得	觉得	to feel	7
juédìng	決定	决定	to decide	7

K

kāi	開	开	to drive; to open; to write (a check, a bill, a ticket, etc.)	6,12
kāichē	開車	开车	to drive a car	6
kāiyáng báicài	開洋白菜	开洋白菜	kaiyang cabbage	11
kàn	看	看	to look, to see, to watch, to visit; to read	4
kělè	可樂	可乐	cola	9
kěshì	可是	可是	but	7
kěyǐ	可以	可以	may, can	3
kèqì	客氣	客气	to be courteous, to stand on ceremony	3
kètīng	客廳	客厅	living room	6
kuài	快	快	to be fast	10
kuài	塊	块	M : (for money)	1
kuài·zi	筷子	筷子	chopsticks	12

L

là	辣	辣	to be hot, spicy	11
·la	啦	啦	a phrase-final particle (denoting a tone of exclamation or interrogation)	12
lái	來	来	to come	3

lái·le	來了	来了	to have come, to have been brought	3
lǎoshī	老師	老师	teacher	4
Lǎo Chén	老陳	老陈	familiar address for a man surnamed Chen	5
·le	了	了	P : (often used after stative verbs, preceded by 太)	2
lěng	冷	冷	to be cold	12
Lǐ Hóng	李紅	李红	a Chinese name	8
lǐmiàn	裡面	里面	inside	5
liǎng	兩	两	two	1
liǎng diǎn bàn	兩點半	两点半	2:30	4
Lín Jīnshuǐ	林金水	林金水	a Chinese name	9
líng	○	○	zero	1
líng	零	零	zero	2
lǐng	領	领	to pick up	10
liú	留	留	to leave; to keep, to save, to reserve	8
liú huà	留話	留话	to leave a message	8
liù	六	六	six	1
liù yuè	六月	六月	June	7
lóu	樓	楼	floor	5
lóu shàng	樓上	楼上	upstairs	5
lóu xià	樓下	楼下	downstairs	5
lù	路	路	road; bus number	5
lùkǒu	路口	路口	crossing; intersection	5
lǔxíng	旅行	旅行	to travel; travel, traveling	3
lǔxíngshè	旅行社	旅行社	travel agency	10
lǔxíng zhipiào	旅行支票	旅行支票	traveler's check	3
lǜ	綠	绿	green	6

M

mā·ma	媽媽	妈妈	mother	9
·ma	嗎	吗	question particle	2
máfán	麻煩	麻烦	to be troublesome; May I trouble you to...; trouble	8
mápó dòufǔ	麻婆豆腐	麻婆豆腐	mapo tofu	11
mǎshàng	馬上	马上	at once, immediately	12
mǎi	買	买	to buy	2
mǎidān	買單	买单	to pay the bill	12
mài	賣	卖	to sell	2
mànmàn	慢慢	慢慢	to be slow	10

mànyòng	慢用	慢用	Enjoy your meal.	12
máng	忙	忙	be busy	4
màoyì gōngsī	貿易公司	贸易公司	trade company	9
méi	沒	没	not	2
méi(yǒu)	沒(有)	没(有)	did not, have not	5
méi guān·xi	沒關係	没关系	It doesn't matter.	10
Měiguó	美國	美国	U.S.A.	2
Měijīn	美金	美金	US Dollar	3
měi	每	每	each, every	7
mèi·mei	妹妹	妹妹	younger sister	9
mén	門	门	door, gate	10
ménkǒu	門口	门口	doorway	10
mǐ	米	米	rice	11
míngnián	明年	明年	next year	7
míngtiān	明天	明天	tomorrow	4
míngxìnpiàn	明信片	明信片	postcard	10
míngpiàn	名片	名片	name card, business card	9
míng·zi	名字	名字	name	10

N

ná	拿	拿	to take	5
náhuíqù	拿回去	拿回去	to take back	7
nǎ	哪	哪	which	4
nǎlǐ	哪裡	哪里	where	5
nà	那	那	that	1
nà·me	那麼	那么	then; in that case; that being the case	3
nàlǐ	那裡	那里	there	4
nán	南	南	south	6
nán	男	男	male (of persons)	9
nánhái·zi	男孩子	男孩子	boy	9
nán	難	难	to be difficult	9
nánkàn	難看	难看	bad-looking; uninteresting	12
·ne	呢	呢	P : (used at the end of a sentence as an interrogative)	4
néng	能	能	to be able to, can, may	8
nǐ	你	你	you	1
nǐ·men	你們	你们	you (pl.)	2
nián	年	年	year	7
niànshū	念書	念书	to study	9

nín	您	您	polite form of you	1
niú	牛	牛	cow, cattle	11
nòng	弄	弄	to make, do, manage, handle	12
nián	年	年	year	7
nǚ	女	女	female (of persons)	9
nǚhái·zi	女孩子	女孩子	girl	9

O

| òu | 噢 | 噢 | Oh! (indicating sudden realization) | 3 |

P

pá	爬	爬	to climb, to crawl	9
pá	爬山	爬山	to climb a mountain, to hike on hills	9
pà	怕	怕	to be afraid of , to fear	8
pán	盤	盘	M: a plate of	12
pán·zi	盤子	盘子	plate, dish	12
péngyǒu	朋友	朋友	friend	7
píxié	皮鞋	皮鞋	leather shoes	5
píjiǔ	啤酒	啤酒	beer	9
piányí	便宜	便宜	to be cheap	2
piàoliàng	漂亮	漂亮	to be pretty, beautiful	12
píngcháng	平常	平常	usually	11

Q

qī	七	七	seven	1
qī yuè	七月	七月	July	7
qíguài	奇怪	奇怪	to be strange	8
qiān	千	千	thousand	2
qiānmíng	簽名	签名	to sign (your name)	10
qiānyuē	簽約	签约	to sign a lease, to sign a contract	7
qián	錢	钱	money	1
Qián Shūyí	錢書宜	钱书宜	a Chinese name	3
qiánmiàn	前面	前面	front, in front of	5
qīng	輕	轻	to be light/gently	10
qīngcài	青菜	青菜	vegetable	11
qīngjiāo	青椒	青椒	green pepper	11
qīngjiāo niúròu	青椒牛肉	青椒牛肉	green papper beef	11
qǐng	請	请	to please; to invite	3,4
qǐngkè	請客	请客	to treat, to host, to be my guest	12

qǐngwèn	請問	请问	May I ask...?	4
qiú	球	球	ball	9
qù	去	去	to go	4
qùnián	去年	去年	last year	7

R

rè	熱	热	to be hot	12
rén	人	人	person, people	4
rènshì	認識	认识	to know, to recognize	9
Rìběn	日本	日本	Japan	2
Rìxīn Bǎihuò Gōngsī	日新百貨公司	日新百货公司	Rixin Department Store	6
róngyì	容易	容易	to be easy	9
ròu	肉	肉	meat	11
rúguǒ	如果	如果	if	7

S

sān	三	三	three	1
sān yuè	三月	三月	March	7
shān	山	山	mountain	9
shàng	上	上	to go up	5
shàng(·ge)	上(個)	上(个)	last	4
shàngbān	上班	上班	to go to work, to be on duty	8
shàngcài	上菜	上菜	to serve the dishes	12
shàngchē	上車	上车	to get on	5
shàng cì	上次	上次	last time; the previous occasion	12
Shànghǎi	上海	上海	Shanghai, China	9
shàngkè	上課	上课	to have class, to go to class	9
shàngmiàn	上面	上面	above, top	5
shàngwǔ	上午	上午	in the morning	4
shāo děng	稍等	稍等	Wait a moment.	8
shāo	燒	烧	to cook; to burn	11
shǎo	少	少	little, few	7
shéi	誰	谁	who, whom	4
shēnfènzhèng	身分證	身分证	ID card	10
shēnshàng	身上	身上	on one's body	12
shén·me	什麼	什么	what	1
shén·me shíhòu	什麼時候	什么时候	when	4
shēngrì	生日	生日	birthday	11

shí	十	十	ten	1
shí yuè	十月	十月	October	7
shíèr yuè	十二月	十二月	December	7
shíyī yuè	十一月	十一月	November	7
shíhòu	時候	时候	time	4
shíjiān	時間	时间	time	4
shì	是	是	be	3
shì	事	事	thing, matter, affair, business	4
shì	試	试	to try	8
shìqū	市區	市区	urban district; city proper	10
shōu	收	收	to receive	3
shǒu	手	手	hand	5
shū	書	书	book	3
shūbāo	書包	书包	school bag, book bag	5
shuākǎ	刷卡	刷卡	to pay with a credit card	3
shuāng	雙	双	a pair of	5
shuǐ	水	水	water	6
shuǐdiànfèi	水電費	水电费	utility fee	6
shuǐfèi	水費	水费	water bill	6
shuìjiào	睡覺	睡觉	to sleep, to go to bed	8
shuō	說	说	to say, to speak	8
sì	四	四	four	1
sì yuè	四月	四月	April	7
sì yuè shíyī hào	四月十一號	四月十一号	April 11	7
sòng	送	送	to send; to deliver; to give something as a gift; to give someone a ride	10
suàn	算	算	to count	6
suànzhàng	算帳	算帐	to compute or settle the bill	12
suì	歲	岁	year, age	9
suǒyǐ	所以	所以	therefore, so	8

T

tā	他	他	he, him	1
tā	她	她	she, her	1
tā·men	他們	他们	they, them	2
tā·men	她們	她们	they, them	2
Táiběi	台北	台北	Taipei	9
Táibì	台幣	台币	(New) Taiwan Dollar	3
Táinán	台南	台南	Tainan	9

Táiwān	台灣	台湾	Taiwan	5
Táiwān Dàxué	台灣大學	台湾大学	Taiwan University	9
Táiwān Yínháng	台灣銀行	台湾银行	Bank of Taiwan	5
Táizhōng	台中	台中	Taichung	10
tài	太	太	too	2
tài·tài	太太	太太	Mrs., wife	2
tāng	湯	汤	soup	11
táng	糖	糖	sugar	11
tángcù yú	糖醋魚	糖醋鱼	tangcu fish (sweet and sour fish)	11
tèbié	特別	特別	specially, particularly; to be special	12
tiān	天	天	day	4
tiānqì	天氣	天气	weather	7
tián	填	填	to fill in	3
tián biǎo	填表	填表	to fill in a form	3
tiē	貼	贴	to paste, to stick	10
tīng	聽	听	to listen, to hear	8
tōngzhī	通知	通知	to notify	10
tōngzhīdān	通知單	通知单	notice	10
túzhāng	圖章	图章	seal; stamp	10

W

wàimiàn	外面	外面	outside	5
wán	玩	玩	to play, to have fun	8
wǎn	晚	晚	to be late	8
wǎn	碗	碗	bowl; a bowl of	12
wǎnshàng	晚上	晚上	evening	4
wàn	萬	万	ten thousand; a Chinese family name	2,6
Wànměi Bǎihuò Gōngsī	萬美百貨公司	万美百货公司	Wanmei Department Store	5
Wáng Jiāmíng	王家明	王家明	a Chinese name	9
Wáng Míng	王明	王明	a Chinese name	9
Wáng	王	王	a Chinese family name	6
wǎng	往	往	toward	6
wàng ·le	忘了	忘了	to forget	10
wéi	喂	喂	a common telephone greeting "hello"	4
wèi	位	位	M : (for a person, in a polite way)	4
wèi ·zi	位子	位子	seat	11
wèishén ·me	為什麼	为什么	why	7
wèidào	味道	味道	taste, flavor	11

wèijīng	味精	味精	MSG (monosodium glutamate)	12
wèntí	問題	问题	problem, question	8
wǒ	我	我	I, me	1
wǒ·men	我們	我们	we, us	2
wǔ	五	五	five	1
wǔ yuè	五月	五月	May	7

X

xī	西	西	west	2
Xīcān	西餐	西餐	western food/meal	11
xīwàng	希望	希望	to hope	8
xīyān	吸煙	吸烟	to smoke	11
xǐ	洗	洗	to wash	5
xǐshǒujiān	洗手間	洗手间	restroom	5
xǐyījī	洗衣機	洗衣机	washing machine	8
xǐzǎo	洗澡	洗澡	to take a bath or shower	6
xǐzǎojiān	洗澡間	洗澡间	bathroom	6
xǐhuān	喜歡	喜欢	to like	7
xiā	蝦	虾	shrimp	11
xiāmǐ	蝦米	虾米	dried and/or shelled shrimp	11
xià	下	下	to go down	5
xià(·ge)	下（個）	下（个）	next	4
xiàbān	下班	下班	to get off from work, to go off work	8
xiàchē	下車	下车	to get off	5
xià cì	下次	下次	next time	12
xiàmiàn	下面	下面	under, beneath, bottom	5
xiàwǔ	下午	下午	in the afternoon	4
xiàyǔ	下雨	下雨	to rain	7
xiān	先	先	first, to be the first (in doing something)	3
xiān·sheng	先生	先生	Mr., Sir	1
xián	鹹	鹹	to be salty	11
xiànjīn	現金	现金	cash	3
xiànzài	現在	现在	now	7
xiǎng	想	想	would like, to want; to think	4
xiǎo	小	小	to be small	7
xiǎofèi	小費	小费	a tip	12
xiǎojiě	小姐	小姐	Miss, Ms.	1
xiǎoshí	小時	小时	hour	6
xiē	些	些	some, several	8

xiě	寫	写	to write	10
Xiè	謝	谢	a Chinese surname	4
Xiè Měiyí	謝美宜	谢美宜	a Chinese full name	4
xiè·xiè	謝謝	谢谢	thanks	1
Xiè Xīnyǔ	謝新雨	谢新雨	a Chinese name	9
xīn	新	新	to be new	3
xìn	信	信	a letter	10
xìnfēng	信封	信封	envelope	10
Xìnyī Lù	信一路	信一路	Xinyi Road	5
xìnyòngkǎ	信用卡	信用卡	credit card	3
xīngqī	星期	星期	week	4
xīngqī èr	星期二	星期二	Tuesday	4
xīngqī liù	星期六	星期六	Saturday	4
xīngqī sān	星期三	星期三	Wednesday	4
xīngqī sì	星期四	星期四	Thursday	4
xīngqī tiān	星期天	星期天	Sunday	4
xīngqī wǔ	星期五	星期五	Friday	4
xīngqī yī	星期一	星期一	Monday	4
xíng	行	行	to be acceptable	2
xìng	姓	姓	surname; be surnamed	3
xué	學	学	to learn	6
xuéshēng	學生	学生	student	6
xuéxiào	學校	学校	school	7

Y

yājīn	押金	押金	deposit	6
yān	煙	烟	cigarette	11
yánsè	顏色	颜色	color	12
yàng·zi	樣子	样子	style, appearance	12
yào	要	要	to want; would like	2
yàoshì	要是	要是	if	7
yě	也	也	also	5
yī	一	一	one	1
yīfú	衣服	衣服	clothes, dress	6
yīguì	衣櫃	衣柜	closet, wardrobe	6
yī yuè	一月	一月	January	7
yídìng	一定	一定	surely, certainly	9
yígòng	一共	一共	altogether	1
yíxià	一下	一下	a moment	3

Appendix I

yíyàng	一樣	一样	to be the same, alike	11
yǐ·zi	椅子	椅子	chair	5
yǐhòu	以後	以后	after	8
yǐjīng	已經	已经	already	11
yǐqián	以前	以前	before	8
yì chéng	一成	一成	ten percent	12
yìdiǎnr	一點兒	一点儿	a little	2
yìhuǐr	一會兒	一会儿	a moment	11
yìqǐ	一起	一起	together	11
yīnwèi	因為	因为	because (of), for	8
yínháng	銀行	银行	bank	5
yīnggāi	應該	应该	should, ought to	5
Yīngwén	英文	英文	English	9
yǐngběn	影本	影本	photo copy	10
yòng	用	用	to use	8
yóujiǎn	郵簡	邮简	aerogramme	10
yóujú	郵局	邮局	post office	10
yóupiào	郵票	邮票	stamp	10
yǒu	有	有	to have; there is /are	2,5
yǒu·de	有的	有的	some, some of	9
yǒukòng	有空	有空	to have time	4
yǒumíng	有名	有名	to be famous	11
yòubiān	右邊	右边	right side	5
yú	魚	鱼	fish	11
yù	玉	玉	jade	11
yùmǐ	玉米	玉米	corn	11
yuǎn	遠	远	to be far	7
yuànyì	願意	原意	to be willing to	11
yuē	約	约	to make an appointment	4
yuè	月	月	month	6

Z

zài	在	在	be in, at, on; Adv: (indicating an action in progress)	4,9
zài	再	再	again; then	4,6
zàijiàn	再見	再见	Good-bye.	4
zāng	髒	脏	to be dirty	12
zǎo	早	早	Good morning.; to be early	2,8
zǎoshàng	早上	早上	in the morning	4

zěn·me	怎麼	怎么	how	6
zěn·me bàn	怎麼辦	怎么办	What can be done about it?	7
zěn·meyàng	怎麼樣	怎么样	How about...?	11
zhàn	站	站	bus stop/to stand	5
zhāng	張	张	sheet (for a form, paper, etc.)	3
Zhāng	張	张	A Chinese surname	4
Zhāng Táishēng	張台生	张台生	A Chinese full name	4
zhàngdān	帳單	帐单	bill	12
zhǎo	找	找	to look for	6
Zhào Qí	趙奇	赵奇	a Chinese name	8
zhè	這	这	this	1
zhèi·ge	這個	这个	this one	1
zhèlǐ	這裡	这里	here	4
zhēn	真	真	very, truly	8
zhèyàng	這樣	这样	such, this kind	7
zhǐ	只	只	only	7
zhīdào	知道	知道	to know	5
zhīpiào	支票	支票	check	3
Zhōngcān	中餐	中餐	Chinese food/meal	11
Zhōngguó	中國	中国	China	2
zhōngwǔ	中午	中午	at noon	4
zhōng	鐘	钟	clock	6
zhǒng	種	种	kind, variety, type	2
zhòng	重	重	to be heavy	10
zhù	住	住	to live, to stay	7
zhuǎn	轉	转	to turn; to pass on, to transfer	6,8
zhuō·zi	桌子	桌子	table, desk	5
zì	字	字	character	5
zìdiǎn	字典	字典	dictionary	5
zìjǐ	自己	自己	self, oneself	8
zǒu	走	走	to walk, to go	6
zū	租	租	to rent	6
zuì duō	最多	最多	at most	7
zuìjìn	最近	最近	lately, recently	12
zuì shǎo	最少	最少	at least	7
zuótiān	昨天	昨天	yesterday	4
zuǒbiān	左邊	左边	left side	5
zuò	做	做	to do, to make	4
zuòfàn	做飯	做饭	to cook	8
zuòshì	做事	做事	to do things, to work	9
zuò	坐	坐	to take (bus, taxi, etc.); to sit	5

Appendix I

-273-

APPENDIX II ABBREVIATIONS LIST
詞類略語表

Adv	Adverb	副詞
AV	Auxiliary Verb	助動詞
Conj	Conjunction	連詞
CV	Coverb	前置介詞
D	Direction	方向
DO	Directional Object	直接賓語
DV	Directional Verb	方向動詞
I	Interjection	嘆詞
IE	Idiomatic Expressin	習慣用語
IO	Indirect Object	間接賓語
L	Localizer	方位詞
M	Measure	量詞
MA	Movable Adverb	可移副詞
N	Noun	名詞
NP	Noun Phrase	名詞短語
Nu	Number	數詞
O	Object	賓語
P	Particle	助詞
PN	Pronoun	代名詞
Proper N	Proper Noun	專有名詞
PV	Post-verb	後置介詞
PW	Place Word	處所詞
QW	Question Word	疑問詞
RC	Resultative Compound	結果複合動詞
RE	Resultative Ending	結果複合詞尾
S	Subject	主語
SP	Specifier	指示詞
SV	Stative Verb	性狀動詞
TW	Time Word	時間詞
V	Verb	動詞
VO	Verb Object Compound	動賓複合詞
VP	Verb Phrase	動詞短語

Appendix II

1 第一课　多少钱？ **How Much?**

Dialogue I　Asking prices

　A：小姐，这个多少钱？

　B：六十块。

Dialogue II　Buying from a Food Stand

　A：先生，你吃什么？

　B：两个包子一杯茶。多少钱？

　A：一共四十八块。

　　　(B pays)

　A：谢谢。

2 第二课　买东西 **Shopping**

Dialogue I　In a Traditional Chinese Market

　A：早啊，太太。你买什么？

　B：白菜好吃吗？一斤几块钱？

　A：好吃，一斤十七块钱。你要几个？

　B：你给我两个。

Dialogue II   Bargaining at the Car Dealership

A：先生，你们有没有日本车？

B：对不起，我们不卖日本车。这种美国车很好。你要不要？

A：多少钱？

B：五十九万九千五百块。

A：太贵了！便宜一点儿，五十万，好不好？

B：对不起，不行。

3 第三课   付钱 Payment

Dialogue I   Making Payments in a Store

A：一共多少钱？

B：两千九百五十块。打八折，两千三百六。

A：可以刷卡吗？

B：对不起，我们不收信用卡。

A：那么，我给你现金。

Dialogue II   Ordering Items in a Bookstore

A：你给我现金，给我支票？

B：我给你支票。噢，对了，那本新书来了，给我打个电话，可以吗？

A：好。你的电话几号？

B：我的电话是三二六八四五七。我姓钱，我叫钱书宜。

谢谢。

A：不客气。

Dialogue III　Exchanging Currencies in a Bank

A：先生，我要换五百美金。一块美金多少台币？

B：二十七点五。请先填表，这两张都要填。

(A fills out the forms)

A：请给我四张一百的旅行支票，五张二十的现金。

B：好。请等一下。（给钱）请点一下。

4 第四课　打电话约时间 Making Phone Calls and Appointments

Dialogue I　Dialing the Wrong Number

A：喂，请问，谢老师在不在？

B：谁？

A：谢美宜老师。

B：对不起，没有这个人。

A：你那里是不是三九五六八二五？

B：不是，你打错了。

A：对不起。

Dialogue II　Leaving a Message over the Phone

小谢：喂，请问，张台生先生在吗？

A：他不在。请问，您是哪位？

小谢：我是谢美宜。我想请他到我家来吃饭。
　　　请他今天晚上打电话给我。
　　A：好。他有你的电话吗？
小谢：我想他有。谢谢。

Dialogue III　Making an Appointment over the Phone

　　小张：喂，请问，钱太太在不在？
钱太太：我就是。你是哪位？
　　小张：我是张台生。我想明天下午三点去看你。
　　　　　可以吗？
钱太太：对不起，我有事。
　　小张：星期四呢？
钱太太：这个星期四、星期五我都很忙。
　　小张：那么，你什么时候有空？
钱太太：下个星期一可以吗？
　　小张：好啊。几点？
钱太太：两点半。
　　小张：好。下星期一见。
钱太太：再见。

5 第五课　在哪里？ **Where Is It?**

Dialogue I　Finding out Locations

　　A：请问洗手间在哪里？
　　B：在楼上，右边第一间。

A：公用电话呢？

B：在对面。

Dialogue II   The Case of the Missing Pen

A：谁拿了我的笔？

B：不知道。我没拿。你书包里面有没有？

A：没有。

B：桌子上面呢？

A：也不在桌子上。……噢，在这里，在字典下面。

Dialogue III   Bus Directions

小钱：老陈，我明天要去万美百货公司买皮鞋。
　　　应该坐什么公车？

老陈：你在我们公司前面坐二七八，到台湾银行那一站，
　　　换十五路就可以了。

小钱：在哪里下车？

老陈：在信一路路口下车。万美百货公司就在对面。

6 第六课   找房子 Looking for a Place to Live

Dialogue I   Asking for Directions

小万：老张，我要去日新百货公司后面看房子。日新百货
　　　公司怎么走？

老张：你开车去吗？

小万：是啊。

老张：你从东三街往南开，过两个红绿灯，到了火车站，
　　　左转，再开几分钟，就到了。

Dialogue II　Renting a Room

小王：请问，你们是不是有个房间要出租？

房东：是啊。你是学生吗？

小王：对。

房东：那么房租可以便宜一点。一个月五千五百块，水电
　　　费不算。

小王：要不要押金？

房东：要，一个月的房租。

小王：有没有电话、家具？

房东：有。房间里，床、桌子都有，还有一个大衣柜，可以
　　　放很多衣服。电话跟电视在客厅。

小王：我可以看看房间吗？

房东：可以啊。

7　第七课　租房子 Renting a Place

Dialogue I　Discussing a Room for Rent with a Friend

小张：你今天去看房子了没有？

小王：看了一个公寓。我不太喜欢。

小张：为什么？

小王：我觉得太小了。

小张：远不远？

小王：很近，去学校很方便。房租一个月六千块，也不贵。可是我的东西很多，房间大一点儿好。

小张：这样的房子不好找。你可以先在那里住两、三个月，不喜欢，再搬。

小王：也好。

Dialogue II Talking with the Landlord about Leasing and Moving in

小王：我决定租了。要不要签约？

房东：要。最少租半年。

小王：如果我只住五个月，押金怎么办？

房东：要是有新房客，就可以拿回去。你什么时候搬来？

小王：这两天每天下雨，不太方便。我朋友也都有事，没办法帮我。

房东：我们可以先签约。等天气好了，你再搬。

小王：好。那我们现在签约。今天是四月十一号。签半年，到十月十号。

8 第八课 真麻烦！How Troublesome!

Dialogue I Discussing Housing Problems with a Friend

A：我想搬家。你知不知道哪里有房子出租？

B：你为什么要搬家？你现在住的地方不好吗？

A：有一些问题。你知道我喜欢交朋友，可是房东怕吵，我不能请朋友来玩。

B：这不是大问题，你可以跟朋友在外面玩啊！

A：对。可是因为房东每天晚上十一点睡觉，所以我不能太晚回去。

B：你也应该早一点回家啊。

A：我可以用厨房，可是不能做饭。我也不能用洗衣机。

B：那真不方便。

A：昨天晚上我要打一个对方付费的长途电话，他也说不可以。

B：嗯。那你搬家吧。

Dialogue II Calling a Friend Who Is Never Home

李红：奇怪，他到哪里去了？打了好几次了，都没人接。我打到办公室去试试。希望他在。

李红：五七一一四三八。

A：大千公司，你好。

李红：请你转二九五四。

A：请稍等。

B：喂？

李红：麻烦你请赵奇先生听电话。

B：他出去了。你要留话还是等一下再打来？

李红：他什么时候回来？

B：他没说。我想下班以前吧。

李红：我打到他家，他都不在。我留了话，他也没回电。

B：那怎么办？啊，等一下，他回来了，你自己跟他说。
赵奇，你的电话。

9 第九课　交朋友 Making Friends

Dialogue I　Meeting a New Neighbor

家明：你好。我叫王家明。你贵姓？

金水：你好。我姓林，我叫林金水。你是学生吗？

家明：是啊！我在台湾大学念书。你呢？

金水：我在一家公司上班。你是哪里人？

家明：我是从美国来的，可是我爸妈都是上海人。

金水：你今年多大了？在美国住了多久？

家明：我下个月就二十岁了。我在美国住了十二年。

金水：那你的英文一定很好。我不太会说英文。
你有空，请你教我，好不好？

家明：好。你是台北人吗？

金水：我家在台南。我爸爸妈妈都还住台南。

家明：你家有几个孩子？

金水：我有三个哥哥、两个妹妹。有的在念书，有的在
做事。

家明：我们家有三个女孩子，只有我一个男孩子。噢，对
不起，我要去上课了。再见。

Dialogue II　Getting to Know Someone

大有：你们大概还不认识吧？来，来，来，我给你们介绍介
绍。这是王明，这是谢新雨。

王明：你好。

新雨：你好。

大有：请坐。你们要喝什么？

新雨：请给我一杯茶。

王明：我要可乐。

新雨：这是我的名片。

王明：噢，你是电脑工程师。我觉得电脑很难，我一点都
不懂。

新雨：那你在哪里工作？

王明：我在贸易公司上班。

新雨：没事的时候，你喜欢做什么？

王明：我常常去看电影、逛街。你呢？

新雨：我也爱看电影。有的时候也去爬爬山、打打球。

10　第十课　寄信 Mailing

Dialogue I　Mailing a Letter at the Post Office

A：请问，寄到日本的航空信要贴多少钱邮票？

B：不超重的话，十三块。每超重十公克加九块钱。

A：几天可以到？

B：快的话，三天就到了。慢的话，大概要五、六天才
能到。

A：这封信要多少钱？

B：四十块。噢，你忘了写地址。

A：啊，我写了名字，忘了写地址。谢谢你告诉我。

Dialogue II　Picking up a Parcel at the Post Office

A：小姐，请问，是不是在这里领包裹？

B：不是。请到一号窗口。

A：先生，我要领包裹。

C：请把通知单跟身分证给我。

(C gets the parcel)

C：这是你的包裹。图章带来了吗？

A：对不起，没带图章。签名可以吗？

C：可以。请签在这里。

Dialogue III　Sending a Fax at the Post Office

小李：旅行社要我五点以前把身分证影本拿给他们。我没有时间送去。你可以帮我传真吗？

小赵：好啊。你把影本拿来。……哎呀！传真机坏了。

小李：那怎么办？

小赵：没关系。邮局也可以传真。

小李：邮局传真费用怎么算呢？

小赵：旅行社在哪里？在市区，还是在别的地方？

小李：在台中。

小赵：台中啊？那传真一张二十五块。

小李：太好了。我现在就去。

11 第十一课　吃什么好？ **What Shall We Eat?**

Dialogue I　Dining with a Friend after Work

王先生：今天是你二十五岁生日，我请你吃饭。

李小姐：你太客气了。不好意思。

王先生：你想吃什么？中餐还是西餐？

李小姐：西餐好不好？

王先生：那我们去吃法国菜，怎么样？这儿附近有一家很有
　　　　名的法国餐厅。他们的菜做得不错。

李小姐：好啊，我们就去那里吧。

(Getting a table at the restauant)

服务生：欢迎光临。几位？

王先生：两个人。

服务生：订位了没有？

李小姐：没有。非吸烟区还有位子吗？

服务生：对不起，已经没有了。得等一会儿。你们愿意等吗？

王先生：要等多久？

服务生：大概二十几分钟。

李小姐：太久了。那就吸烟区吧。

服务生：好，请跟我来。

Dialogue II   Ordering from the Menu

服务生（拿水来）：两位好，这是我们的菜单。请看一下。

陈先生：谢谢。你们餐厅哪些菜比较有名？

服务生：宫保鸡丁、麻婆豆腐、开洋白菜都不错。

李小姐：开洋白菜是什么啊？

服务生：就是把虾米跟白菜放在一起烧。

李小姐：味道怎么样？很咸吗？

服务生：不咸，跟平常的菜一样。我想你们会喜欢的。

陈先生：好。谢谢。我们先看一下菜单。(对李小姐说)
　　　　你想吃什么？

李小姐：我想试试开洋白菜。你呢？

陈先生：宫保鸡丁太辣了。你也喜欢吃鱼，我们点一个糖醋
　　　　鱼，再叫一个青椒牛肉吧。

李小姐：好啊。

陈先生：三个菜够不够？

李小姐：够了，够了。不够再点。

陈先生：要不要喝汤？玉米汤，好不好？

李小姐：好。就这样吧。

12 第十二课　在餐厅吃饭 Dining at a Restaurant

Dialogue I   Making Small Talk at the Table

Philip：我们好久不见了。最近怎么样啊？

赵小姐：还不错。欸，你看我刚刚买的这件衬衫怎么样？

Philip：颜色很漂亮，样子也不错，穿在你身上非常好看。

赵小姐：真的啊？谢谢。

服务生：对不起，上菜。

Philip：先生，麻烦你给我刀叉。我不太会用筷子。

(过了一会儿)

服务生：菜都来了吗？

赵小姐：都来了。

服务生：喜欢我们的菜吗？

赵小姐：每个菜都做得不错，就是味精多了一点儿。

服务生：不会吧？一点儿都不放也不好吃。下次你先告诉我，我就叫厨房少放一点儿。还要不要加菜？

赵小姐：我想够了。麻烦你给我们一壶热茶。还有，这个盘子脏了，也麻烦你换一个。

Philip：请再给我一碗饭。

服务生：好，马上来。请慢用。

Dialogue II　Settling the Bill

小钱：吃饱了吗？

小林：饱了。今天吃得特别高兴。

小钱：我们算帐吧。

小林：好。

小钱：先生，我们要买单。

服务生：要不要分开算？

小林：一起算。

服务生：好，马上来。

小林：今天我请客。

小钱：那太不好意思了。

小林：没关系啦。

小钱：好吧，那下次我请你。

服务生：这是你们的帐单，请到门口柜台结帐。
　　　　要不要把这个菜包起来？

小钱：好，麻烦你打包。噢，对不起，帐好象算错了。我
　　　　们没点这个菜。

服务生：是吗？我再看看。噢，对，是我弄错了。
　　　　真抱歉。我再开一张给你。(服务生走开)

小林：要不要给小费？

小钱：不必啦。已经加了一成服务费了。

小林：那就走吧。